Outer Search
Inner Journey

An Orphan and Adoptee's Quest

Peter F. Dodds

Foreword by
Nancy Verrier, M.A.

Aphrodite Publishing Company
Puyallup, Washington
United States of America

Outer Search\Inner Journey:
An Orphan and Adoptee's Quest

Although the following account is true, the names of certain persons have been changed to protect their privacy.

Cover and interior design by Sarah Toll, Fremont, California
Front cover photo — the author the day he was adopted
Back cover photo — the author 1996, photo by Gary McCutcheon, Puyallup, Washington

Publisher's Cataloging in Publication
(Prepared by Quality Books Inc.)

Dodds, Peter F.
    Outer search, inner journey : an orphan and adoptee's quest / Peter F. Dodds.
    p. cm.
    Preassigned LCCN: 96-97016
    ISBN: 1-889702-24-2

    1. Dodds, Peter F. 2. Intercountry adoption--Germany--Personal narratives. 3. Intercountry adoption--United States--Personal narratives. 4. Adopted children--Germany--Personal narratives. 5. Birthparents--Germany--Identification. I. Title.

HV875.58.G4D64 1997   362.7'34
                                       QBI96-40390

If unavailable in local bookstores, additional copies of this publication may be purchased by writing the publisher at the above address.

Acknowledgements

I wish to publicly thank the people who helped me along the writing journey.

To Marcia Holland, my dear friend and mentor, who for three years encouraged and guided me as I journeyed through the ups and downs known by all writers. A heart-felt thank you to my gifted friend Christie McIntyre, for her support and considerable editing skills. I am grateful to Elizabeth Lyon and Penny Lent for their taking time to help polish my work. To William Gage for introducing me to the German-born adoptee population in America through his newsletter *Geborener Deutscher*, and Irene Maria Plank who edited the German portions of this book.

Grateful acknowledgement is made for permission to reproduce the following material: excerpts from *Nemisis at Potsdam* by Alfred M. de Zayas, published by Routledge & Kegan Paul Ltd. Copyright 1977, 1979 by Alfred M. de Zayas. Reprinted by permission. All rights reserved.

This group of people have given me much and I am grateful.

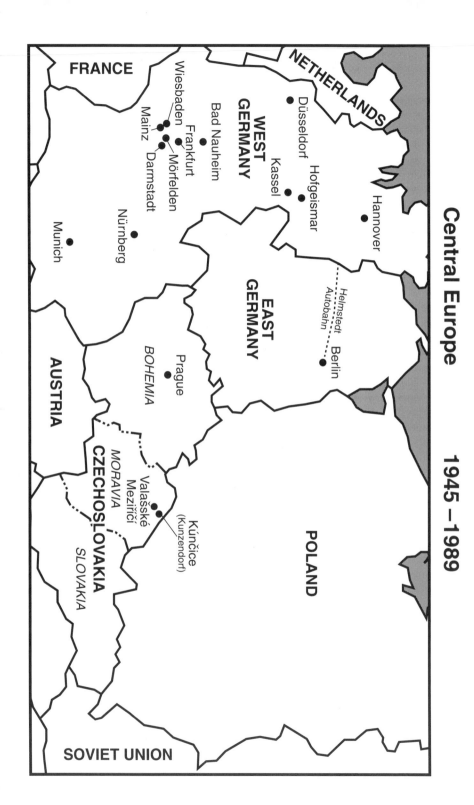

Central Europe   1945 – 1989

Outer Search\Inner Journey:
An Orphan and Adoptee's Quest

For All Those Who Search

Foreword

For too long adoption has been seen by society as the altruistic rescuing of children whose parents are unable to care for them. Embedded within this view is the expectation that these children should be grateful for this humanitarian effort on their behalf. The children's feelings about being separated from their biological parents and genetic heritage have seldom been considered. The children themselves have felt that these secret feelings were abnormal and that they were bad for having them. Now, with more international adoptions taking place, there is the added deficit for these children of being separated from their country and culture, as well as their family. Without bitterness or blame, Peter Dodds has written a personal account of his experience with international adoption, which will shed much-needed light on this subject.

It will probably come as a surprise to many people that between the years 1963 and 1981, United States citizens adopted 6,578 German children. Although adopted before such statistics were kept, *Outer Search/ Inner Journey: An Orphan and Adoptee's Quest*, chronicles the experiences of a little German boy named Peter who was "rescued" from an orphanage at age three and adopted by American parents. The account of his experience is especially powerful, because he suffered no outwardly visible wounds. His parents were good, solid, middle-class people. As a family they ate their meals together, took outings together, and went to mass every Sunday. Although not overtly affectionate, his parents nevertheless gave Peter a stable upbringing; yet he never felt as if he belonged. His story is both a search for roots and a parallel inner journey for healing.

Upon learning of his adoption at age five, Peter built a castle "dark and foreboding...from the stones of grief, sorrow, helplessness, guilt, fear, embarrassment, rage, rejection, anger, shame, inferiority." This castle was for years to serve as protection against further devastation. Yet, it was also a prison for which Peter had no key. The key to this castle, he thought, was with his birth mother.

Two decades later Peter's quest leads him back to his native Germany. It is here that he hopes that reuniting with his birth mother will restore his sense of belonging: "The dreadful realization that I'd been torn away from my mother resulted in a yearning, a primordial ache, to find the woman who had given me life... The search was more than a simple journey to discover my mother. It was also a voyage of inner faith. I felt if I could find out who my mother was, then I would find out who I was." Despite the more public reasons given for searching: medical records, curiosity about heritage, etc., Peter's poignant words most closely describe the true reason so many adoptees search: a primordial aching need to find the Self, as well as the mother to whom they were connected.

Yet the journey is hazardous and strewn with victims. In his search for himself and for a sense of belonging, Peter finds love, only to sabotage the relationship by acting in a hostile and uncaring manner toward the very person he cares about the most.

To dull the pain stemming from adoption, he turns to alcohol. Peter's account of his struggles with alcohol is impressive, because he so candidly describes his behavior and how it affected his relationships. Peter's honesty about his inner and outer struggles in his relationships with his birth mother and his adoptive parents, with the sabotaging of relationships with women, as well as his struggles with alcohol will give courage to those struggling with these same issues.

People often say they want to write a book about their adoption experience, especially the reunion experience. Everyone's story is sacred to him. There is no doubt that the writing of these stories has great potential for healing. But to be appealing to people beyond the bounds of birth/adoptive family about which it is written, it must support, educate, and inform in a way which can be both meaningful and helpful to others struggling with the wounds of separation and loss. It should help those not directly affected by adoption to understand the emotional, psychological, and spiritual pain caused by separation from one's biological roots and growing up without seeing oneself reflected anywhere. This book not only fulfills those requirements, but fills a gap in adoption literature by being the first personal account to examine the life-long emotional impact of adoption, as well as the only narrative on international adoptions. To make this process more interesting, the author writes in a flowing, narrative style that engages the reader in the adventure and romance of his story.

But perhaps the most important aspect of *Outer Search/Inner Journey* is that while recounting a tale of loss, guilt, shame, and alienation, it offers the hope that love, faith, and forgiveness can help heal the emotional wounds of adoption as one proceeds on the journey toward wholeness.

Nancy Verrier, M.A.
Lafayette, California

The Hidden Castle

I always knew I was adopted. It settled in my consciousness at the age where memory first collects imprints of smells and people and places. My birth parents left me at the age of one and an orphanage became my second home. The uprooting continued when a man and woman from a foreign country adopted me a year-and-a-half later.

I've always had an exaggerated ability to feel. The loss of my birth parents, time in an orphanage and exile to a foreign country acted as a series of injuries that left me emotionally devastated. My life became a search, a quest to heal the suffering that stemmed from those early events.

Most people, from the time they are born, grow and develop in the shadow of their parents. For others, like myself, birth parents disappear and life drastically changes at a very young age. Why did they give me away? Where do I come from? Where do I belong? Is there anyone who looks like me? Who am I? Am I worthy of being loved and can I love in return? These questions haunted me into adulthood, questions with elusive answers.

I don't consciously remember anything about my birth parents, the orphanage or the day I was taken out of the home for forsaken children. When I turned five, my second set of parents decided to tell me I was adopted. But part of me already knew.

I was in my bedroom, crouched on the floor playing with my little Matchbox tin racing cars. My parents called from the living room for me to come and join them. "I'll be right there," I said and pulled the red car back along the hardwood floor, gave it a shove and shouted, "Vrooom." It rolled across the floor and stopped just short of the dresser. Then I raced the blue car. "Vrooom." It sped from my hand and veered sharply to the left before crashing against a wall. "Red car won; red car won." I stood up cheering and went to join my parents.

I knew something serious was going to happen as soon as I entered the living room. Neither of my parents said a word. I sensed danger and was afraid.

"Sit down, Peter. We have something very important to tell you," my father said while pointing to a big, blue, upholstered chair across from the sofa where he and my mother sat.

I did as I was told, moving cautiously across the room while looking at the carpet, too frightened to talk. After I climbed into the chair, my father spoke in a tone fit for a lecture. His voice wasn't comforting; he sounded serious, and it increased my anxiety. My mother sat close by his side and held his hand. A coffee table stood between their sofa and my chair, a huge barrier separating parents from their child.

"Your mother and I love you very much. We want you to understand that you're very special to us. This is the story of how you came here to live with us. We wanted a little boy but weren't able to have one ourselves. Then we found out about a place where little boys and girls live who don't have any parents. It was the orphanage where you lived. Do you remember the orphanage?"

I shook my head no and felt blood rush to my face, making it hot. My heart hurt and my wide-open eyes began to moisten.

"Your real mother and father couldn't keep you. They couldn't give everything a good little boy like you deserves. When you were one-year-old they had to put you in the orphanage. That's where you were before you came and lived with us."

I felt they were going to tell me I was bad and then give me away. I could barely see them because tears clouded my eyes. My insides hurt, but I didn't move. My parents' voices sounded far away as if they were speaking from another room. What would happen next? Were they going to abandon me?

"Before we chose you we visited the orphanage many times and watched all the boys and girls playing. You were always by yourself and never played with the other children. You looked so sad. We wanted you to be happy, so we picked you to come and live with us. You were almost three-years-old then."

They weren't telling me something new; part of me had always known. But to hear the words from them, from grown-ups, from the people I thought were my parents, terrified me. My eyes could no longer hold the tears. Drops leaked, one by one, and trickled down my burning face. I didn't say a word, didn't make a sound and sat motionless in the big chair. Tears from my face splashed onto my lap. Where were they going to put me?

My mother spoke for the first time, still holding my father's hand. "We love you and want you to be happy. You're part of our family now. Why are you crying, Peter?"

I couldn't say anything; fear prevented me from speaking.

"It's all right son," my father broke in. "Be strong. You're the little man of the house. Big boys don't cry."

Remaining silent, I moved for the first time since sitting in the chair and used both hands to wipe the wetness from my face. I dropped my hands back to my sides, moist from an outpouring of grief and fear. I lowered my head and couldn't look at them any longer.

My mother continued talking. "Everything's fine, Peter. After we adopted you, we kept your first two names but changed them to English. We changed your last name to Dodds so you could have the same name we do. That's how you got your name—Peter Fredrick Dodds. Oh honey, why is he crying?"

"Why don't you go back to your room, son?" my father said. "You'll feel better in a little while. Your mother will make you dessert for supper. Go on to your room now."

I slid off the chair and the jolt of my feet hitting the floor jarred more tears loose. I left the living room, trying hard not to cry, and looked at the floor so my parents couldn't see my face. I walked to my bedroom as fast as I could, locked the door behind me and threw myself face-down on the bed. I pulled back the bedspread, buried my head in the pillow. I sobbed uncontrollably, tears and fluid spewing out my nose and mouth. I didn't have any thoughts, only an awareness of a deep ache searing my body with each sobbing shudder. My hands shook from the force of squeezing the pillow against the sides of my head. Fear and sorrow raged inside until the churning pain erupted in an involuntary howl. My screams continued until I went limp from exhaustion. I don't belong to the two people in the living room. They don't want me. They wanted a new toy and got a hand-me-down instead. Anger flared again and I opened my eyes to see the white pillowcase pressed against my face.

Why didn't they leave me in the orphanage? I gripped the pillowcase again, knotting it in my hands. I remembered their words. They picked me because they felt sorry for me, like I felt sorry for the puppy I saw in the pet store last week. I'm not a dumb dog.

I kicked my feet again and again against the end of the bed. I hated them for adopting me; I hated them for taking me away. I hate them... I hate them... I want my real mommy. Finally, the thought of her melted my anger. I wanted her arms around me, holding me. I wanted her to say she wouldn't leave. Where are you mommy? Where are you daddy?

Later in the afternoon, after the tears had crusted on the pillowcase, I slowly rolled out of bed and played with the cars. When my parents came into the room with a bowl of ice cream, I put on my strong little-boy mask and pretended everything was okay.

But everything wasn't okay. Something was terribly wrong. Why would parents give their child away? Mothers and fathers keep their children if they're good, so I must be bad.

There was no escaping the dreadful feelings that came with knowing I was adopted. It resulted in the destruction of my self-esteem and I needed protection. So during my childhood, I created a refuge for self-preservation from the devastation of knowing I was adopted. In the interior of my being, I sifted through the debris of my shattered self to look for material to build a protective fortress. Tossing aside fragments that couldn't be used, I mentally stooped down and with two hands picked up a stone, the heavy stone of *loss*. Struggling with the weight, I carried it to my far-away interior and set it down as a castle's foundation, a foundation without love. I brushed the dirt from my hands, pants and shirt, then went back to adoption's devastation.

In my mind, I pulled a charred, wooden board from a pile of rubble and beneath it saw another stone, the stone of *abandonment*. I carried this also back to the foundation and set it beside the stone of *loss*.

While growing up, I encountered everything needed to construct my castle: *grief, sorrow, helplessness, guilt, fear, embarrassment, rage, rejection, anger, shame, inferiority*. With each experience, my fortress grew stronger. Stones were cemented together with the mortar of belief that I was a mistake, that I didn't belong and couldn't be loved. My castle walls stood thick and high and strong. No one could hurt me when I hid inside where I was safe from the outside world.

However, the lonely structure within me was no picturesque, fairy-tale castle. It stood cold and menacing, a citadel designed to defend against outside attacks. It became my protection but also held me prisoner.

The only way out was through the door, but it was locked. And I didn't have a key. To open the door, I needed to find the key or have someone on the outside bring me a key to escape. My birth mother would have a key; she could let me out of the castle. She would free me from the miserable enclosure I had built. Dear mother, where are you? Father, will you come and help? Why did you leave? Didn't you care? What did I do to cause you to abandon me?

Sometimes I wanted badly to escape my self-made prison. I wanted friends, to be understood, to give and receive love, lead a normal life. I'd go into a frenzy and ransack my fortress, searching for the key, any key that might open the door. It was terrible to be trapped inside. I couldn't get out. Help! Please let me out! But there was no escape, and the desire to break out slowly withered, replaced by the silent calm of chilling loneliness.

Isolation

My adopted parents raised me in a solid, middle-class home. We ate our meals together, took family trips to the zoo, and I rode in the back-seat of the station wagon every Sunday morning, wearing a white shirt and tie to Catholic mass. Neither of my adopted parents drank excessively; my father didn't beat my mother, and I suffered no physical, emotional or sexual abuse. My adopted parents enrolled me in swimming lessons, signed me up to play little league baseball, let me go to the Saturday matinee and made me do my homework. They often told me, "We love you very much."

But I didn't believe them. My adopted parents would have told any little boy or girl they picked out of the orphanage that they loved them and I might have believed them if they'd held me in their arms and said they'd never leave me, but they weren't the touching kind. Since I'd learned early in life to judge people by actions, instead of words, my parents did little to ease my fears of abandonment and rejection.

My adopted parents told me, "Little boys should be seen and not heard," nearly as often as they said they loved me. They wanted an obedient, happy child, instead of one filled with sadness and anger. Their good intentions had an ill effect; by the age of five I had learned to bury my feelings and didn't trust people who said they loved me.

My father, Francis Xavier Dodds, grew up during the Great Depression in a working-class neighborhood on the tough streets of Philadelphia. The army drafted him at the end of World War II; he completed his military service and went to college on the G.I. Bill. After graduation he earned a commission as an army officer in the infantry and fought in the Korean War. Consequently, my father ran the household like an army unit and demanded instant obedience to his every order. He viewed his family role as the disciplinarian and provider. He expected me to excel in school and sports, taught me to be fair and instilled a sense of right and wrong.

My mother, Jean Ann Mulraney, grew up on a dairy farm near Scranton, Pennsylvania. She left for college after high school and became a registered nurse. The army needed nurses in the early 1950's, and she served in a M.A.S.H. unit during the Korean War. She met and married Francis X. Dodds after returning to the States, then resigned her commission with the rank of captain and became Jean M. Dodds.

Mother was the model homemaker of the 1950s and 60s. Every morning she had breakfast on the table and sent me off to school with lunch packed in my tin pail decorated with cartoon characters. She kept the house spotless, prepared three meals each day, did the household laundry, grocery shopped and nursed me when I scraped my knees.

My parents often read to me after they tucked me into bed. Therefore, reading became an activity I enjoyed—as long as it was a book I wanted to read. School work often bored me, and instead of homework, I wanted to read books about dinosaurs or baseball players. Jack London, Jules Verne and history books replaced dinosaur stories as I grew older. I imagined myself a wolf while reading *The Call of the Wild.* I was in a submarine sailing the world's oceans when devouring 20,000 *Leagues Under the Sea.* Reading sparked my imagination and allowed me to escape difficulties and problems.

My parents never said another word about adoption after they told me how they found me. Perhaps they believed it satisfied their obligation as adopted parents. I didn't want to talk about adoption because it hurt, and I was never allowed to cry or show anger. Adoption became my darkest secret, even though my parents told their adult friends.

Social get-togethers were a frequent part of army life, and my parents often hosted parties. Shyness pushed me into my room before guests arrived because I didn't like people showering me with attention. It made me feel awkward, as if I were on display. My parents always gave guests a tour of our house at the beginning of their parties, and I'd hear a knock on my bedroom door. I'd open the door and see my parents standing in front of a crowd of strangers. "Oh, this is Peter. He's so cute." The strangers smiled and my face turned red as my emotions secretly ran inside "the castle." Sheltered safe behind its walls, I watched my body move as if in a dream. I politely shook the hand of each man and woman parading through my room, and only after the crowd left did my feelings venture back out of the castle.

During one of these social affairs, someone knocked on my bedroom door. "Who's there?" I asked, kneeling over parts of a model airplane scattered on newspapers strewn about the floor.

"It's one of your parent's friends," a female voice answered. "We met earlier. Can I come in?"

"Yes, but be careful. I'm building a model and don't want you to step on any of the pieces."

"I'll be careful," she said as the door slowly swung open. I looked up to see one of the women I'd been introduced to earlier. She walked inside and I watched her high heels take baby steps across the floor.

The woman looked down at me. Her mouth stretched into a smile that wasn't matched by her prying eyes. "I'm taking a break from the party. Do you mind if we talk a little bit?"

"No," I said, immediately sensing danger and running back inside the safe confines of my hidden castle. I focused on the pieces of the disassembled plane instead of her.

"What are you building?"

"It's a B-17 Flying Fortress," I said, without looking up and wishing she would go away. I knew she wasn't interested in my model airplane.

"That's great, can I see it when it's done?"

"Yeah," I said, trying to glue a wing to the fuselage.

"You know, you're so special that your parents picked you from all the other children in the orphanage. You were chosen. I've always thought adopted children are the luckiest children in the world."

I tensed and focused hard on inserting the wing's pins into the holes of the plane's main body. Picked like a dog at a pet shop flashed through my mind. I knew she felt sorry for me and I didn't want her pity. Shame and anger tried to grab me, but I hid safe behind the thick castle walls. She might go away if I ignored her.

She paused, looking at me kneeling on the floor. She didn't know what to say or do. I could tell she was surprised I didn't say anything. "Can I help?" she finally asked.

"No, thank you," I didn't want her touching my model.

"Okay. Well, come and show everybody your Flying Fortress after it's finished."

"Okay," I said, knowing I would never show her the plane after it was built.

"Have a good night," she said, and closed the door which shut with a soft thud as I snuck back out of my castle.

I wished, I prayed and desperately hoped she wouldn't tell her kids I was adopted. I wanted so badly to be like all the other children who had their real parents. Terror loomed in the back of my mind that one day my friends might discover the truth.

I looked nothing like my adopted parents. Francis X. Dodds was 5'8", stockily built with blond, wavy hair and sky blue eyes. Tatoos covered the biceps of his muscular arms and he had a pug nose. My mother was small— 5'2", plain looking with a long nose, medium build, brown hair and hazel eyes. I would grow to be 6'1", had angular facial features and a Roman nose beneath dark blue eyes and straight dark hair. Our physical differences glowed like a neon flashing sign; we weren't the same blood.

Boyhood friends sometimes asked why I didn't look like my parents. Sweat poured from under my arms, and I'd feel my body tense as if waiting for the first stroke of a spanking. I'd tell a hasty lie and quickly steer the conversation in a different direction before the subject could turn to adoption.

"I take after my grandfather. You guys wanna go play kick-the-can?" I never wanted anyone to know I was adopted.

I felt different from everyone and believed I didn't fit in the little world where I lived and played. No one, not my adopted parents, friends or teachers could get close. It didn't matter what I did or how hard I tried, nothing would ever be good enough to prove to myself that I was an equal. An iron belief that I wasn't loved or wanted fed my low self-esteem.

I wasn't like my childhood playmates. Although I pretty much looked like everybody else on the outside, on my insides an infinite gulf kept us separated. They had their birth parents; mine had abandoned me.

As a child I never met another kid who had been adopted; I thought I was the only one who'd been rejected. My feelings of isolation might have ended if I'd known another boy or girl who had also been adopted, but feeling alone, I stuffed my damaged feelings. The only way I knew to deal with my shame, anger and loneliness was to escape to the castle. Inside, I was alone and a stranger to the outside world. But I knew my real mother would have the key to unlock the massive, wooden door. She could let me out of the castle and make everything okay.

I discovered my fears were real on a hot summer afternoon between second and third grade. A windowless side of an apartment building provided a backdrop for a game of dodge-ball. The kid who was "it" stood with his back against the wall trying to dodge balls thrown by the rest of the group. Like everyone else, I wanted to be "it" and ran to the front of the wall when my turn came.

I turned to face the others who were fighting over balls before they finally decided everyone would get two balls to throw. They spread into a line ten steps away, but before the first ball was thrown, one of the kids yelled out, "You're adopted."

"No I'm not," I yelled back, devastated that he knew.

"Yes you are, my parents told me you are." His teeth glistened, looking like a wolf about to devour its prey.

"Its a lie. I'm not adopted." I shouted, trapped like a hunted animal with my back against the wall, forced to face my attacker.

"You don't have your real parents. Peter's adopted, Peter's adopted, Peter's adopted," the entire pack joined in, howling the mocking chant.

I was enraged, ashamed, embarrassed. No one had thrown a ball, and I glared at my tormentors with feverish eyes. I would have given anything to disappear.

I had to get away. Pushing my way through the pack as fast as I could, I fled into a nearby forest. Running down a deserted path deep in the thick woods, I looked over my shoulder to make sure they weren't giving chase. When I was sure I was alone I slowed to a walk. My chest heaved as I gulped air, and tears streamed down my face. Why can't I just be like the rest of them? I couldn't help being adopted. It isn't my fault. Something was terribly wrong, and I didn't know what to do. I was ashamed. I was frightened. And I felt alone, so very alone.

Surrounded by towering evergreen trees in the midst of a cool, dark forest, I stopped walking and cried using the bottom of my t-shirt to wipe away the tears. No one could help me. I was too scared to talk about adoption with my parents. All my teachers were gone during the summer. I didn't have any brothers or sisters, and my friends had just ridiculed me. The sense of isolation and helplessness was overwhelming. I promised to keep my adoption secret and never to let anyone get close because that might lead again to ridicule or rejection. Never again would I be abandoned. My castle grew stronger.

The Foreigner

Another part of my adoption experience deepened every feeling of being uprooted, of not belonging and being different. I always knew I wasn't American. My birthplace was in a cold and distant land, a country envied and at the same time hated by Americans. My adopted parents brought with them a new life, a different language and a foreign culture. Francis and Jean Dodds took me from the land of my birth, blood, language and heritage when they adopted me out of a German orphanage while they were stationed in the Federal Republic of Germany. I became a naturalized American citizen and later in my youth felt a deep sadness on being taken from my home and forced to live as a foreigner in a different country. Adoption created a schism, a change from the original to the imitation. It confused me, divided my heart and split my loyalties.

Every feeling of separateness from the people I grew up with was intensified because I was German and they were American. I suffered layers of wounds from being adopted. The first occurred when my birth parents put me in an institution for forsaken children. Then, adoption severed the relationships I had developed during my year-and-a-half in the orphanage. A third blow struck when I was ripped out of Germany and torn from my roots.

I don't remember the day my American parents took me from the orphanage, but the transition isn't difficult to reconstruct. A boy just learning to speak was one day uprooted from his daily surroundings and placed with two strangers, in a different environment. The boy, at best uneasy in his new home, couldn't talk to the two adults because they didn't understand his language. The boy couldn't understand the strangers because they spoke in a tongue he couldn't comprehend either. For the boy, it was an experience of complete isolation.

Being German and raised in the American culture further stripped me of my identity. Adoption destroyed another part of me when it shredded the connection to my heritage. Foreign parents robbed me of my native language when they taught me English, and I lost the ability to speak German. Adopted at the age of two-and-a-half, it took months before I completely lost my German vocabulary. Jean and Francis Dodds probably breathed a sigh of relief when *no* replaced *nein* and the last trace of my mother tongue disappeared.

As I grew older, I felt great pride in being German but didn't tell any-one. That would have forced me to talk about my birth family, and I vowed to keep my adoption secret after the dodge-ball incident. A second reason for hiding my Germanic pride was that Americans hated Germans. At that time while growing up, I saw constant signs that Germans were bad people. Schools taught that the United States had to fight and free the world from German evil, in two world wars. Derogatory words like Hun, Nazi and Kraut were a part of every kid's vocabulary. While growing up, I can't remember anyone saying a good word about Germany, and it added to my belief that I was somehow defective. No one—not teachers, friends or adopted parents—told me any different.

I was at the kitchen table doing my fifth-grade history homework one evening and couldn't answer a question. I asked one of my parents to come and help.

"Why are American soldiers in Germany?" I asked my adopted mother.

"The Germans started a war and we want to make sure they don't do it again," she answered.

I didn't feel any part of the *we* in her last statement. It added to the barrier already dividing us. "Aren't the Germans good people?" I asked.

"No, I don't trust them."

I felt a dagger pierce my heart. What I felt her say was that she didn't trust me.

The trauma of adoption didn't heal with the passage of time. The wounds wouldn't mend, sometimes slipping into quiet remission, other times flaring with nasty ugliness.

"You can't go out and play until you clean your room," my mother said one day while sitting on the living room sofa. Not bothering to look up, she turned a page of her magazine and reached out for her morning cup of coffee resting on the coffee table.

"I cleaned my room," I said, standing at the opposite side of the table.

"You'll have to do a better job. I looked at it five minutes ago and your toys are thrown all over the closet. Clean up the mess and you can go out and play." Then she took a sip of coffee while flipping a page of the magazine.

"I cleaned my closet." The words came out heated and fast. "I want to go and play." I clenched my hands into fists and challenged her with an icy glare. "Let me go out and play. They're waiting for me."

She put the coffee cup on the table and looked up from her magazine for the first time. "Young man, get in your room and do as I say," she said pointing a finger, as a stiff look cut across her face.

"No!" My shoulders and head lurched forward when shouting the word. Venom had replaced defiance.

She sprang off of the sofa and in a flash came around the coffee table, catching me by the arm. I quivered as I saw her raise a hand and felt a searing slap on my bottom.

"Let me go," I gasped, struggling to break free. But she was too big and strong and led me to my bedroom. "Now clean up your closet, and you're not going outside to play at all this morning. Wait until your father gets home for lunch." And the door slammed shut.

My breaths came short and fast, and my clenched fists turned white. "Why did you take me out of the orphanage?" I shouted through the door. "I don't belong here. If you loved me you never would have taken me away." I felt my eyes bulge and blood vessels pop out on my temples.

I waited for her response, but she didn't say anything. My anger simmered until it ignited the fuse of locked-up adoption-feelings and the bomb exploded. I screamed as my face twisted in rage, "If you loved me you would have left me where I belonged. You're not my real mother." I stomped to the dresser, grabbed the model airplane and broke both its wings as the fuselage fell against the floor. Rage blinded me against all thoughts, except the obsession to pulverize the B-17 Flying Fortress. I threw one wing against the bed, then the other. My chest heaved with each gasp for air. A fire inside me burned, from my stomach to my eyes. Tears streamed down my face. I raised a foot and crushed the plane's broken body. Nothing could stop the spewing volcano. I rushed across the room and snatched one of the broken wings. With a vicious growl I snapped the wing in two, slamming both pieces to the floor. Tears seared my eyes as I grabbed the second wing. Its jagged edges cut into my hands before I threw it against the floor. I stood above the broken pieces, raised a knee and slammed down my foot, feeling the plastic crunch. Again and again I stomped the broken plane. It disintegrated into unrecognizable pieces. The model destroyed, I threw myself face-first on the bed and screamed with all my strength into the pillow. Screams were the only medicine to soothe adoption's pain. I screamed uncontrollably until the pillow became soaked. Finally, my rage melted to grief, a sorrow so deep that it punctured the marrow in my bones. Crying and exhausted on the bed, thoughts of my real mother materialized, and I longed for the day when I would find her.

Still, I cried until the pain subsided. Guilt crept in and I slid off the bed to sweep-up the pieces of smashed plane. The dresser mirror threw back bloodshot eyes, and my voice turned hoarse as I whispered regrets over destroying a model I'd lovingly built. I heard my father come home and tip-toed to the bedroom door, pressing my ear against the frame.

"He had another temper-tantrum. I don't know what to do," my mother said.

My father took a deep breath and blew out of his mouth. "I don't know either," he sighed.

Army boots marched down the hallway and I scurried from the door to earnestly clean my closet. A couple of knocks sounded on the door. "Time for lunch," my father said, and the boots marched away.

I put down the toys, slid past the bedroom door and slithered down the hallway. I stared at the floor and headed to the dining room where I took my assigned seat. We ate lunch, but my parents didn't mention my temper-tantrum. They ignored it, as if it never happened.

My adopted parents didn't know how to resolve my emotional upheaval. To their great credit, they never once threatened to put me back in an orphanage, although they certainly must have privately second-guessed their decision to adopt me. My temper-tantrums continued until they sought outside help.

I didn't know the bearded, bald-headed man wearing thick-rimmed glasses was a psychologist. My parents stayed in the reception area as I followed the weird looking man into his office. He sat behind a wooden desk, a desk so shiny that it reflected his face. I sat on a large, wooden chair, terrified of the man to my front. I retreated deep inside the castle, to protect myself from fear. He asked a lot of questions and, too afraid not to reply, I answered with subdued yes's or no's, while keeping my eyes glued to the floor. Was this stranger going to take me away? I hated the bald-headed man, and he only reinforced my belief that something was terribly wrong. I only saw him once, but afterwards buried all signs of emotions caused by adoption. It was safer to hide my feelings.

Every day while growing up, every single day, I thought about finding the woman who carried me for nine months and brought me into the world. Some mornings she was the first thought that popped into my head, other times the last hazy reflection before falling asleep. The idea of finding her would materialize while I sat in a classroom or when I rode in a car. Not one day passed where I didn't think of finding my birth mother.

I didn't have any expectations about who or what she might be, no fantasies about my birth mother being an aristocratic duchess or a beautiful movie star. A blind passion filled every fiber in my body and pushed me toward her. Nature filled me with an all-powerful desire to reunite with my own flesh and blood, just as Nature drives salmon to return to the river where they were spawned. The fish dies at the end of the journey, but the force driving the salmon back to its birthplace is stronger than death.

The invisible bond between mother and child blazed inside me like a roaring furnace, but the desire to find my birth father became almost an afterthought. I felt no scorching compulsion to discover him, as compared to the obsession to find my birth mother. Reuniting with her was a desire that distance and time could not diminish.

The first clue to finding the key that would open the castle door came when I was twelve years old. My parents left me alone in the house when they departed for a Sunday afternoon drive. My stomach tingled with excitement as I watched them drive away. It felt strange being in an empty house, but at the same time the freedom was electrifying. I turned the television on to a football game, grabbed a pop from the refrigerator and kicked back in my father's easy chair, pretending to be grown-up. It was boring. I turned the TV off, guzzled the rest of the pop and burped. Afterwards, I realized I didn't have to put my hand over my mouth because my parents were gone. Flexing new found muscles of independence, I thought about forbidden places to explore, things I could do since they weren't home. Where would I start...?

I headed to my adopted parents' bedroom to uncover the mysteries hidden in their dresser drawers and closets. Doing the forbidden excited me, but the great secrets I'd hoped to uncover turned out to be pretty boring stuff—clothes. Their dresser drawers didn't contain any great discoveries, only socks, a jewelry box, underwear, gloves, sweaters. What's the big deal I wondered? In the bottom drawer, hidden beneath a pile of neatly folded clothes, lay a large brown envelope. It looked strange and out of place, so I had to discover its contents. I carefully slid the envelope out of the drawer and sat on the edge of their king-size bed, unwinding a thick string binding the packet. I peeled back the flap and peeked inside—only a bunch of official-looking papers. I stretched the opening of the envelope wider to get a better look but still saw only papers. There weren't even any photographs. How boring.

Wanting to see what the papers were about, I shook the envelope a few times and dumped the contents onto the bed. The pages were different shapes and sizes, all typewritten with some in English and others in German. Suddenly, I lost sight of everything but the papers strewn on the bed.

The envelope contained documents about my birth and adoption. My hands trembled as I gazed at each piece of paper, and I breathed in short, fast gasps. I couldn't understand the papers written in German. But I read my birth certificate that had been translated into English. Other papers discussed my adopted parents' good character saying they were well qualified to adopt children. What if they walked in? I took a risk and continued examining the remaining documents.

I picked up a piece of yellow paper that had writing on both sides. The document had been translated from German into English. It read:

CERTIFIED TRUE TRANSLATION
First Copy

No. 1019 Year 1956
the Document Register   Gross-Gerau on 7 July 1956.

Declaration Of Consent

Before me the undersigned Notary Public Dr. ARTHUR KEIL with offices at Gross-Gerau appeared today:

Miss Ilse Sander, a clerk, born at Kunzendorf on 31 December 1920, residing at 64 Frankfurter Strasse, Mörfelden.

The identity of the party was ascertained by presentation of her German Federal Identity Card with photograph NO. HE 089596, issued by the mayor of the Community of Mörfelden on 22 November 1955.

The party states:
I am the mother of the illegitimate child PETER FRIEDRICH SANDER, born at Darmstadt on 23 June 1955.

As the mother of the child I give my consent that the child may be adopted by a couple appointed by the Gross-Gerau Youth Office.

I give this declaration towards the adopters as well as towards the competent court and other offices irrevocably. I grant first copy of this statement to the adopters and all concerned offices.

I give up claim to be notified of the confirmation of the guardianship court and of the decree regarding the acknowledgement by the guardianship court resp. district court.

I, hereby, state that I was informed of the irrevocability of these declarations.

The party states that she is a German citizen. The acting notary made sure of this by inspection of her Federal Identity Card with photograph.

Read aloud and approved by the party and personally signed by her and the notary as follows:

t/ILSE SANDER
t/Dr. KEIL, Notary Public.

My heart beat wildly, and breaths pounded in rapid bursts so loud that I became aware of my breathing. I didn't look at any other paperwork and hastily stuffed all the documents back into the brown envelope. I shoved the packet into the bottom of the dresser drawer and covered it with a pile of neatly folded clothes. I shut the drawer and raced from the bedroom to look out the living room window. Good, my parents' car was still gone.

I didn't know what illegitimate meant so I pulled the dictionary off a living room bookcase shelf. Fumbling through the pages, I went to the "I" section, found the word illegitimate and read its definition: 1. Against the law; illegal. 2. Born out of wedlock; bastard. 3. Not in correct grammatical usage. 4. Incorrectly deduced.

I traveled back to adoption's wreckage and found the stone of *illegitimacy*. I picked it up and carried its stone to the castle. I added *illegitimacy* to the walls.

Adoption's Tragic Flaw

Growing up in a military family meant constant change as my adopted family moved to a new army post every two or three years. What I needed most was stability, but instead grew up with a steady series of uprootings and constant change, which fed my insecurities. We moved from Germany to Georgia after I was adopted. Then to Texas, back to Germany, then Missouri and arrived in California by the time I was eleven. Living in a variety of places exposed me to a diversity of kids and survival meant learning how to blend in with new groups. This lifestyle offered other pluses too. I developed a worldly view, excelled in geography and knew how to get along with kids of different personalities, races and backgrounds. But life as a transient came with a major price tag—instability—and it added to my emotional upheaval. I never had long-term friends, and it hurt every time we moved. At our new home I picked up the pieces of my wounded heart and started another life. Shyness was the by-product of strange surroundings, but as I settled into my new environment I gradually attained a comfort level and made new friends... until we moved again a few years later. My boyhood was an extended experience of loss. The major lesson I learned was an emotional one—people to whom I became attached always left. I feared growing close to anyone.

My parents adopted a second child when we returned to Germany. Michelle was adopted from a German orphanage while still an infant. Unlike me, she seemed to adjust well to her new home. The age difference when we were adopted—six months verses two-and-a-half years—may have accounted for some of our dissimilarity. My sister and I lived in the same house but may as well have lived on different planets. Michelle tended to be quiet, artistic and dedicated to her studies, while I was outgoing, athletic and not much for school. Besides our dissimilar interests, a six-year age gap resulted in us having separate friends. We had little in common except growing up in a home with parents to whom we weren't connected biologically. There was little sibling rivalry for our parents' love as I never bonded to my adopted parents and had nothing to compete for. Michelle could have their affection as far as I was concerned. My sister and I weren't close and didn't talk about adoption until we reached adulthood.

We had lived in Missouri for little less than a year when my father received orders to Vietnam. While he spent a year in Southeast Asia, my mom, sister and I lived with an aunt in Los Angeles.

I was in the sixth grade that year and enrolled in a Catholic school where strict nuns demanded the most from every student. I liked the challenge, did well academically, and after coming out of my shell, made good friends.

What should have been my reaction to God at the age of eleven? Devout parents who adhered to every ritual of the Catholic faith raised me. But the strict environment of the Catholic school ran counter to my independent nature. Nuns never spared the rod for my slightest misbehavior. Mass was said in a language I didn't understand—Latin. I learned to count each of my sins and knew God was angry every time I did something wrong. He would get even by making me burn in purgatory or sending me to hell. But, instead of fearing or hating God, I loved Him.

I liked the nuns, or rather, I liked the habits the nuns wore. Although I can't consciously remember, I'm certain it was a Catholic orphanage where I lived for eighteen months. During my time there, I bonded to the sisters who gave me nurturing and unconditional love. My unconscious memory never forgot the black and white garments worn by those selfless women.

In the sixth grade I decided to become an altar boy. During lunch or after school I sometimes snuck into the empty church at the edge of the schoolyard. Careful to ensure no one watched, I slid past the door and slowly walked to the front row pew. Giving one last look to make sure the church was empty, I knelt in front of statues of Christ and the saints. My favorite was the Blessed Virgin Mary holding the baby Jesus. Mary looked beautiful and serene while peacefully gazing down at her son. It made me feel good to look at Jesus so happy in His mother's arms and clutching her garments with tiny hands. Soft waves of light from groups of candles in devotion boxes seemed to bring the statues to life. After kneeling a few minutes, I'd stop reciting Our Fathers and Hail Marys to stare upward and gaze into the face of the Madonna who held her only son. My boyhood troubles vanished into a wonderful calm, and I knew Jesus and his mother wanted, accepted and loved me. I didn't think it or want it; I *knew* it.

The same feeling descended on me the second time I served a mass as an altar boy. It was more than a feeling; it was an understanding that I was loved no matter what I did or what had happened to me. I felt a warm and tranquil sensation spread throughout my mind, body and heart. For a few moments life became pure joy. I couldn't control that feeling; it wasn't like turning a light switch on and off. But the same awareness visited me often the first month I was an altar boy. I connected it to God and the Catholic Church and decided I wanted to become a priest. My mother didn't like my idea of joining the clergy, and I was surprised when she told me she hoped I'd instead become a doctor or a lawyer. The idea of entering the priesthood eventually faded, but I never forgot the love I experienced during those moments in the sixth grade.

My father returned from Vietnam at the end of my sixth-grade year. We left Los Angeles for Bozeman where he served his last tour of duty as an R.O.T.C. instructor at Montana State University. Once again I had to leave my friends and start a new life. I reverted to a shy, quiet boy, until I made friends. Then I became my more natural, extroverted self.

In Montana, I was enrolled in another Catholic school and tried out for the basketball team in the seventh grade. In practices I ran quicker and faster, jumped higher and shot better than most of my counterparts. I made the team and became one of the starting players. Basketball was fun and gave me a healthy outlet for my energy. Sports provided incentives and a sense of direction, taught discipline and brought friendships at the vulnerable age when I began adolescence. Without basketball, I might have fallen into juvenile delinquency because my buried, chaotic emotions demanded release. Instead, I discovered the value of teamwork and found comradery based on mutual respect for each other's talents and skills. I liked the discipline sports required, the locker room pranks, the excitement and competition of games. It offered the opportunity to set individual goals and work with others to achieve team goals. Progress depended on my work ethic. I could regularly make six out of ten free throws, but I wanted to do better and stayed in the gym after practice, shooting free throws until I consistently made seven out of ten shots. That made me feel good and imparted a sense of achievement.

I respected the coaches and to this day can remember every one by their first and last names. Basketball gave me self-esteem and positive recognition from my friends. It was also the first activity where I stood out, in a positive manner, from my friends. I loved to practice and play in the games, not to mention the attention it drew from girls. I played basketball all year long and dreamed of one day becoming a college basketball player.

Coaches said I had natural talent when I was a high-school freshman. During practices and games, I instinctively knew how to glide between players and make a seemingly impossible shot. I loved it when I'd snatch a rebound from the outstretched grasp of an opposing player, block a shot or make a pass that led to one of my team-mates making an easy shot. Self-consciousness disappeared when I played basketball, and it was the first time in my life I felt totally free. Yet, when I stepped off the basketball court the feeling of belonging left me, and emotional insecurities resurfaced.

We were still living in Montana during my sophomore year in high school, a special year when I experienced my first love. She was a freshman named Jean Daems, and she caught my eye during the chaotic first week at the start of the new school year. I couldn't approach her though. I didn't know what to say and was frightened she might know I liked her. I did nothing except try to catch glimpses of her during the opening weeks of school and found myself liking her more and more, even though we had never said a word. One night, after mustering all my courage, I called Jean and asked her to the Homecoming football dance. I'd never been that scared in all my life and would have been devastated if she said no. To my immeasurable relief, she accepted.

Jean was my first real date. My dad chauffeured us to and from the Homecoming dance, since I was too young to drive. I had never been as nervous as I was during that date and didn't know what to do or say. Jean didn't seem to mind, and we managed to start talking at the end of the night while my dad drove us back to her house. I walked her to the door with the car's headlights shining in our faces. We didn't touch or even hold hands. I certainly wouldn't try to kiss her—God, I'd never kissed a girl before. We said goodnight, and I bashfully walked back to the car.

"Nice girl, son," my dad said as he pulled away from her house.

"Yeah," I responded, not wanting him to know that I really liked her.

Jean and I saw much more of each other after the Homecoming dance. We'd meet between classes, or I'd help carry her books while walking her home after school. We had two more formal dates—both meetings at a local hamburger stand for milkshakes on Saturday nights. As I got to know her better, I felt something new tugging at my heart. It was warm and made me tingle with excitement, but I fought to bury the new feelings inside. Jean made me feel good, but at the same time I was scared of her. Besides, what if she didn't really like me?

She invited me to her house on a Saturday afternoon later in the fall. We hung out in the living room for a couple of hours playing silly games and laughing the entire time. The hours quickly passed until I had to leave to go home for dinner. Jean walked me to her front door where I put on my coat and stood silently looking at her with one hand gripping the door-knob. Surely she knew how much I liked her, and my face flushed red with embarrassment. Panic started to overwhelm me, and I decided to bolt saying, "I'll call you tomorrow," and turned the doorknob.

"Wait," Jean said. "The Sadie Hawkins dance is next weekend. I wanted to ask if you would go with me?"

Did I hear her right? Did she ask me to the girl-ask-boy dance? My heart felt like it was going to leap out of my chest. Everything around me seemed to whirl. The redness of embarrassment disappeared as blood drained out of my head, and I turned ashen white. My head didn't feel like it was attached to my body, and I was numb all over. "S-s-sure," I replied, wondering if I'd answered a question that she really asked.

"Great," she said smiling, and moved past me to open the door. In the swell of excitement I hadn't realized I'd dropped my hand off the doorknob and both my arms hung limp at my sides. Jean looked so calm, in contrast to the typhoon that roared inside me. I walked out the door barely feeling my body and moved as if in a dream.

"Call me, and we can work out the details," she said. I listened while walking backwards on the porch, keeping my eyes glued to her foggy form. I missed the first step and clumsily stumbled to both hands and a knee.

"I meant to do that," I joked, quickly regaining my balance and standing straight. Heat flashed across my face from embarrassment.

"Sure you did. Talk to you tomorrow," she said closing the door with a grin.

"See ya." I carefully turned around on the porch steps, stuffed both hands in my jeans and tried to walk casually down the remaining steps.

I had to concentrate just to walk in a normal manner. Was I dreaming? I felt light-headed and a wonderful explosion erupted in my chest as I realized Jean really liked me. At the bottom of the stairs I turned right and started running down the sidewalk. A block away, when I knew she couldn't see me if she looked out a window, I screeched to a stop. I yanked both hands out of my jean pockets and threw them into the air hollering,"Yeeaaah." When the sound of my voice stopped echoing down the quiet residential street, I tucked my elbows tightly against my sides and clenched both fists to my front like a boxer. Then I danced in a small circle on the corner sidewalk. Jean had asked me to the Sadie Hawkins! Jean asked me to the Sadie Hawkins! Unable to contain my joy, I threw both arms into the air and let loose another, "Yeeaaah."

Jean's request filled me with an inexhaustible energy, and I started running home. I felt like I could fly and leapt from the sidewalk, galloping over the tops of cars parallel-parked on the street. Automobile hoods, roofs and trunks thumped beneath my feet as I sprinted down the line of cars. Every thought and ounce of energy I had was aimed at Jean. She asked me out! She likes me! I arrived home, out of breath and walked into the kitchen. But I didn't say a word about Jean to my parents.

Jean and I became better friends as we spent more and more time together. I was first string on the Junior Varsity basketball team and she was a
cheerleader. I knew she had to cheer for everyone on the team, but in my
heart I knew she cheered loudest for me. During the games I never thought
of her, I couldn't. I was too intense and focused on playing. But after the
game we'd sit together and watch the varsity play. She always gave me a
critique of the J.V. game and said she was proud to be my girlfriend.

After one of my basketball games, I bought two sodas from the conces-
sion stand before going inside the gym to find Jean. She was sitting in the
bleachers with the other cheerleaders and waved at me as I searched the
stands from the ground level. I saw her and immediately smiled, then
danced up the bleachers, careful not to spill any pop from the cups. Before
I sat down she asked, "Can we go and sit on the other side of the gym
where there aren't as many people? I don't feel very good."

"Sure," I said, and an ache of sadness ricochetted through my heart as I
watched her stoop to pick up her gym bag. We walked to the other side of
the gym and sat on an empty bleacher.

"What's wrong?" I asked.

"I've got a bad headache." She rubbed her temples with both hands
while looking down at her saddle shoes.

By now I knew her well and could tell she was in pain. She looked pale
and didn't have her usual spunk. I felt terrible and my heart ached as I
watched her suffer.

"Drink this coke; it might help." I offered her one of the cups. "Do you
have any aspirin?"

"I took some after your game, but it didn't do any good."

We sat and watched the varsity play as I raked my mind trying to figure
out how I could make her feel better. It was the first time I understood the
meaning of powerlessness. I could do nothing except offer feeble words, "I'm
sorry you feel so bad. I wish I could have your headache so you wouldn't
have to hurt. I'd gladly take your pain if it would make you feel better."

She turned her head toward me and softly smiled. "Will you walk me
home?"

"I'll do anything for you," I said.

Still, after six months of dating, I hadn't told Jean that I loved her. I couldn't. The irrational fear of abandonment and rejection was too deeply planted in my emotional makeup. Telling Jean I loved her was too great a risk. Part of me knew that if I grew to love people, they went away. So if I didn't tell her what I truly felt, she would stay.

Jean never told me she loved me, and I was happy she didn't. Maybe she was waiting for me to say it first. Perhaps she was too young to express her heart's sentiment verbally, or she might have known how terrified I was of those three words. Still, we had a tremendous unspoken love.

Although I couldn't tell Jean I loved her, I wanted to tell her I was adopted. With a copy of the Consent of Release form tucked into my flannel shirt pocket, I set out for Jean's house on a Saturday morning, determined to tell her my darkest secret. I planned to hand her the paperwork, ask her to read it in my presence and take my chances with her reaction. The morning passed without me giving Jean the piece of paper. Then the afternoon streaked by. The moment never seemed quite right, and the adoption paperwork remained buttoned inside my flannel shirt pocket. Darkness fell, and I had to go home. I held her while we said goodbye as my every thought and ounce of willpower yelled for me to give her the paperwork. My mind screamed, give her the paperwork. Give her the paperwork. But I didn't do it. I was trapped inside the castle and held back by shame, guilt and embarrassment.

In early April Jean and I agreed to meet at the University fieldhouse and watch Montana State play a basketball game. Jean had arrived earlier and rushed out of the stands to greet me. She grabbed me by the hand and led me to our seats. She smiled, a smile that glowed and lit up her entire face. Hand in hand we walked up the bleachers with Jean looking at me the entire time. I felt her beautiful warmth cascading out her hand and knew in my heart of hearts that she loved me. We sat down, with Jean still looking at me as we continued holding hands. She was bursting with happiness and energy and started telling me all the little things she had done that day, her words interrupted only by flashes of her sparkling smile. As she talked, I took my hand away from hers, sat back in the bleacher and crossed my arms.

She continued talking but a questioning look replaced her lovely smile. "Are you okay?"

I didn't look at her and stared stone-faced at the basketball court without even comprehending a game was being played. Ice ran through my veins as I sat inside the castle walls.

"Well don't saying anything then," and she put an arm around my shoulder, leaned forward and kissed my cheek.

As she sat on the bleacher with her arm draped around my shoulder, she didn't know I was locked away, a prisoner from the outside world. I knew Jean only loved a part of me, the part of me I shared. She couldn't love all of me because I wouldn't share my terrible secret. If she knew I was adopted, she'd leave. I withdrew into the castle for protection.

I sat on the varnished pine bleacher and barely felt the weight of Jean's arm pressed against me. How did I get into the castle? I wanted out. I wanted to feel. I wanted to tell my beautiful girlfriend sitting beside me that I loved her. I wanted to share with Jean my deepest secret. Yet I stood inside the castle, pounding my fists against the massive wooden door. But it was fruitless. Inside the castle there was no passion, no emotion and no feeling. The protecting walls were made of my own sentiments, and I had no feelings on the inside.

At the age of fifteen I didn't have the ability to probe my emotions and search out reasons for my behavior. I didn't know why I was destroying the relationship with the girl I loved. My mind was shocked at my behavior. If someone had suggested that my being adopted was the reason for my destructive actions, I wouldn't have believed them. But it wouldn't have mattered, even if I had understood my behavior. I had no tools for healing.

Jean and I continued sitting together on the bleachers, but I no longer felt expressions of her emotion because the protective fortress I'd constructed blocked out all emotions. Her warmth, energy and love were on the outside of the castle and couldn't penetrate its heavy walls. I could sense her thoughts though. "Please come out, Peter. What did I do?" She hadn't done anything except love me, and I didn't believe I was loveable. Despite my best efforts, I couldn't stop from sabotaging our relationship. I had to withdraw inside the castle where I was safe. Finally, Jean left at halftime because I hadn't said a word to her. That night was the end of my first love.

The Quest Begins

We left Montana for Pensacola, a city located on Florida's northwest Gulf Coast, after I completed my sophomore year. The move uprooted me again as I left friends and stable surroundings behind. I spent my junior and senior years in a public high school with 1600 students, an enormous change from the Catholic high school in Bozeman with a student body of only 100. I ached for my friends in Montana and insecurities again resurfaced, the same insecurities that appeared every time we moved. I thought everyone was smarter, that all the guys were better looking and that everyone fit in—except me. I felt unwanted and believed that no matter what I did to try and be accepted, it would never be good enough. I reverted back to a shy and quiet loner. This time I wouldn't break out of my shell for several years.

The move had one positive effect, however: I got serious about academics. Not knowing anyone, and being too reserved to make new friends, I had nothing to do after school except study. Later in the school year I tried out for basketball and made the team. I wasn't first string, but sports continued to provide a positive activity and kept me away from drugs, alcohol and gangs. The basketball team gave me a good group of guys for friends, but girls frightened me, and I didn't go out on a date my entire junior year.

The Navy trains its pilots at Pensacola, and sleek military jets often roared overhead. I watched open-mouthed as the Blue Angels, the Navy's precision aerial stunt team, practiced their daredevil maneuvers at incredible speeds. The planes criss-crossed overhead, roared by upside-down at altitudes so low I could see the pilots' helmets, and flew in formations so tight it seemed as if their wing-tips touched. Sleek, fast and free, I thought. It made my blood pump with excitement, and I decided to become a Navy fighter pilot. I imagined flying my jet far above the earth and escaping my feelings of loneliness.

At the start of my senior year, I applied for admission to the United States Naval Academy. Graduating from Annapolis would allow me to begin my dream of flying. But first, I planned to take a trip to Germany during the summer between high school graduation and the start of the Naval Academy. I imagined finding my mother and then returning to America to start my studies at Annapolis.

Making plans to find my mother filled me with hope, enthusiasm and confidence. Instead of only dreaming and wishing, I was taking action to achieve my goals. My dreams would soon become reality, and the anticipation of finding the woman whom I had thought about every day my entire life kept me awake many nights. My parents encouraged my efforts to enter Annapolis, but I never told them about the plan to find my birth mother.

But events didn't unfold the way I expected—the Naval Academy didn't accept me. So I developed a second plan to get into flight school and decided to go to college for an engineering degree. I enrolled at Auburn University, located in Alabama, and began studying industrial engineering. At Auburn I joined a Navy program that would send me to Officer Candidate School and then to flight school. My second plan also failed. After taking a battery of tests, I received a letter from the Department of the Navy thanking me for my interest in aviation but stating I failed to qualify for their flight program.

The content of the letter crushed me, but I knew how to handle feelings of rejection—I stuffed them and didn't tell anyone about my failure. Only my adopted parents knew, but like their love, I emotionally rejected all their letters and phone calls offering consolation and support.

I discovered later that the dark cloud of shattered flying dreams had a silver lining. When one door closes, new ones open. I pursued other options that gave me new hope. Engineering seemed dry and boring, so I changed my major to history, a subject I'd always enjoyed. An insatiable curiosity about people and past events drew me in this direction. I wanted to know how people lived in the past, what they thought and how they viewed the world in which they lived. I focused on middle-European history and concentrated on Germany. Studying history increased my longing to return there and fueled the yearning to renew my heritage. History majors were required to study one year of a foreign language. Naturally, I chose German. I learned basic grammar and vocabulary, skills I hoped would one day help in the search to find my birth mother.

Still wanting to become a military pilot, I investigated Auburn's Air Force ROTC program. There weren't any openings, so that ended my attempts to pursue a career in military aviation. But I still wanted to serve in the Armed Forces and become part of any exciting, adventurous and challenging military option still available. Infantry in the Army sounded as if it would meet my needs. I enrolled in Army ROTC and would be commissioned a second lieutenant after earning my college degree. Like father like son, I entered the profession of the man who adopted me.

At the end of my sophomore year in college I joined a fraternity. Auburn had over 16,000 students, and I felt more lost than when in high school. I needed a small group to associate with because I hadn't established many friendships. I still hurt from the Montana uprooting and thought joining a fraternity would provide opportunities to find new friends and enrich my academic, athletic and social life.

The desire to join a fraternity was also a quest to belong. I struggled with my identity, but my efforts to fit into groups never worked. I didn't know who I was, so I played the role I thought others wanted of me. Living a facade wasn't comfortable. Emotionally immature and socially underdeveloped, I thought joining a fraternity would lead me to myself.

I joined Pi Kappa Phi and discovered companionship based on bonds of mutual academic, athletic and social interests. I took part in small study groups and played basketball for the fraternity intermural team. But the bonds I developed with my fraternity brothers, like the links with high-school basketball teammates, weren't deep. Although we played and studied together, a chasm still separated me from them. The fear of ridicule and rejection again prevented me from honestly expressing myself and caused me to conform to a group culture. I never discussed my feelings about being adopted and remained a quiet loner.

My fraternity had an active social program with a party nearly every week. I drank my first beer in my college fraternity and hated the taste but loved the effect. Insecurities evaporated when booze numbed my mind. Drinking caused my loneliness to vanish. While under the influence of alcohol, I thought everyone liked me, and I was handsome, charming and irresistible to women. The terrible separateness dividing me from others also seemed to disappear. I drank excessively at every party because I wanted a stronger connection with people. Intoxication provided an unexpected key to open my castle door. It allowed me to step outside my fortress walls. Beer drinking gave me what I had always wanted—release from negative emotions that had resulted from childhood abandonment and rejection. Drinking made me feel like I belonged. When drunk, I was transformed from a quiet loner to an obnoxious hellraiser.

I grew to love the taste of beer and drank as much as I could whenever I could. I created occasions to drink because I constantly wanted to escape feelings of isolation and loneliness. Soon, my fraternity brothers unanimously elected me social chairman because of my social and drinking prowess. They couldn't have made a better choice. I excelled at planning and organizing the social calendar. Every party and dance I scheduled gave me the opportunity to bond with my fraternity brothers, drink beer and chase women. Pi Kappa Phi had a busy social calendar while I was the social chairman.

But, of course, drinking had negative side effects. I lost control nearly every time I drank and often passed out or blacked out. On mornings after a drinking spree, fraternity brothers often asked if I remembered what I had done the night before. Always too embarrassed to say no, I laughed with them as they told what I believed were exaggerated tales about my exploits. I soon realized drinking had became a problem and tried to control it. Before parties I often vowed to drink only three beers, but despite my good intentions, I went on to drink a fourth, and a fifth, and once again make a fool of myself. Then suffering a hangover the next morning, I swore I'd never drink again, but at the next party I'd go off on another binge. During this time, I stopped going to church, too hungover on Sunday mornings to get out of bed.

While I played the role of the fraternity clown, part of me liked it because it brought attention. But inside I still felt separated from others. I knew there was more to me than just being a clown. So I rationalized my drinking as just a passing phase and believed my problems with alcohol would eventually go away.

Sometimes I drank by myself, getting rid of the haunting loneliness that continually plagued me. Sitting alone in my room with a six pack, I'd listen to Neil Young sing about loners, isolation and grief. I lived the words he sang and often cried in a drunken stupor, finishing one beer and opening another. In my alcoholic daze, I occasionally glimpsed a ray of happiness shining in the distance as if reflecting from a mirror. I tried to concentrate on that beam of happiness and in my mind reached out to grab it. But instead of capturing the feeling I hit the solid glass and felt that happiness remained locked behind the mirror's surface.

I couldn't understand why alcohol caused me problems. My adopted parents were social drinkers and didn't have any problems with their drinking. What I had first thought was the key to open the castle door turned out to be nothing more than an illusion. Booze provided only a temporary cure for my inadequacy because once the drunkenness wore off, I was still the same man.

A passion for basketball remained, and I became a gym-rat, playing four or five nights a week. Guys showed up at the gym and we'd play until eleven o'clock when the doors closed. One night, in the fall of my last year at Auburn, I finished playing and dribbled a basketball on the walk back to my fraternity house. Passing some of the dorms on the way home, I caught sight of a coed leaning out a third-floor window. Darkness obscured my view, and it looked as if she wore a white towel around her head. I thought she was looking at me so I stopped, cradled the ball in my arms and asked, "Why are you wearing a towel around your head?"

She laughed. "You must be blind; I'm not wearing anything on my head. Come closer and see for yourself."

I left the sidewalk and moved to the edge of the building to get a better view. What I had mistaken for a towel turned out to be her thick, platinum blonde hair. "Gosh, I'm sorry. I thought your hair was a towel," I said feeling awkward at my mistake.

She laughed again, "It's okay and nothing to worry about. Why are you out so late?"

"I just finished playing basketball and am on my way back to my fraternity house. Why are you hanging out the window?"

"I just needed some fresh air after studying and didn't feel like going outside. What fraternity are you in?"

"Pi Kappa Phi. What's your name?"

"Karen Rice. What's yours?"

We talked for an hour as I looked up from the ground with Karen leaning out the window. She and I went out a few nights later and dated the entire year. Karen was a true Southern Belle from Mountain Brook, Alabama. She talked with a lovely Southern accent and was 5'6" with sky-blue eyes. Karen was pretty, athletic and outgoing. She had been a cheerleader in high school and was in a sorority. Her good looks, energy and extroverted personality attracted me, but we didn't have a deep relationship. I never grew to love Karen, but she was a lot of fun. That suited me just fine, since I was fraternity social chairman and a consummate beer drinker.

I kept my adoption a secret throughout college and had no intention of ever telling anyone. Again, things didn't work out as I planned. One evening Karen and I played pool at a local tavern. I was drunk when we left the tavern. We went up to my fraternity room, and Karen lay on my bed. I turned the stereo on low and slumped into a chair by my desk. Nervously rubbing my hands together, I sat facing her.

"There's something I have to tell you," I said, in a voice just barely louder than the rock and roll playing on the stereo. I turned my head from her and stared out the window. Alcohol started breaking the defenses that shielded my insecurities.

Karen picked up my serious mood and sat up on the bed. She looked at me with a blank stare. "What is it?"

I didn't respond immediately. Seconds seemed to stretch into minutes as I considered a way to tell her my terrible secret. Blank thoughts raced through my mind, but my heart forced words into my mouth.

"I don't know; I've never told anyone," I said. Despite my desire for self-control, I felt tears forming in my eyes. I hated to feel that way. I hated having the emotions of a little boy but couldn't deny my painful feelings. Sitting straight up in the chair, I stared a hole through the window while clasping my hands between my legs.

Karen realized I wasn't my normal self. "It's okay; you can trust me," she said, leaning back on both arms. What's bothering you, Peter? Do you want another beer?"

It was the rare occasion I turned down a drink. "No thanks, I've had too much. There's something you don't know about me." I stopped. Despite the stereo music, a roaring silence engulfed the room as Karen waited for me to continue.

"I'm afraid if I tell you, you'll leave me, that you won't want to see me any more. I've never told this to anyone—ever," and the first tear dropped from my eye and slid down my cheek. I wiped it away and shook my head in disgust because I was allowing myself to be vulnerable.

"You can tell me; it's okay."

Even in my intoxicated cocoon, shame filled me as the emotional memory of the dodge-ball incident raised its ugly head. I didn't love Karen, but I trusted her. She had a warm and kind heart. "My parents in Florida aren't my real parents. They... they... they adopted me from a German orphanage. My real parents didn't keep me," and I looked at her for the first time since sitting down. I expected her to run out of the room and slam the door shut saying she didn't want anything to do with me.

"Is that it? Is that what's been bothering you?" Karen smiled, got off the bed and went to the refrigerator to grab a beer. "It's no big deal." She opened the beer and took a swallow.

"You mean you're not going to leave me?" I asked, looking at her in disbelief.

"Of course not. You should have told me sooner and saved yourself a lot of grief. Now, do you want to go to the street dance next weekend? I heard there's going to be a great band playing, and it ought to be a lot of fun."

Telling Karen my secret changed the way I felt about revealing my adoption to others. She didn't leave me after I shared my greatest sorrow. She didn't reject me, and the memory of the dodge-ball affair began to soften. Karen helped me to realize I could discuss my adoption background without feeling shame or guilt.

Army ROTC proved exactly what I had hoped it would be—rigorous and challenging. I learned to fire a rifle, to navigate in the woods with only a map and compass and to rappel off of cliffs. Between my junior and senior years I volunteered for Airborne training, the Army's three-week parachute school. I parachuted five times—three from propeller-driven aircraft and twice from jets. My father had been a paratrooper, and he attended my graduation ceremony, pinning silver parachute wings to the chest of my khaki uniform. Army ROTC gave me confidence and a sense of accomplishment. I realized I could make something of myself.

The Army also gave me a direction in which to focus my attention and energy. I accepted the belief that the Soviet Union was an evil empire and I was going to become part of a military force to keep them in check. Studying history taught me about the long-standing animosity between Russia and my beloved Germany. The Army gave me a purpose. I'd be protecting both the United States and the country of my birth when I began my service as an Army officer. I needed an outlet for repressed feelings and began to focus my anger on the Soviet Union. It was easier than keeping it bottled inside.

The Army required its senior ROTC cadets to fill out what was known as a dream sheet. On the dream sheet I listed the three locations where I wanted to be stationed after attending my basic training. I listed Germany as my first choice. If the Army sent me to Germany, I'd be there for three years and could finally undertake the search for my mother. I also completed paperwork requesting my branch assignment and picked infantry from one of 23 army specialties.

I received a letter from the Army a few weeks before graduating from Auburn University. The letter stated that I'd been selected for the infantry and, after my initial training, would be assigned to Germany. I was ecstatic and threw the letter onto the desk in my room. I ran to find Karen to share the good news. Then I called my parents and everyone else I knew. It marked the beginning of my search to find my birth mother.

Initiation into Manhood

Four months after graduation I reported to Fort Benning, Georgia to attend the Infantry Officer Basic Course. I joined 200 young men who had also been commissioned second lieutenants after graduating from colleges and universities throughout the United States.

In the military, I broke out of my shell of loneliness. During officer basic training, I discovered the bonds of Army comradery and wholeheartedly embraced that fundamental piece of military culture. I made the best friends and formed the strongest partnerships I'd ever known. All my fellow lieutenants were college educated, well traveled and athletic. Infantry drew aggressive men who approached life with reckless abandon. We had a zest for living, and it was not a place for the meek or mild. Even the robust friendships I was part of as a member of a high school basketball team paled in comparison to the forged iron of army brotherhood.

The Basic Course was physically demanding and mentally challenging. It wasn't a nine-to-five job. The typical day started at 6:30 a.m. and usually finished at six in the evening. One or two nights a week were spent on ranges firing rifles, machine guns, grenade launchers, mortars, exploding demolitions or practicing maneuvers. The hazards involved never crossed my mind. I found the danger exhilarating. Life in the Army was never routine or boring.

We studied "the threat," a military force the United States was most concerned about defeating in case of war. Although the instructors never named the country, we all knew "the threat" was the Soviet Union. We learned their tactics and how they were equipped and organized. Our training focused on how we would fight the Soviets, or an army modelled after the Soviets, if a war broke out. The maps used in classroom exercises were always of the German countryside and it put my training in perspective—I would soon face a very real and lethal army in Europe.

The Basic Course also emphasized equipment maintenance. An infantry platoon couldn't function if its equipment didn't work. For a few weeks we became grease monkeys and tore apart engines, weapons and communication equipment. I enjoyed the mechanical challenge and physical labor of maintenance training.

The last month we trained on tactics: planning, organizing and conducting mock battles. After graduation from the Basic Course, every lieutenant was expected to have acquired the necessary skills to lead an infantry platoon during war.

The Army issued pinpoint orders specifying where lieutenants would be stationed after completing basic training. I was assigned to Mainz, a choice duty location because it was located near a large metropolitan area that offered plenty of social and recreational opportunities.

Every lieutenant was also offered the opportunity to attend Ranger School. But there was no pressure to volunteer for the army's most gruelling and demanding training. Ranger School, an eight-week course simulating war-time conditions, taught small-unit leaders how to conduct operations behind enemy lines. Soldiers who had served in Vietnam said Ranger training was their best life insurance policy. It offered extremes of adventure, challenge and excitement. Along with half of my class, I volunteered.

We all heard stories about the exhausting physical and mental ordeals, where for eight solid weeks, Ranger students were placed under constant stress to test and build their leadership skills. Stress was created through a combination of harassment, physical exertion, and deprivation of food and sleep. Over time, even the strongest men reached their limits.

At the age of 22, I was in splendid physical condition. A high level of stamina, endurance, strength and discipline were my rewards for having played basketball since the seventh grade. Still, I trained extra hard the weeks leading up to the start of the course. My required butch haircut was obtained two days before Ranger School, and that night while lying in bed, I laughed listening to the scratching noise the nubs made as I moved my head against a pillow. It would be one of the last times I laughed for two months.

Most lieutenants going to Ranger School spent the last night of "freedom" in their quarters, partying. The studios and hallway of the section I lived in transformed into an oasis of wildness. Stereos blasted rock music, beer flowed and Rangers-to-be conducted themselves in foul ways. We drank excessively and performed the sacred rituals associated with male bonding in the military. Arm-in-arm, we held our beer cans high and toasted the Army, God, America, our mothers and each other. You name it, we toasted it. We danced and sang, changing the word cowboys in Willie Nelson's song to, "Mamma don't let your babies grow up to be Rangers." Two rugby players jumped on my bed and led the crowded room in choruses of limericks, always followed with good swigs of brew. Some self-appointed dramatists re-enacted the many ridiculous and hilarious events that happened during our basic training. We joked and laughed until it hurt.

A couple of guys rappelled out of a third story window. Two lieutenants paraded through my room wearing only their skivvies stuffed with leaves, and with smeared green and brown camouflage paint over their bodies. "We're, ready! We're ready for anything during Ranger School!" they yelled. Many guzzled beer after beer, ran outside to throw up, then re-turned to start again. A lieutenant who wasn't going to Ranger School made the mistake of dropping by my room. We grabbed a coil of rope and hog-tied him, then kicked him as if he were a soccer ball. After untying the unfortunate soul, and to show there weren't any hard feelings, we baptized him in beer. After he got off the floor, we all locked arms and drank to all the non-Ranger pukes in the army.

Mike Smith, who lived down the hall and would join me the next day at Ranger School, strode into my crowded room. He walked inside holding a can of shaving cream and yelled out to get the room's attention. Everyone became silent and fifteen pairs of drunken eyes squinted at Mike. He put the can's nozzle to his lips and sprayed his mouth full of shaving cream so that his cheeks puffed out like an inflated balloon. A guy to my left ran up to Mike and stood directly to his front. He then slapped both sides of

Mike's cheeks and instantly became the proud recipient of a volcanic shaving cream eruption.

I grabbed a bottle of liquid boot dye and used the applicator to write obscenities all over Mike's bald head. The dye wouldn't wash off the next morning and Mike had hell to pay explaining to the Ranger School instructors why four-letter words were painted on his head. It's a miracle the military police weren't called, but I loved the craziness and sense of belonging the Army provided. I had finally found the brothers I'd always wanted.

The next morning I reported to Fort Benning's isolated Ranger Camp along with 150 other men. About half the students were comrades from my basic training class, and the remainder were enlisted men, a couple of Force Recon Marines and Canadian Airborne troopers. No one wore rank or insignia as officers, and enlisted were treated exactly the same.

We had to run at all times. We formed two columns and double-timed to the mess-hall for lunch, after storing equipment and personal gear in drab, two-story wooden barracks. The head of the columns stopped fifteen yards outside the mess-hall doors. One-hundred-and-fifty men divided into two lines stood waiting like statues with their hands clasped behind their backs. Talking was strictly forbidden. On a command, the two Rangers at the front of the columns sprinted toward the mess hall and, without stopping, threw open the building's screen doors. Inside they came to a screeching halt and snapped to the position of attention. Behind a rickety wooden table sat a grim and powerful looking Ranger Instructor (RI). The two students yelled out their names, serial and Ranger class numbers and requested permission to eat. If either made the slightest mistake, both were kicked back outside to the end of the line. More than just a form of harassment, it taught that our lives depended on each other. A mistake by one could be fatal for others.

Once inside, we had exactly five minutes to eat. Food was served in a cafeteria line and I quickly learned to start eating as soon as I was handed a plate. This was a luxury. The meals were hot and we ate inside a building.

After lunch, we double-timed half-a-mile to a one room wooden classroom. We dropped our rucksacks to the ground in perfect alignment and ran inside the building carrying only our rifles. Each man stood behind a desk at the position of attention yelling at the top of his lungs. A Ranger Instructor walked to the front of the class, and with a wave of his hand the room fell to instant and complete silence. He then commanded, "Take seats." One-hundred-fifty voices screamed in perfect unison— "RANGER!"—and then everyone smartly sat down. The immaculately dressed RI gave a block of instruction on the long and colorful history of the United States Army Rangers, the Ranger Code and what being a Ranger meant. He reminded us that we had volunteered for Ranger training and could quit at any time. He was followed by an RI dressed in combat fatigues who taught movement techniques while operating behind enemy lines. He finished his instruction and ordered us out of the building. Seconds later, we stood outside at the position of attention wearing 70-pound rucksacks. A group of RI's then led us at double-time to a large, open field and gave a demonstration on what had been taught in the classroom. Then we broke into groups of eleven and practiced movement techniques.

An RI closely observed each group. If he didn't like what he saw, he yelled for everyone to hit the dirt and crawl. "Crawl on your fat bellies until I'm tired," he barked with a sarcastic grin. Then he ordered the group to turn around and crawl back to him. I was surprised how draining it was to crawl, keeping my stomach flat against the ground.

Every few minutes and, for no apparent reason, a student would be singled out and ordered to do push-ups until he couldn't push himself off the ground again. The RI hounded him. "Don't like this training, maggot? Then quit and go home to mama." The unfortunate student, arms turned to jelly, kept trying to push himself up until ordered to rejoin his group.

We stayed in the field until dark. The RIs ordered us to the mess hall and we went through the same routine as during lunch—in 20 minutes everyone had eaten. Back in the classroom we had an hour-long block of instruction on moving at night. The class finished and we endured constant screams, threats and insults while scrambling out the building. Minutes later we were back in the field to practice night movement behind enemy lines. We practiced until midnight when the RIs ordered us to stop. They screamed we were the worst soldiers ever to put on Army uniforms and that we were disgusting. Then they ordered us to the barracks until morning.

We quickly washed, shaved and went to bed. Most simply lay on top of their bunks so time wouldn't be wasted making them in the morning. Before I crawled on top of my bunk, I looked around the darkened room with orderly rows of bunks and metal lockers. The room where fifty men slept was quiet, except for an occasional cough or squeaking bed. The open room imparted a sense of comfort that I'd known before—safe, clean and warm. At some level it triggered memories of the eighteen months I lived in an orphanage. I took one last look, hopped onto my bunk and covered myself with a poncho-liner. I fell asleep instantly. The first day of Ranger School had come to an end.

It seemed seconds later when the RIs entered the barracks. Ceiling lights glared in my face, and I heard rough shouts, "Get out of bed you lousy maggots." The RIs kicked over metal trash cans and lockers, and overturned bunk beds. They yelled to get the barracks ready for inspection and for everyone to be standing outside in formation within five minutes. I looked at my watch. It was 4:00 a.m.

I ran outside with the others into a pitch-black morning. We stood silently in formation, dressed only in combat boots and olive-green fatigues. I shivered in the early March cold and waited to begin physical training. One group of RIs inspected the barracks while another group led us through conditioning exercises. We did a variety of calisthenics and then began a four-mile run, singing jodies for cadence:

> One, two, three, four-hey,
> Run a little, run a little, run a little more-hey.
> Two old ladies laying in bed,
> One rolled over to the other and said,
> I want to be an Airborne Ranger,
> I want to lead a life of danger.
> I want to go to Vietnam,
> I want to kill the fucking Cong.
> One, two, three, four-hey...

A few students hadn't physically prepared themselves and fell out of the formation. They were dropped from the course that same morning.

We moved to a confidence course after the run. Streetlights hung from scattered telephone poles and washed an area the size of two football fields with eery, yellow light. Despite the cold, sweat poured through my fatigues and steamed into the cold air. Before I could catch my breath, I started running, crawling and climbing through a variety of obstacles.

We reformed for the last event of the confidence course, *the worm pit*. A rectangular mud-filled hole the size of an Olympic swimming pool lay directly to our front. Intermittent strands of barbed wire stretched a few feet above a thin layer of ice that coated the mud hole. We formed into eight columns and faced the pit. In the quiet pre-dawn darkness, every man clapped and chanted. It wasn't the beautiful melody of a medieval Gregorian Chant; the sounds we made would have pleased any self-respecting Neanderthal.

An RI issued a command and the men at the front of each column sprinted toward the worm pit. The veneer of ice cracked as the men dove into the pit and worked their way through the lanes. A few seconds later eight more men sprinted forward and dove into the mud. My turn came and I ran to the edge of the pit and slithered into the frigid glop. Ice cold mud covered me from head to toe and I felt the ooze seep through my uniform and into my boots. The icy muck forced short breaths. I had to keep my head and body low in the mud, or else be cut by the barbed wire overhead. I slid to the other side and stumbled out of the frigid swamp. I rejoined the others and resumed the barbaric chanting until every man came out of the pit. We double-timed back to the barracks and my confidence grew. I'd survived another test.

The instruction at Ranger School was the most professional of any school I've ever attended, military or civilian. We were told exactly what was expected and nothing less was accepted. Book knowledge wasn't enough. Evaluations took place outside, in the rain, when it was dark and students were dog-tired and hungry. It didn't matter what you looked like or where you came from. All that mattered was your ability to perform. Success was measured by what you did, not by what you said. Tests were clear-cut, black and white. We had to work as a team to survive. Those who couldn't pull their weight were weeded out.

At the end of the first week, trucks carried us from our barracks to a remote bivouac site. No more mess hall, no more buildings. Every 24 hours we were issued only two C-ration meals, starting the slow process of forced starvation. I began to feel the strain brought on by constant physical exertion and lack of food and sleep. It was hard to concentrate. I had to force myself to think. But I learned to push through self-imposed limits and found that I could function with little food and less sleep.

We learned to move and operate behind enemy lines with someone trying to kill us. We became expert at camouflage, used black tape to deaden equipment noise and traveled during the hours of darkness to conceal our activity. We seldom talked during patrols. Instead, we communicated using arm and hand signals during the day and blinks from red-filtered flashlights at night. If the patrol got lost or the plan wasn't being executed to the satisfaction of the RI we did it again, not stopping until the RI was satisfied. A few nights we didn't sleep and the class continued to shrink as students quit.

It all seemed overwhelming. I had to think and function despite being hungry, cold, tired and wet. Every day and night I trained with a group of men who faced the same hardships. Survival meant everyone had to sacrifice for the good of all. The only external motivation came from the connectedness we had for one another. From common suffering sprang mutual respect. I was part of a group of strong individuals, made stronger by a collective will to succeed no matter what the cost.

At the end of the second week my patrol was ordered back to the bivouac site. It wasn't a leisurely return stroll. We moved in tactical formation in a pouring night rain. Single file, rifles at the ready, faces and hands smeared with camouflage paint, no talking, no lights. Eleven men moved carefully through dense underbrush with only a compass for a guide. Never, ever, did we walk on roads, paths or trails. To hide our movements and avoid detection we stayed in the most difficult terrain filled with wait-a-minute vines. We arrived at the bivouac site at dawn and silently packed our gear in the pouring rain. Rain trickled down the back of my neck and underneath my t-shirt. My entire body shook. I had difficulty tying my bootlaces because my fingers were numbed from the wet-cold. We climbed on the back of open trucks for the return drive to the barracks. Despite the cold and rain, I fell asleep.

Back at the barracks, we were given our first eight hour break in two-and-a-half weeks. No friends or family were allowed at the compound so we drove our cars back to "the world." The lucky ones had wives or girl-friends waiting for them. I wasn't one of the lucky ones and arrived at my empty studio. I took a long, hot shower, did laundry, paid bills and joined a few other Rangers for a steak dinner.

In the blink of an eye it seemed, I was back standing in formation in front of the drab barracks. Our class of 150 had been reduced to less than 120 as injuries, sickness and weakness caused many to fall by the wayside. We boarded buses and were transported to a base camp near Dahlonega, Georgia, at the southern end of the Appalachian Mountains. I slept the entire way, and the muscles in my legs and shoulders ached when I stepped off the bus to start the Mountain Phase of Ranger School.

Thankfully, most of the harassment had ended, and the first few days we ate three hot meals and slept four or five hours a night. This wasn't out of the RI's kindness but to somewhat rejuvenate us to reduce injuries while undergoing dangerous mountaineer training. Despite the danger, moun-taineering provided a refreshing break from the strain of patrolling.

After mountaineer training ended, we were taught how to patrol and fight in that environment. In Georgia, we learned how to pull-off ambush patrols, and daily rations were cut again. We conducted airmobile opera-tions for the first time, using helicopters to transport us behind enemy lines and pick us up after the mission. The mental strain increased.

Twenty-hour days resumed for the duration of the Mountain Phase. The RIs continually stressed that an in-depth, well-rehearsed plan was crucial for a successful patrol. Plan, rehearse, conduct—plan, rehearse, conduct. Day and night, rain or shine, tired, hungry and cold. All the while the respect I had for my peers and myself grew. I could function despite extreme physical and mental hardships.

On the third straight night of patrolling we moved seven kilometers up and down mountains and arrived at a small valley. We set up an ambush along a bend in a dirt road. At 2:30 a.m. we lay hidden on the frozen ground, expertly camouflaged. Twenty-two men, paired in groups of two or more, were spread out over an area the size of two football fields. Intelligence reports said a convoy would come down the road, and we silently waited for the enemy to enter the kill zone.

The entire patrol had set up on high ground, five meters inside a woodline paralleling one side of the road. Security teams, positioned 100 meters at opposite ends of the road's L-shaped curve, would radio the main body when an enemy force approached. The fire support team with the patrol's two machine guns waited along the base of the curve. Once the enemy entered the kill zone they would initiate the ambush by detonating mines and firing their machine guns. I was part of the twelve-man assault team positioned along the stem of the L. After the machine guns stopped firing we were to run into the kill zone and search enemy personnel and destroy any weapons or equipment we couldn't take with us.

Time crept, if it moved at all. In the pitch black night I looked at my watch—6:00 a.m. I trembled in the early morning April air and the cold earth sapped my body heat. For nearly four hours I had been lying on my stomach wearing only my uniform. I pressed close beside another assault team member; our body heat provided the only warmth. Survival meant sharing a physical closeness we never would have allowed ourselves in civilian life. He and I took 10-minute turns: one slept while the other kept watch. Sleep finally overwhelmed me despite the tormenting cold and a gnawing hunger.

We had been at the ambush site for over four hours when first light approached and the sky began to leak a murky gray. It was absolutely still— no wind, no birds, no nothing. I ached from the cold, and my swollen joints became numb from inactivity. It seemed like we had been waiting forever. I started second-guessing the decisions of the patrol leaders. Did we set the ambush in the correct location? Was this patrol only a test of endurance to see how much pain we could take? Did the security teams fall asleep and let the enemy pass through the kill zone? Maybe there wouldn't be an enemy force coming through. For four weeks I'd been slowly starving. Hunger forced my body to consume muscle as reserves of fat had long before been depleted. My head hurt. I couldn't stop shaking and it felt like the marrow in my bones was freezing. Sleep crushed me.

Before I could sink deeper in despair, I thought I heard the faint sound of engines. Was it real or was I imagining? I nudged my sleeping comrade and asked if he could hear anything. We lifted our heads and strained our ears to pick up any distant noise.

Minutes later the patrol leader rushed down the assault line saying the security teams reported a jeep and a truck moving down the road. The vehicles were moving slowly from south to north, without lights, and would soon enter the kill zone. The patrol leader left and I lifted my rifle butt into the hollow of my shoulder. I flicked the safety to the automatic fire position and stared at the curve in the road where the vehicles would soon appear. My heart pounded, and I wasn't cold, tired or hungry anymore. Every nerve in my body came alive. My senses awakened to a keen state of awareness.

We heard the vehicles slowing as they crept toward the curve in the road. In the murky gray dawn, a truck and a jeep appeared from around the curve and entered the kill zone. Mines detonated and flashes of brilliant light momentarily blinded me. Concussions from the explosions ripped the air as machine guns fired. Seconds later, a green and white flare erupted overhead, signalling the machine guns to stop firing and for the assault team to enter the kill zone.

My comrade and I, along with other members of the assault team, leapt up off the ground and sprinted to the vehicles, twenty paces up the road. Simulated dead and wounded enemy soldiers littered the area. We took their weapons and searched the vehicles for documentation, weapons, maps, special equipment and food. Within two minutes we completed our search and quickly placed dummy explosives on the engine blocks of both vehicles. A red flare erupted overhead, signaling the explosives would soon blow and for the entire patrol to rendezvous at its previously designated rallying point, a stream junction one kilometer east of the ambush site. After throwing smoke grenades to conceal our withdrawal, I ran as fast as I could to the stream junction.

After the patrol assembled at the rally point, two RIs called an administrative halt and gave a critique of the patrol's operation. They completed their critique, and two fresh instructors took their places. New student leaders were assigned, and the patrol prepared for another mission. And so it went, day after day, night after night.

I didn't think I could feel any worse, but I was wrong. I got sick the next night. Some kind of flu overcame me, and I couldn't stop shaking from a fever; my throat hurt; I was dizzy and nauseous. My comrades saw I was sick and told me to suck it up and gut it out. That night we trudged up and down mountains, and I looked down into a valley, glimpsing a few faint lights flickering. I knew normal people slept inside houses, in warm, dry beds. In the haze of my sickness, I fantasized about being in a warm house, asleep in a bed, with a full stomach. For the first time, I thought about quitting.

We continued moving through the mountains, and all night I thought about quitting. Although, I would still have to walk five or six miles to the base camp if I did quit. Medevac helicopters were only used for emergencies, and the flu wasn't an emergency. If I quit, I wouldn't be able to live with myself because I would be separated from my comrades. I'd be considered an outcast and would lose the bonds of belonging. The need to belong proved greater than hunger, exhaustion and sickness. Ranger School taught me how far I'd go to satisfy my need to be accepted. I viewed it as my initiation into a life-long goal. I kept putting one foot in front of the other and knew I'd either collapse or recover from my illness. I walked with the others in single file and focused my mind on the patrol's mission instead of on my physical pain. Thankfully, whatever I had lasted only 24 hours. My self-doubt faded along with the illness.

At the end of the Mountain Phase, helicopters picked us up in a farmer's field and flew us back to the Dahlonega base camp. We cleaned our filthy bodies, wolfed down a hot meal, and buses returned us to Benning for our second and final eight-hour break.

The third and final phase of Ranger School, the Florida Phase, started with a parachute operation into the enemy's rear camp area. First, we went through a quick refresher course on parachuting, and those who completed a grueling three-mile run were considered medically fit to jump.

One-hundred men put on combat gear, strapped weapons into special leg-harnesses and donned main and reserve parachutes at Benning's airstrip. Painted with camouflage, and wearing hundreds of pounds of equipment, each man waddled on board a cargo jet. Inside, we packed ourselves into four long rows of canvas-covered, aluminum-framed seats. Soon the jet sped down the runway and we were quickly airborne. Immediately I fell asleep, and didn't wake up until hearing the "10 minute to jump" warning. Twin doors at the rear of the aircraft opened filling the interior with a deafening roar. I stood, along with the others sitting on the inside rows, and hooked the cord of my parachute to the static lines running overhead. Crammed together in a single line, we started pushing toward the open door. The plane pitched left and right as it lurched up and down. With nothing to lean on for support, it required the agility of a mountain goat to stand without falling. The human line's momentum pushed me toward the open door at the rear of the pitching plane. Light glared in from the outside and suddenly the guy in front of me disappeared. I took two small steps and leapt out of the plane into a quiet, blue sky. In addition to fear, the sensations of exiting a jet and flying in excess of 130 knots, are severe turbulence and being blown backwards. Counting to four, I looked up and checked my parachute canopy to ensure it had inflated properly. Then I looked down, still 400 feet in the air. Seconds later I hit the ground, landing surprisingly softly as Florida's sand cushioned my impact. I got out of my harness, simulated burying my parachute and ran into a nearby woodline to join the others.

My patrol moved quickly to raid an enemy command post seven miles from the drop zone. We raided the command post and moved to a base camp.

Spending the first few days in the compound, we slept in beds. The Florida RIs taught raiding tactics, how to move through swamps and rivers, tracking an enemy force, prisoner interrogation, and first aid for heat injuries and snake bites. One reward of Ranger training was having the best at their craft for instructors. Along with the others, I had a deep respect for the Ranger Instructors.

We conducted raids in Florida, attacked command posts or missile sites, and snatched high-ranking enemy officials out of their compounds. Patrols increased to thirty men for these risky operations. Rations were cut to one meal a day, and it seemed like we never slept. We moved in stinking swamps all night, conducted a raid at the crack of dawn and then moved to a dry area to prepare for the next operation.

My mind-set had changed. I knew I could fight in a war. With the discovery of new abilities I believed I could do anything. My self-confidence now bordered on arrogance. Before Ranger School, I never believed I had a killer instinct but in Florida I looked forward to the violence. Along with hardship, Ranger School provided challenge and clear purpose. The training had the feel of athletic competition, and I wondered if somewhere on the other side of the world a group of Soviet soldiers were undergoing similar training. Would we meet one day?

On the ninth night in Florida my patrol received orders to raid an enemy communication site. The mission was to kill everyone, destroy all their equipment and then move to a pick-up site where helicopters would fly us to a new location. After moving through five miles of jungle, we reached our objective. Unlike every other raid we had conducted, this one would be different—no prepatory fire. Instead, we would sneak up on the communication site in two waves and engage the enemy in close combat. I was part of the first wave that would kill anyone guarding the perimeter. The second wave would follow close behind, killing any remaining enemy and exploding demolitions to destroy the communication equipment.

About a half mile from the objective we hit high ground and moved out of the swamp. Thick jungle gave way to thin ground vegetation under towering pine trees. We spread out in two straight lines, one behind the other, separated by a distance of twenty paces. I crouched forward in the front line, an arm's length apart from the men to my left and right. Then I spotted a camp fire burning 100 yards to my front—the communication site. The men in both lines started crawling forward.

I cradled my rifle in my arms and crawled closer to the enemy. Twenty-five yards away we came to a roll of concertina wire and cut our way through, after first making sure it wasn't booby trapped or mined. We continued crawling forward, 20, 15, 10 yards from our target. The sounds of a generator helped conceal our noise, and I saw a large truck with a radar dish by its side. Five yards to my front I saw the silhouette of an enemy soldier. His back was turned, and he sat on a log, warming himself by a fire. Strength and energy surged through me as I raised off the ground. Hunched over, I inched my way toward him. It was hard to keep quiet, and I thought the sound of my heavy breathing might startle him, but the noise of the generator acted as a muffler. I wanted to take my rifle and knock his head off with a baseball swing. Only the dim realization that it was a training exercise kept me from doing it. Our entire line was a single step from the communication site perimeter. I sprung at the soldier sitting on the log and grabbed his throat in an arm lock. He gasped for air as I flexed my arm and squeezed his throat. "You're a dead son-of-a bitch," I yelled in his ear. The rest of my comrades attacked other soldiers, and the second wave sprinted past firing their weapons. They rushed to the truck and radar dish, killing anyone in their way. At that point, I knew if a war came, I could kill.

Ongoing stress, constant physical exertion, and lack of food and sleep combined to create a different dimension of existence. Hormones raged in my twenty-two year old body, but I hadn't thought about sex for weeks. It was the same with my Ranger comrades. We were too busy, tired and hungry to think about women. But while moving single file through the jungle at night, my mind sometimes wandered to showers and beds. In Florida I made mental lists of what I would eat after Ranger School: candy bars, steak, hamburgers, fresh vegetables, peanut butter... Then the squelch of a radio or the kick of a comrade would stir me out of my stupor.

The biggest scare I'd had during all of Ranger School came one night when moving under double-canopy jungle through a stinking swamp. Thirty men travelled single file in pitch blackness which prevented me from seeing the man to my front. I had to keep one hand on his shoulder to follow him even though he was only a foot or two away. The water, higher than usual, wavered from chest to neck deep. Submerged logs made it easy to trip and drowning posed a constant hazard. Soft trickling sounds of water as the patrol made its way through the swamp broke the otherwise still air. Without warning and a rock's throw to my left, a gruesome deep bellowing rang out. I heard a thrashing noise in the water followed by a large splash. It was a bull alligator in a nearby slough.

And it wasn't a simulated alligator, this one was real, one who kills its prey by drowning. My muscles tensed, expecting at any moment to feel an alligator's teeth rip my leg and pull me under the water. But no soldier said a word. No one acted any differently. Maybe I was hallucinating. We kept moving single file through the swamp as if nothing had happened.

After twelve straight days and nights in the swamps we returned to base camp. The RIs served us a ceremonial "super supper." I weighed myself before eating and discovered I had lost 15 of my 170 pounds. We consumed all the food and beer we could. But I couldn't keep regular food down, and like many of my comrades, I lost my "super supper," throwing it up an hour later.

On May 10, 1979, I graduated from Ranger School and joined the elite ranks of the United States Army. It stood as the biggest accomplishment of my life up to that point. With the passage of an initiation rite, I gained priceless skills, developed a powerful new confidence and a belief I could accomplish anything. I felt ready to go to war. More importantly, I had gained what I'd always wanted—the acceptance and respect of my peers.

Home Again

An RI pinned the coveted black and gold Ranger tab to my uniform at the Fort Benning Ranger School graduation ceremony, and I returned to my quarters. My comrades who shared neighboring rooms had long since departed. Such was the culture of the Army: make best friends in a very short time with guys you'd never known before only to say goodbye a few months later and never see them again.

I spent the day in my room, surrounded by a case of beer, candy bars, a giant bag of potato chips, jars of peanut butter and packages of junk food I so desperately craved during Ranger School. The food didn't taste all that great, now that I could have as much as I wanted. I spent the day alternating between eating, packing, sleeping and sitting like a vegetable in front of a television set.

The next day I began a two-week vacation. I checked out of my quarters and drove to Auburn University to say goodbye to college friends and fraternity brothers. Later, I left Auburn feeling a bit sad, knowing I had closed the door on my college experience. My remaining days in America were spent back home in Pensacola, where I hung out at the beautiful, sugar-white beaches of Northwest Florida.

The beach atmosphere was the very opposite of Ranger School. I found it difficult adjusting to the sluggish pace. Civilian life seemed to move in slow motion and appeared boring and empty after the excitement, danger and clear purpose of the Army. I couldn't fathom living life with only the empty goal of making and spending money. I was anxious to get to Europe and take my place squaring off against the Red Army. I wanted to join the Guardians at the Gate and keep the Soviet hordes in check so others could make and spend their money.

My parents were proud of my graduating from college and becoming an Army officer. My father was not only proud; a part of him lived vicariously through his young lieutenant son. With nostalgic enthusiasm, he saw himself in the mirror of my uniform and reminisced about the highlights of his 22-year military career. My mother, the former Army nurse who had served in a M.A.S.H. unit during the Korean War, was equally pleased. She waited on me hand and foot and although I initially resisted, I saw it made her happy to wash my laundry and prepare my meals. I succumbed and let her take care of me. In my parents' eyes, I couldn't have made a better son. I was a symbol of their having successfully raised a child.

However, an ever-present danger threatened to diminish my adopted parents' joy. To me, their happiness was superficial. Unresolved issues begged for enlightenment but instead were pushed into a dark closest. The secret hidden in the closet bred fear—a fear that stemmed from our refusal to acknowledge the reality of past events. Not once during any conversation with them did the subject of my biological parents arise. Adoption issues hadn't been discussed since they took me to see a psychologist when I was a boy. My American parents also didn't note that I was going back to the country where I was born. Certain it would result in nothing but ill will, I too kept quiet about my adoption. Never did I mention my deeply felt desire to find my mother nor the immeasurable yearning to know where I came from.

At the end of my vacation, on a hot and humid Florida morning, the day came to say goodbye. I was leaving for three years, but it wasn't a heartfelt, tearful parting. I wasn't sad because I had still never emotionally connected to my adopted family. Despite their kindness, I did not develop an attachment and felt more sadness at leaving Auburn than leaving them. Whether my parents had connected with me I didn't know. Despite their wonderful qualities, they weren't able to talk from the heart and express their innermost feelings. That last morning, my father gave a firm handshake and told me to do my best. My mother offered a placid hug and asked that I write. My sister wished me luck and offered her hand.

After the formalities, I drove to the Port of Charleston, South Carolina, to put my car on a boat and have it shipped to Germany. I handed my car keys to a longshoreman and changed from civilian clothes into my Army Class A uniform—dark green coat and pants, black tie, khaki shirt, patent leather black shoes, saucer cap—and caught a taxi to Charleston Air Force Base. I had a few hours to kill before the plane departed and passed the time reading at a picnic area outside the terminal. Music blared from a nearby soldier's portable radio as he stood leaning against a tree. He played a tape by Grand Funk Railroad with the song *I'm Your Captain*. The repeating chorus, "I'm getting closer to my home ... I'm getting closer to my home," played over and over again. An appropriate piece of music for my homecoming.

The airport P.A. system announced it was time I board my plane. I walked onto the chartered jet whose passengers were either uniformed soldiers or their family members. It felt strange getting on an aircraft and knowing I wouldn't parachute out of it.

During the eight-hour flight to Germany, I spent a lot of time thinking about how to find my biological mother. How could I find the woman I had thought of every single day for as long as I could remember? I had little information. I knew my mother's name, her age, German identification number and the address where she lived in 1956. That was it. No picture or physical description, nothing about my father, no names or addresses of relatives, no family or medical histories, and nothing about the orphanage were I had lived. I figured my best bet was to find a German government agency and ask for assistance.

The plane landed mid-afternoon, German time, at the U.S. Rhein-Main Air Force Base located near Frankfurt in central Germany. I stepped off the plane and retrieved my luggage at the terminal's In-processing Office where newly arrived military personnel reported. While I stood in line, a sharp-looking army major dressed in a khaki uniform passed by and noticed the 8th Infantry Division patch on my left shoulder.

"What unit are you assigned to, lieutenant?" he asked.

"2nd Battalion-28th Infantry in Mainz, sir," I answered in a manner fitting for addressing a field-grade officer.

"Great outfit; I'm driving right by Mainz. C'mon, I'll give you a lift. Let's go."

Before I could answer, the major grabbed one of the suitcases resting at my feet and with a reassuring smile told me to follow as he headed out the building.

"All they'll do at In-processing is make you wait around and then put you on some old army bus for Mainz. This will save you a couple of hours." We left the terminal and headed to his Datsun 240-Z sportscar. The major drove through the streets of Frankfurt at a fast clip. He told me he was the operations officer for an air cavalry regiment and flew Cobra helicopter gunships. We turned at a traffic light and accelerated onto the famous German Autobahn from which the Americans copied their Interstate system. One big difference between the two: no speed limits on the Autobahn.

"Best damned drivers in the world," the major said as he shifted from third to fourth and merged into traffic. His eyes had narrowed as he focused on the traffic. Visualizing him in the cockpit of his helicopter, I felt safe. He was in total control of the automobile and the speeds were thrilling.

"Most disciplined people on earth," he went on. "They drive fast as hell but follow the road rules to the letter." He shifted into fifth gear, hitting 85 m.p.h. as a BMW blew by and left us shaking in its wake. He looked over at me, cracked a joke and we both laughed.

We got off the Autobahn at Mainz-Gonsenheim and drove into Lee Barracks, home to 1st Brigade, 8th Infantry Division. The major stopped in front of the headquarters building and helped me unload my gear. He wished me luck and drove off. I never saw him again.

I reported to the battalion's adjutant, the personnel officer, who was another infantry lieutenant. He welcomed me and said the battalion commander wanted to meet with me at 6:00 a.m. the following Tuesday. It was the last Friday in May, the start of Memorial weekend, and the adjutant said I had the next three days off. He called the duty sergeant who drove me to a hotel in Wiesbaden for newly arrived U.S. military personnel. After unpacking, I took a shower, changed into civilian clothes and hurried to the hotel restaurant.

An older German woman who spoke English, laden with a heavy accent, acted as my server. Could this woman be my mother? I didn't think so. My mother was thirty-five when I was born and would be fifty-eight today. The waitress appeared to be in her mid-forties.

After eating dinner, I decided to walk to the downtown area located about six blocks from the hotel. Wiesbaden was a medium-sized city, and I figured something would be going on in the city center.

Outside the hotel, I walked along a sidewalk in a residential area toward the city center. Cool and clean spring air, perfumed from blossoming flowers and shrubs, refreshed me. Immaculate houses with well-kept yards hid behind iron lattice fences on both sides of the street. Birds sang, adding music to the twilight atmosphere. Towering deciduous trees grew on each side of the street and spread their branches to form an arc overhead. An occasional car passed by, and only a few other people walked in the area. Stopping along the sidewalk to absorb my surroundings, the full impact hit me that I'd actually made it back to Germany. An indefinable sense of belonging swept through me as I felt I had returned to where I was meant to be.

This is the country where I was born. I have German parents, German blood and never should have been taken from Germany. I had finally come home after years of dreaming about returning. I stood still on the sidewalk and basked in the warm glow of realizing a deeply felt and life-long goal.

The considerable mental discipline and physical toughness I had acquired did not heal the emotional wound of my adoption experience. Uprooting from my biological parents and the subsequent removal from the orphanage left a gaping hole in my psyche. All my positive life experiences—a proper home, a good education, friends, sports—did not put an end to my feeling of sorrow. Part of the quest to find my mother was somehow to change my feelings and stop the pain.

Where would I be if my mother had raised me? Where would I be if I had stayed in the orphanage or if German parents had adopted me? Would my personality and emotional make-up be any different? What would have been ...? If only I knew. These somber reflections were based more on emotion than intellect. The laughter and shouts of a couple of kids kicking a soccer ball down the street put an end to my introspection, and I resumed walking toward the downtown area.

Crossing a street, I left the residential area and entered Wiesbaden's business sector, filled with people out to enjoy a pleasant Friday evening. Drifting through the crowd, I picked up occasional words or phrases spoken in my native language. I wondered how much German I spoke at the age of three and wondered how much I retained in my subconscious memory.

Immersed in the crowd of my countrymen, my mood shifted to one of enthusiasm. I wanted to yell, "I've been gone 20 years. I didn't want to leave; it wasn't my fault. I had no choice. I've always wanted to return and live as a German."

I kept quiet though and observed the people walking along the streets. I looked for anyone with similar physical characteristics and noted tall and slender people with blue eyes and dark hair. There, across the street, a tall man and woman were window shopping. Could they be my parents? The young man with angular features and dark hair who just walked by —a brother I'd never known? A teenage girl with large blue eyes laughing and holding hands with another girl—a younger sister I would never grow up with?

I walked aimlessly and eventually ended up on an avenue for pedestrians only. The cobblestone walkway was as wide as a two-lane street and lined with specialty shops, restaurants, wine cellars and beer halls. Twilight had turned to darkness, but outdoor streetlights illuminated the walkway. Laughter, spirited music and the smells of food and alcohol poured out of the festive establishments. I wanted to be part of it.

The pedestrian way wound through the downtown area and emptied into a huge, open square with a massive cathedral at its center. Tables and chairs overflowed with people; food and drinks filled the square and surrounded the centuries old church. The excitement of my quest prevented me from stopping. I continued toward the cathedral, fueled by a dreamlike hope. Did my mother live in Wiesbaden?

If my mother lived, or had lived in Wiesbaden, there might be records of her whereabouts in the cathedral's administrative files. Not caring that it was after normal business hours, I decided to go to the cathedral and ask for help. I jogged up the front steps of the immense church only to find its huge wooden doors locked. I went back down the steps and followed the structure's facade until I arrived at what I knew must be the rectory. After two or three rings of the buzzer, an older man appeared in the doorway. He spoke in German and asked what I wanted. Stammering back in atrocious German, I explained that I wanted to find my mother and hoped he might have records of where she lived. Halfway through my explanation, he curtly interrupted and asked that I speak in English. I continued, giving my mother's name and saying in 1956 she lived in the town of Mörfelden. He shrugged his shoulders and suggested I go to Mörfelden. Then he wished me goodnight and closed the door.

As he shut the door in front of me, a door opened in my mind. A clear sign pointed the way along an obscure trail. Of course, I'll go to Mörfelden. Back on the pedestrian way, I walked a few blocks and decided to go inside a beer house.

People packed the room; noise and cigarette smoke filled the air. Across the room I spotted an empty barstool which I took and ordered a beer. "What kind?" asked the bar tender, a man about my age.

"What kind do you have?" I said responding in German, determined to practice and re-acquire my Mother tongue.

"I'll bring you a Pils," he said in English and returned a few minutes later with a glass mug of beer, topped with a foamy head. He stopped me as I reached into my wallet to pay.

"In Germany, one pays for their drinks when one departs for the evening," he said, placing a round cardboard coaster beneath the mug. Did I have "I am American" tattooed on my forehead? Raising the mug to my lips, I took a big swig of the room temperature beer and swallowed. My first taste of German beer went down deliciously smooth. I never again drank an American beer while living there.

German, English and American songs played from a corner jukebox, adding to the chatter of couples and small groups busily engaged in conversation. No one paid any attention to me. I ordered a second beer as my thoughts again turned to finding my mother. Memorial weekend gave me three free days. Why didn't I think of going to Mörfelden? I'll take a train and go there first thing in the morning. But where's Mörfelden?

The waiter returned with the second beer and made a mark on the coaster to keep count. He cocked his ear toward me as I explained my situation. He listened more attentively than the man at the cathedral and said Mörfelden was a little town about an hour's train ride from Wiesbaden. He took a coaster off a nearby stack and drew a map showing Wiesbaden-Frankfurt-Mörfelden. Then he handed the coaster to me across the counter. The helpful waiter recommended I go to the train station for more detailed information. When he finished giving advice, I lurched out of my stool and stood up, throwing my hand across the counter to thank him. I did it with so much exuberance that he took a few steps backward and looked at me a little anxiously. Finishing the beer, I paid the nervous waiter and departed for Wiesbaden's train station.

The trail in my mind now became more distinct. Mörfelden is near, better than being tucked away in Germany's farthest corner. But it wouldn't matter if my mother was shoved away in Germany's most remote location; I would have traveled anywhere to find her.

I left the beer hall and walked four more blocks along the pedestrian street. It came to an abrupt halt and I stared at a four-lane boulevard with Wiesbaden's train station on the opposite side. Crossing the busy street, I walked up an entryway concourse to the station's main entrance. Above the building's double-wide entrance doors a pale light illuminated yellow letters—Hauptbahnhof. Then I walked inside the main train station.

A few people milled about. High school and college travellers rested against backpacks; a wino sang and danced before a flock of pigeons. Travel-oriented shops decorated both sides of the lobby. Banks, an information office, a restaurant, gift shops and book stores were all closed for the evening. On a wall outside the information office, behind a glass window case, stood a large map of the Federal Republic of Germany. Using the sketch the waiter had drawn for orientation, I looked at the map and found Wiesbaden. I then moved east and spotted Frankfurt. From Frankfurt I looked in a southerly direction, looking... looking... there... Mörfelden. The waiter was right; it must be a small town, judging from its thin font compared to the heavy marks labeling other towns and cities. With nothing else to do, I decided to return first thing in the morning and buy a train ticket for Mörfelden.

Energy built as I realized tomorrow might be the day. Was my mother still living in Mörfelden? Was she living at all? Could I track her down after a 22-year separation? If I found her, would she welcome me or scorn my arrival? Would my father be there? Did my parents marry later in life? Did I have brothers or sisters? Would I look like them, have similar personality traits? Would the puzzle come together, questions answered and the past revealed?

Making my way out of the railroad station, I retraced my steps back to the hotel. Back along the pedestrian way, I wandered into another beer hall. This time I ordered a Pils and remarked to the bartender that German beer tasted much better than American beer.

"Ja," he replied with a disinterested smile. "Amerikanisches Bier ist Pinkelwasser." I knew enough German to understand what he meant. After two more mugs I was quite drunk. I paid the bill, left a tip and headed for the hotel.

It was after 2:00 a.m. and the once-crowded walkway was deserted. Passing the hall where I had my first German beer, I walked through the open square with the huge cathedral. A few more blocks and I'd arrive at the residential section of town. A little farther ahead I saw a man standing alone on a street corner. He seemed to be waiting for someone. Filled with drunken excitement, I walked up to the stranger and attempted to initiate a conversation. I saw the man as a gift. Besides him being another opportunity to improve my German skills, he might provide a tip on how to conduct tomorrow's search.

The man looked slightly older than I was—late twenties perhaps. He might have been an inch or two taller if he stood up straight, but I probably outweighed him by ten pounds. His oily, stringy shoulder-length hair swished each time he jerked his head to look in a different direction. An unkempt beard hid most of his face. He smoked a cigarette with one hand and stuffed the other in the pocket of his dark jacket that gave way to frayed blue jeans and dirty tennis shoes.

I stood a few paces from the live scarecrow and tried to explain my life's story. He wasn't at all interested. He kept quiet, shifted his weight from foot to foot and scanned the streets. Shamelessly, I continued trying to get a response. Instead, he threw his cigarette butt into the street and turned his back on me. He certainly must have wished I would go away.

Then without warning, two large men came quickly from around the corner and pushed us up against a wall. In authoritarian German voices they demanded identification. I reached inside my back pants pocket and pulled the military ID card out of my wallet. A minute later I got it back and was told to leave. I moved a few steps away to slide my wallet back in my pants while the scraggly man was still detained. He either refused to answer questions or didn't give the right ones because the two men started punching and kicking him. I didn't stick around to see what would happen next. I learned the lesson that you don't fool around with German police.

About a year later, the German equivalent of the F.B.I. contacted me and questioned me about that night's events. They asked how I knew the nervous man with the long hair and unkempt beard, what our relationship was, and what we had talked about. I explained what had happened and the German F.B.I. told me he was a member of the Baader-Meinhof terrorist gang, a splinter group of the Red Army Faction. They were notorious for blowing up cars and buildings and killing people in the name of peace and justice. I realized my homeland was not a utopia.

Mörfelden

Sunlight poured through the windows of the hotel room and baked my motionless body sprawled on the bed. Before collapsing the night before, I hadn't bothered to undress or even close the drapes. With my eyes still shut, I slowly began to regain consciousness. The heat of the sun told me it was late morning. In a split second a foreboding fear flashed that I had overslept and would never be able to launch my search. I popped up in bed like a jack-in-the-box and in a panic looked at the clock perched on the dresser. It read 6:00 a.m. That couldn't be right. I frantically called the front desk but the monotone voice on the other end assured me that it was indeed six o'clock in the morning. The hotelier hung up after saying it sometimes took visitors a few days before adjusting to Germany's early summer mornings.

The reason for panic proved false, but there was no mistaking a real hangover. A fog enveloped me as I stumbled to the bathroom with every footstep magnifying a pounding headache. My mouth remained parched even after gulping three full glasses of water. I looked into the mirror and a hideous man stared back, with road maps having replaced blue eyes. I wobbled into the shower stall and took solace by reflecting how much worse I had felt during Ranger School when dementia had taken hold during the Florida phase. The last minute of the shower I turned the water ice cold, and that jolted me out of my stupor. I completed the morning bathroom ritual with my stomach growling. I dressed in faded blue jeans, penny loafers and a dark blue sweat shirt, then packed a suitcase for a three day trip. Before leaving, I took another look into the bathroom mirror. As I had done countless times throughout my life, I stared at the face in the mirror and wondered if I were looking at the reflection of my birth father. Was I looking at my mother's eyes? After breakfast in the hotel restaurant, I changed two hundred dollars into Deutsch marks and headed for Wiesbaden's train station.

A clear sky and cool morning air greeted me on the walk to the Hauptbahnhof. Not a trace of humidity as compared to the oppressive heat on a May's morning walk back in Florida, Alabama or Georgia. I was invigorated by the time I reached the Hauptbahnhof.

The Information Office provided detailed rail schedules where I purchased a one-way ticket and soon boarded an eastbound train. After an hour's journey, I stepped out of the train onto a concrete loading dock adjoining a small train station. For the benefit of travellers, a sign providing the station's location hung beneath the building's upper facade. A single word was painted in black letters against a white background, and I looked at it with a mingled reverence, wonder and expectation. The sign read Mörfelden.

After a conductor's shrill whistle blast, doors closed and the electric train snaked along steel ribbons, rounded a curve and disappeared behind a grove of trees. Surveying the scene with impassioned eyes, I slowly set the suitcase down without removing my gaze from the surrounding area. Though always considering adoption a mark of inferiority, I had imprisoned the feelings during military training because frailty had no place in the life of an infantry officer. Standing alone on the empty dock, I allowed my life-long craving for my birth mother to slowly emerge. Here in Mörfelden it was safe. The call rose from the depths of my soul and spilled into my heart with every breath.

As far back as I could stretch my memory and revisit the past there wasn't a time when I hadn't known I was adopted. The dreadful realization of being torn from my mother resulted in a yearning, a primordial ache, to find the woman who had given me life. Every day while growing up, every single day as far back as I could remember, I thought about her and about reestablishing nature's bond that connects mother and child.

As a boy, I learned to live with the suffering and anger of abandonment like one who slowly disciplines themself to accept the perpetual pain of a debilitating physical injury. My uprooting had shattered the protective shield that safeguarded my psyche, and only by discovering my mother could I hope to understand the adoption experience and find inner peace. In essence, I had never accepted my role as an adopted child or the life that came with it. I had never felt I belonged, was accepted by others, or was loved for who I was. Emotional serenity was foreign to me, and I believed healing would only come through union with the woman who had given me life. I didn't know how inner healing would take place, but I was certain Ilse Sander would mend the wound and stop the pain.

The search was more than a simple journey to discover my mother. It was also a voyage of inner faith. I felt if I could find out who my mother was, then I would find out who I was. By discovering my birth mother, I would accept my role in life, become capable of receiving and giving love, and gain a sense of belonging.

Why did she give me away? Where do I come from? Where do I belong? Is there anyone who looks like me? Who am I? Am I worthy of being loved and can I love in return? These questions constantly haunted me.

Standing on the railroad dock at Mörfelden, I grasped for the first time the reality that I might actually find my mother. It felt strange after so many years of only wishing and hoping to realize my dream might come true. A separate part of me awakened at the same time and questioned why I searched. The questioning voice was *reason*, and it came to challenge the inborn bond that linked me to my birth mother. For the first time, I had doubts about my desire to find her. Did I truly want to?

Reason asked: What, if any, positive outcome might result from a successful search? Wasn't it enough to appreciate life as an adoptee and to enjoy the many gifts I had been given? *Reason* went on to compare the life of an adoptee with that of an orphan. In all categories—wealth, education, opportunities—an adoptee came out ahead, and it logically followed that a second set of parents were far better than none.

Sentiment came forward and offered a different point of view: *Reason's* evaluation was based only on material criteria and failed to recognize emotion. The origins of human behavior often begin with the invisible stirrings of feelings. *Sentiment* said that a child could grow up in the house of the wealthiest family in the world, attend the very best schools and be given every available material gift, but that would never be enough. Without love, a child cannot know inner peace, and he remains forever incomplete. If love was the chief criterion on which to evaluate life, *sentiment* viewed a penniless orphan, who knew love, as better off than a loveless adopted child surrounded with material riches.

Reason argued back with a different question encouraging me to stop my search: By simply finding my birth mother, how would my life as an adoptee change? After all, what difference would it really make? Why not simply bury the past and get on with life?

Instinct stepped in to respond: Adopted parents can never claim that they are the natural parents. This biological chasm which cannot be bridged has special significance for adopted children regarding their mothers. The unseen bond originating in the womb at the time of conception, a link that forever connects mother and child, doesn't exist between adopted children and adopted mothers. If this link is broken, it shatters the natural order of life. When separated, an inherent reaction is for a mother and her lost offspring to search for one another.

Reason again objected. Hurling a series of "what ifs," *reason* suggested that a successful search could do more harm than simply not knowing. What if my mother rejected me a second time? What if she was an impoverished old maid? What if my sudden reappearance had a detrimental impact on her? What if my mother was dead?

Curiosity answered the last of *reason's* challenges: adopted children usually don't look like their adopted parents. That was certainly true in my case. I yearned to find my own flesh and blood, to see someone who looked like me. I wanted to know about my birth family, where they came from and to learn their history. I wanted to know why I wasn't kept by my birth parents and put in an orphanage instead. My mother would answer these questions, I thought. The urge to discover her outweighed any fear of possible rejection. I didn't care what she looked like, where she came from or what her position in life might be. I simply wanted to know, and *curiosity* drove me to find out.

Reason admitted more to the human condition than what could be compartmentalized within the confines of rational thought. Emotions fall outside the scope of logic and are unknowable to *reason*. *Sentiment, instinct* and *curiosity* were real, although they defied the five physical senses. Proof of the bond connecting mother and child was my arrival in Mörfelden, because I had no logical basis for being there. Conquering doubt, I returned to the task at hand.

Picking up my suitcase, I moved toward the aged building that served as the town's railroad station. The faint odor of disinfectant greeted me when I opened the door, reminding me of a hospital. An old man sitting behind a yellowing glass ticket counter was the only person inside. I quickly exited the other side of the building and entered the town where my mother had lived 23 years earlier.

The railroad station sat near one end of town. Mörfelden looked about 10 blocks long, with three-story buildings the tallest in town. A corner street sign indicated I was walking along the main street, Hauptstrasse, a two-lane road where an occasional car passed by. I walked inside a hotel two blocks from the train station and found a stout woman with graying hair busily dusting furniture in the foyer. She stopped when she heard the door close behind me and clasped the feather duster in both hands. In German, I asked for a room for one night, and the heavy-set woman threw a steely glance my way. Without a word, she shoved the feather duster on a table and marched to a tiny office. She thrust a registration form printed in German at me. I completed it as best I could. She examined the completed paperwork as I stood nearly at the position of attention.

"Eine Nacht?" she asked.

"Jawohl," I answered, my body straight as an arrow.

She ordered me to follow her to a single room on the second floor. I trailed behind as she showed me the community bath and handed me the room key before marching back downstairs.

With her footsteps echoing through the hallway, I closed the door and set my suitcase on the bed. I unzipped the suitcase cover and sifted through its contents, removing a yellowed piece of paper that had been translated from German to English. Carefully unfolding the document, I once more read the words that provided the only link to my past, "... Miss Ilse Sander... a clerk born at Kunzendorf on 31 December 1920... residing at 64 Frankfurter Strasse, Mörfelden... give up claim to be notified... irrevocability of these declarations..." Committing the street address to memory, I refolded the yellowed piece of paper and carefully tucked it into my back jean pocket. After locking the door to my room, I left the hotel.

Outside, the sun burned directly overhead and the warm air caused drops of perspiration to trickle down my chest and press against my long-sleeved sweatshirt. For an instant, I thought about returning to the room to change into a pair of shorts and t-shirt, but that would take time. I was in a hurry, so I continued along the Hauptstrasse and soon came to a bakery with its door swung invitingly open. Inside, I asked for directions to Frankfurter Strasse. A rotund baker with a gentle face and wide grin greeted me. He didn't speak English, but drew a map showing his shop and a route to the street where my mother had lived when she signed the Consent of Release form. Ten minutes after leaving the bakery I stood in front of a two-story house along Frankfurter Strasse. The numbers 64 were posted on its side.

I didn't spend time looking through the windows to catch a glimpse of someone inside. Instead, I hurried past the waist-high iron gate and walked up to the front door. Would anyone be home? I hadn't prepared a speech and didn't know what I'd say if my mother answered. Could this be the moment I had dreamed about?

My breathing became forced and blood throbbed in my temples with every racing heartbeat. I lifted a sweaty palm and without hesitation pushed the buzzer. The doorbell chimed. Footsteps thumped toward the door. Someone was unlocking the bolt. With eyes stretched wide, I watched the door slowly swing open. A female figure appeared in the doorway, a nice-looking woman in her mid-thirties. Instantly, "not my mother" flashed in my brain.

"Yes," she said in German. "What can I do for you?"

"Does Ilse Sander live here?" I stammered back.

She shook her head from side to side and answered no.

"Ilse Sander lived in this house in 1956, and I was hoping to find her."

She repeated that she didn't know Frau Sander and it was clear the name meant nothing to the woman standing in the doorway. Certain I had gained all that I could, I gave a dampened thank-you and left, closing the iron gate behind me.

Beforehand, I knew the slim possibility that my mother would still live at 64 Frankfurter Strasse. Still, I felt disappointed. On the return trip to the Hauptstrasse my body and confidence grew limp as adrenaline and intensity ebbed. Nothing had materialized from the only clue I had to my mother's whereabouts. Heaven only knew where she was.

Somewhere in Mörfelden there had to be proof she once lived here. I had to uncover that information and hope it would somehow lead me to her. Where would records of Mörfelden's citizens be stored? It was Saturday afternoon, so the townhall would be closed. What other organizations would keep documents of people who live, or had lived, in Mörfelden? Energy surged as a thought came. The police, of course.

I returned to the bakery. After a muddled conversation, the baker drew a second map. This time it contained directions to the town's police station.

Minutes later I entered Mörfelden's police station with renewed hope of obtaining the next clue. I must have been an unusual looking man to the three uniformed police officers and female secretary who sat behind a partition, separating them from the entryway lobby. They saw a young man hesitantly approach, who had a dark tan, and a quarter inch of hair. I wore faded jeans, scuffed penny loafers and an Auburn University sweat shirt. Certainly not the look and dress of a German. Their assumption proved correct when I spoke.

Though I tried my best to speak German, their looks changed from amused curiosity to icy stares as my rough sentences betrayed my Germanic roots. They thought I was a foreigner—an American. One of the policemen marched to the entryway door, opened it and motioned for me to leave. Remembering the prior evening's late night activities, I knew better than to press my case and skirted out the door, feeling a combination of humiliation barbed with anger.

They thought I was some stupid American and didn't even try to help. Disgusted with my lack of German-language proficiency, I nearly ran back to the Hauptstrasse to begin developing Plan C.

Along the main thoroughfare, now becoming quite familiar, I thought hard for options and pushed away the bitterness over the police station incident. I racked my brain for possibilities and refused to become discouraged by the setbacks. I was determined to come up with another idea. Using every bit of creativity, imagination and intelligence I possessed, I tried again to piece a picture together. My mother was born in a town called Kunzendorf, a town I had never heard of. When did she move to Mörfelden? One of the few facts I had was that my mother lived here when she was thirty-five. What year she moved here and when she left, if she left, were missing parts of the puzzle. Did she move to Mörfelden as a child? If not, what would make her come to this little town that didn't seem to offer much opportunity? Maybe she moved here only to give birth.

The possibilities seemed endless. I had drifted back to the train station and wandered inside. Unconsciously, I had retraced my steps as if I had forgotten something and had returned to retrieve the lost article.

Only the ticketmaster, rummaging through a cabinet behind the counter, was inside the station. Sparse furnishings decorated the interior. A pair of chipped wooden benches sat back to back in the center of the room. Pushed against a far wall stood a large oak table under a wide open rectangular window. The stale smell of disinfectant lingered, despite ceilings that must have been 14 feet high. I moved forward; the only sounds were my shoes knocking against the linoleum floor and echoing with a hollow resonance as I headed toward the table.

A telephone sat on top of the table, and beside it lay the object I didn't realize I had overlooked—a half-inch thick telephone book. I opened the frayed book and thumbed through the pages until I found the section listing last names beginning with the letter S. I examined the pages over and over, but there was no Ilse Sander. That meant she didn't live in Mörfelden any longer, or if she did, and my heart sunk with the idea, she had changed her last name. That would add another barrier to a quest already filled with significant obstacles. To make matters even worse, no one with the last name of Sander was listed in the book.

I racked my brains and paced the empty room until I finally came up with one last possibility. For the second time that day I walked out of the train station and headed back to the bakery to get directions to the biggest church in town. The mild-mannered baker picked up a piece of paper and pencil when he saw me enter his shop. "Church?" I asked while folding my hands together and gazing at the ceiling as if engaged in prayer. He drew a third map and handed it to me. Away I went. The baker had the disposition of a saint.

The church where he directed me wasn't far. Everything was within easy walking distance in this town where no more than 10,000 people lived. The church stood off on a side street, surrounded by beautiful grounds of flower gardens intermixed with shrubs, and evergreen trees that provided a refreshing coolness. An attached house adjoined the backside of the church. I picked up my gait and headed toward the house, thinking it had to be the rectory.

A few steps in front of the building, a medium-built man rounded a corner of the church and shouted my way. A black, broad-brimmed fedora partially obscured his clean shaven face. His solid black clothes were topped at the neck with a Roman collar. The image gave a me feeling of trust and calm as I watched the uniform draw closer. As always, the attire of a priest or nun gave me the same warm sensation. Time didn't diminish the emotional attachment I had developed for those selfless and kind religious people who had run the orphanage.

"The building is locked," he said in German. "Is there something I can help you with?"

"I wish to speak with the parish priest," I said, frustrated again by my poor grasp of German.

He continued walking and stopped directly in front of me. "I am the priest assigned to this parish. Are you British or American?"

"American," I answered.

"Very good," he said, switching from German to English. He explained he had visited both Great Britain and the United States.

"I'm always pleased to have an opportunity to maintain my proficiency with foreign languages. English is such a splendid language, don't you think?" With far-away eyes he reminisced about some bygone pleasant experience. But he caught himself and came back to the present. "Now, how may I be of assistance?"

I was grateful to speak English and told my story, saying I had traveled to Mörfelden to find my mother. I ended by sharing the day's earlier events at 64 Frankfurter Strasse and at the police station.

"Ah yes," he answered thoughtfully, while slowly rubbing his chin and looking at his black shoes. "The police have had many problems with American soldiers, but it is still too bad they didn't assist you." The priest stopped rubbing his chin, crossed his arms over his chest and looked at me. "Have you examined a telephone book to see if your mother is listed?"

"Yes. I've tried that too, but without success. There wasn't a Sander in the book. I'm afraid she might have changed her last name." I stopped there, unwilling to admit the terrible possibility she might be dead.

The priest's eyes narrowed behind silver-rimmed glasses, and wrinkles creased his forehead beneath the brim of his black hat. I sensed he didn't entirely trust the foreigner's story, and it seemed he tried to decide if my story was genuine or forged. I wondered how anyone could make up a story like mine.

After I finished, he turned his head to one side and resumed rubbing his chin. Then the priest turned his gaze toward me and offered help after a few moments' pause. "We have records stored in the church, and if your mother was a parishioner, she'll be listed in our historical files. Unfortunately, I'm leaving town in a few hours and won't return until tomorrow evening. But if you come back on Monday morning I'll examine the files to see if your mother was a member of the parish. We might have information that could be helpful."

I desperately wanted to ask if he could look before leaving for his trip. Instead, I thanked him and tried to present an air of gratitude while masking the disappointment at having to wait. The church archives might contain a valuable clue, and I didn't want to damage any chances of gaining access to those records. Still, Monday seemed a long way off. I felt as if I was standing outside in a freezing rain with my face pressed close against a window, craving the warm comfort of the room inside. I didn't want to wait anymore. With the future showing more uncertainty than promise, I shook the priest's hand and told him I'd come back on Monday morning.

On the return route to the main street an empty bus stop offered a welcome bench and I slumped onto the wooden planks. Leaning forward, bringing both elbows to rest on top of my knees, I dejectedly lowered my head into the palms of my hands. Closing my eyes, I cut off the outside world and let my imagination run free.

Spiralling within the depths of fantasy, I find myself the only person sitting in a darkened theater. A projector starts and fills the room with a whirling click..click..click.. and casts shadowy figures with its flickering light. The clicking noise fades to a soothing hum. Numbers alternately fill the screen in a countdown, 5-4-3-2-1, and a blurry picture encased in large black borders appears. The film's dark edges recede and give way to a black and white motion picture of Mörfelden—the train station, hotel, bakery, then to Frankfurter Strasse. The scenes are from 1956.

No sounds interrupt the silent theater as the picture zooms in on a woman in her mid-30s. She's carefully walking on a sidewalk along Frankfurter Strasse, face obscured, height and weight indistinct. The woman directs her entire attention to a baby cradled in her arms. Arriving at a cross street, she stops and looks down to the bundle at her breast. Pulling back the head garments, she smiles softly and caresses the baby's fine hair.

The picture frame freezes and I long to address the image:

Oh dear mother, why did you abandon me? Was I too much for you, more than you were able to care for? Was I an inconvenience and you rejected me to continue life without the hardships of raising an unwanted son? Was my conception an accident, a gross mistake, and you got rid of me to get rid of a constant reminder of some unpleasant experience? Was your rebuff an attempt to forget? Or, could your decision to put me in an orphanage have been a selfless act because you believed an institution for forsaken children would offer more opportunity than you could provide?

Still mentally sitting in the empty theater, looking at the picture, my thoughts continue:

Did you know the haunting pain and loneliness our separation would cause? Did you know that grief, spurred from not knowing you, would mercilessly follow me, no matter where I went or how much time passed?

The screen remains frozen, with the woman gently smiling at the baby clutched in her arms.

The reason for your decision isn't important, because if you feel guilt, I'll forgive and be grateful if your motive was unselfish and for my benefit. It doesn't matter why you put me in the orphanage. I will find you no matter what it takes, because you are my mother.

Outside the theater a car horn blows, and the picture disintegrates. I'm back sitting on the bus stop bench, staring at the ground beneath my feet. The horn blows a second time. Raising my head out of my palms, I looked up to see a taxi, with the driver shrugging his shoulders and raising his hands asking if I want a ride. I shook my head no, and he drove away.

What can I do? I didn't know what to do. Remain in Mörfelden until Monday and visit the priest? Stay around waiting for the townhall to open, hoping they'd have records providing additional information? Maybe the church and townhall archives wouldn't even mention Ilse Sander. Either way, a timeless abyss separated me from Monday. I didn't want to keep on waiting... waiting... waiting...

Echoes of a remote valley in the far away mountains of north Georgia swept through me. As I lay on the frozen ground it seemed as if I had been waiting forever. Am I in the right place? Is waiting merely an exercise to test my endurance? Once again, I had reached that place where the night is darkest, and I was forced to draw on all my mental strength to resist the idea that I might never find my mother.

I was so close but couldn't bridge the invisible barrier that cloaked the past. She walked these very same streets 23 years ago. If only I had a time machine. I'd set the controls to 1956 and sail backward along the continuum of time and find her.

Undeniably, the candlelight of hope flickered, and one more gust of wind might forever extinguish the flame. Before I could sink deeper into self-pity a new idea began to materialize. Gradually it coagulated, slowly took shape and crystallized into a coherent thought. The idea was so bizarre that it just might work, and it filled me with fresh confidence and renewed energy. My body once again pumped adrenaline. Suddenly I didn't feel despair or sadness. Every nerve in my body came alive; my senses awakened to a keen state of alertness.

No time machine existed to take me to 1956 Mörfelden, but I had another way to travel to the past. If I could find someone who had lived in Mörfelden during the mid-1950s they could carry me back in time through their experiences. My time machine would be someone else's memory. I would ask elderly people if they had lived in Mörfelden in 1956 and if so, had they known Ilse Sander.

A few people walked on the street, going about their Saturday afternoon business. Getting off the bench, I headed for an aged woman a block away who moved slowly, using a cane for support. I rapidly overtook her and glided past, a couple of steps. Then I turned around and looked at her.

"Excuse me gnädige Frau. I am looking for a woman named Frau Ilse Sander who lived here in 1956. Do you know her?"

She stopped, leaned forward on the cane with one hand as the other trembled involuntarily at her side. Despite the warm temperature she wore a dark woolen sweater and covered her head with a gray cloth kerchief. She arched her head upward, and I saw surprisingly clear blue eyes, in stark contrast to her bent body and wrinkled face.

"No, I don't know her," was all she said and hobbled away.

Adrenaline formed a protective shield, so I was unscathed despite another set-back. Determined to find the trail, I continued searching, like a hunting dog that madly sniffs the earth to pick up the scent of its quarry.

A man pushing a bicycle, accompanied by a woman carrying a canvas bag by its straps, appeared from around a corner. They walked toward me and looked to be in their fifties, maybe sixties—suitable candidates. I approached them and forced myself to remain calm. They talked to one another and didn't seem to notice me.

"Excuse me," I interrupted.

They stopped.

"Did you live in Mörfelden in 1956? Did you know Ilse Sander?" I blurted out the words without thinking how crazy it probably sounded to total strangers.

"Ilse Sander?" the woman answered with a question.

"Yes, I'm looking for Ilse Sander who lived here in 1956. She was my mother and put me in an orphanage. I was adopted by American parents and grew up in the United States. I have come to Mörfelden to find my mother. I was hoping you might know her."

They listened without interrupting and turned to each other after hearing my impassioned plea. How clear it was in German I didn't know and only hoped they understood the key points. It was my turn to listen.

The man and woman engaged in a short dialogue that I couldn't understand, except picking out the name Sander, mentioned several times. Their conversation ended abruptly when they turned my way. My eyes looked at them and begged a favorable response.

The man spoke fast so that I struggled to understand what he said. They didn't know my mother but thought they knew a woman with the last name of Sander. But the woman named Sander didn't live in Mörfelden. They wanted me to follow them home where they would try to contact her by telephone.

I agreed, and we left for their house. The couple talked excitedly between themselves, and I understood little of what they said. A few times they stopped talking and looked at me, as if expecting a response. I nodded my head and said "Ja," hoping it was an appropriate answer.

We arrived at their modest home and went into a parlor where they asked me to sit. The woman disappeared into the kitchen. The man shuffled up a wooden staircase and soon returned, accompanied by a boy who looked to be in his mid-teens. After a quick introduction, they all sat side-by-side on a sofa.

The youth had the look of an angelic warrior—startling blue eyes beneath golden hair, rosy cheeks along with an athletic build. The miniature archangel spoke in English saying the man and woman were his grandparents, and they wanted him to act as a translator. The grandfather looked on admiringly and put his arm around his grandson.

The woman reappeared, having donned a white apron, and carried a tray holding a porcelain pitcher of coffee, matching saucers, cups, cream and sugar containers, silver spoons and cloth napkins. She set the tray on a coffee table, served the adults, and took a seat in a wooden rocking chair. The grandparents began talking, and the boy, who spoke the beautiful Queen's English, translated.

"My grandparents have lived in Mörfelden all their lives, but neither recognize the name Ilse Sander. They knew a couple by the name of Kauer who had moved to Mörfelden in the 1950's. A husband and wife along with their three or four children. The woman's name was Maria."

I sat on the edge of my chair and held the coffee cup with both hands. Silently I nodded.

"The Kauer family only lived in Mörfelden a few years, but during that time they established a friendship with my grandparents. Since they left, my grandparents and the Kauer's have maintained their friendship through letters and phone calls."

I remained quiet. How was this going to tie into my search?

"My grandmother isn't sure, but she thinks Maria Kauer's maiden name is Sander. If so, she hopes there might be a connection between her and Ilse Sander. She will try to call Maria after we are done talking. Is there anything you wish to add?"

"No," I said, stunned at the possibility. "Please tell your grandparents I am very thankful for their help."

He relayed my statement and his grandparents acknowledged it with a nod of their heads. They put their cups down and went into an adjacent room to make the telephone call. The boy and I stayed in the parlor and, thankfully, he was quiet. I stretched my ears to the bordering room but couldn't make out what his grandparents said.

Time flashed by as I tried to analyze this new information. Before I could put anything together the couple returned to their seats in the parlor. Another exchange took place, with the boy continuing to translate in his wonderful British-German accent. His grandparents stared at me with wide-open eyes of astonishment.

"Maria Kauer lives with her husband in a town called Hofgeismar, about 150 kilometers from Mörfelden," the archangel said. "My grandmother was correct. Marie's maiden name is Sander and she has a niece named Ilse Sander. My grandmother wrote Maria's address for you."

The woman leaned forward in her rocking chair and smiled while handing me a slip of paper. I took it and was so excited that I only read the name written on the top line. I tried to think of what to say but couldn't in English, much less in German, find words to adequately express my gratefulness.

They said I could take a train from Mörfelden to Hofgeismar and walked me to their front door. We all shook hands as I continued thanking them, and they wished me luck. I ran back to the hotel, grabbed my suitcase and checked out. The same drill sergeant made me pay half a night's lodging. I would have gladly paid a full night's bill.

The old ticketmaster still sat behind the counter with yellowing glass. I took the slip of paper from my pocket and read the name of the town where Maria Kauer lived. Soon after, the train for Hofgeismar pulled away from the loading dock. I stared out a railroad car window, looking at a sign painted Mörfelden.

Following the Trail

The train sped north through the farmlands and forests of central Germany. A man and his son sat opposite me in a compartment as I half-heartedly tried to read a paperback book. Turning page after page without remembering the words, I finally put the book back inside my suitcase. Outside the railroad car window the fading sun painted streaks of blue, gray and crimson on the canvas sky. I wasn't tired. Sunset always brought me new energy. "Peter, the wolf, comes alive at night," I laughed. Hunger gnawed at my stomach and I remembered I hadn't eaten since breakfast.

Excusing myself past the man and boy, I slid out of the compartment and made my way to the diner car. After my meal I studied a map of Germany to find where I was going. The conductor who checked my ticket when boarding had said I would have to change trains at Kassel, a city about 30 miles south of Hofgeismar. The timetables said I'd arrive in Hofgeismar around midnight, but I planned to go straight to the Kauer's residence.

Before leaving the diner car, I read the slip of paper the woman had given me in Mörfelden:

> Maria & Hieronymus Kauer
> 1600 Hemminger Strasse
> Hofgeismar

Assured that I wasn't dreaming, I put the slip of paper back into my wallet.

Back in my compartment I reviewed the day's events. I felt a great relief from the pressure of not knowing if I would find my mother. Despite all the difficulties I had somehow made the right connections. God, I was lucky to run into that man and woman in Mörfelden. What were the odds of finding people who knew my great-aunt and remembered her maiden name? Divine Providence seemed to guide me along my journey.

Still, a bit of uneasiness remained. What if I was on track to meet the wrong Ilse Sander? Was Sander a common German surname? Was it the American equivalent of Jones or Smith? If Maria Sander Kauer wasn't really my great aunt, then her niece wouldn't be my mother. I'd soon learn if Maria Kauer's lineage would perfectly match the facts I knew about my past.

The train pulled to a stop at a station too small to be Kassel. The man and boy gathered their belongings and left the compartment. The conductor slid open the door a few minutes later.

"All passengers must exit, " he said.

I stared at him in disbelief and asked, "Excuse me but could you repeat yourself?"

"I'm sorry but you have to get off," he answered. "This train is out of operation for the night."

I got up out of my seat and gave him my ticket. "I bought a ticket to Hofgeismar. You told me I had to change trains in Kassel. Is this Kassel?" I asked, thinking perhaps I had mistaken the town outside.

The conductor took my ticket. "No this isn't Kassel," he said, examining my ticket. He pulled a fat schedule book out from his navy-blue vest pocket and leafed through the pages. "The next train to Kassel departs from this station tomorrow morning at 5:45. At Kassel you can catch a train to Hofgeismar."

I grabbed my suitcase and stepped off the train. If push came to shove, I'd go to the edge of town and sleep in a field until morning. The weather was warm, and I was used to sleeping outdoors in only my clothes.

Thankfully, I didn't have to undergo another night of infantry training and checked into a hotel a block from the train station. It was nearly midnight by the time I made my way to a tiny, second-floor hotel room. Setting the suitcase on a chair crammed into one corner of the room, I brushed my teeth, washed my face and hands, set the alarm clock for 5:00 a.m., and sat on the bed. Anticipation and excitement energized me. I felt caged. Looking out the room's only window, I saw nothing but an empty street below. A red-neon "Gäste" sign glowed above a building doorway on the opposite side of the street. Thinking that might be a place to unwind, I headed for the neon light.

The "Gäste" in the small town had a different atmosphere compared to the beer halls in Wiesbaden: quieter, three-quarters empty, breathable air, and only German music played on the juke box. I took a seat at a table and ordered a Pils.

Another night's wait wasn't going to kill me. I wanted to relax, but the day's events kept me in a state of excitement. Hunger again gnawed at my stomach, and I ordered the only food available, a couple of bags of peanuts. I sat in my chair and ate one peanut at a time, realizing I was tired, not physically but emotionally and mentally. The roller-coaster in Mörfelden had drained me. My problem-solving abilities were stretched to their limits, and continually communicating in a language I barely knew added to the mental drain. My brain felt tired, like muscles the day after vigorous exercise. I was alone and didn't have anyone to share my experiences with, no conversation to help diffuse the tension. Emotional and mental fatigue, coupled with the language barrier, discouraged me from striking up a conversation with a stranger, and the "Gäste" didn't have a television to offer a distraction. So I did what I always did, I internalized my thoughts and emotions.

I reviewed the day's events, too drained to contemplate what might happen next. Then I got the distraction I wanted. In fact, two distractions. They walked in and sat a couple of tables away—two German women about my age. Instantly, they became the center of my attention. Their natural beauty and expressive mannerisms kept me captivated. I alternated glances between the two women and the lip of the beer mug where I ran the edge of my index finger. For the first time, I viewed German women in a romantic manner. We shared a common ancestry, heritage and culture. By the time I finished the peanuts and beer I had imagined myself courting, marrying and living happily ever after with one of the women sitting at the table. But the romantic interlude didn't last long. Low self-esteem still kept me emotionally separated from people and overpowered my romantic fantasy. My insecurities said I didn't deserve the women I desired, and I again experienced the same lonely feelings I had known since childhood. Finishing the beer, I paid the bill and walked out of the "Gäste" without saying a word to the women. Back in the hotel room I rechecked the alarm and fell into bed.

The next morning the alarm sounded at 5:00 a.m., jolting me out of a deep sleep. Thirty minutes later I stood panting and out of breath at the railroad station. I'd run from the hotel, afraid I'd miss the train. But I needn't have

panicked because exactly at 5:45 a.m. the train for Kassel screeched to a halt at
the passenger loading dock. The timely precision of German trains amazed me;
they arrived and departed exactly as printed on the schedule. Forty-five
minutes later I changed trains at Kassel and soon after arrived in Hofgeismar.

The sleepy town was barely waking. A few people went about their
Sunday morning business as I walked toward the center of town with suitcase
in hand. It was another beautiful day with not a cloud in the sky. My senses
never seemed as keen, and I effortlessly absorbed my surroundings. Birds
sang; the air seemed perfumed with the fragrance of flowers; dew clung to
the morning grass, and a distant church bell chimed seven times. I felt alive,
calm and confident with the sun's warmth against my body.

Sixteen-hundred Hemminger Strasse was a newer two-story apartment
building set off the street by a sidewalk and narrow strip of manicured
grass. The Kauers lived in the apartment on the bottom, far left-hand side
of the long, white building. I walked up three steps to the building's
entryway door and rang the buzzer. Then I back-pedaled to the base of the
steps, holding my suitcase, waiting for the door to open.

No forced breathing, sweaty palms or racing heartbeat this time; only a
calm confidence. A minute passed, and I started back up the steps to ring
the buzzer a second time when I heard the sound of a window unlatching
to my immediate left. The first-floor window swung outward. It didn't have
a screen, and a woman was visible only from the waist up. She leaned out
the window with both her hands planted on the sill. She had obviously just
gotten out of bed; her silver hair was slightly disheveled and she was
wearing a silk robe over a nightgown. She looked stately and kind.

I felt awkward, knowing I had wakened her. She straightened the robe
tighter around her waist and poked her head outside. "Yes," she said. The
friendliness in her voice surprised me.

"Are you Maria Kauer?" I asked in German.

"I am." She replied in German.

"Do you have a niece named Ilse Sander?"

"Yes."

"Did she have a son who was born in June of 1955?"

"Yes," again. Her voice gave no sign of impatience or waning interest.

"Was his name Peter Friedrich Sander?"

"Yes," she said nodding her head.

"I am that boy."

Maria Kauer's jaw dropped as she put both hands to her cheeks. "Moment, moment. I'll be right there." She closed the window and disappeared. As I waited for her to come to the door I realized her answers matched my past. I was on the right path and felt a quiet relief, like men who have just survived a battle on the winning army's side.

She opened the door and extended her arms to give me a warm embrace. "Welcome Peter, welcome." She was the first blood relative I had seen or touched in 22 years.

Maria Kauer smiled at me while still holding my arms with her hands. I returned a nervous grin. "Come this way, come this way," she said excitedly, and I followed her down a narrow hallway and through a door that opened into a small living room. Oak furniture sat over a rich red Persian rug. Oil and watercolor paintings hung on the sky-blue walls, and the morning sun streaked through white lace curtains, filling the room with light and warmth. I stood in the living room while Maria looked me over from head to toe. She asked me to sit, after her inspection.

"I am very happy to see you," she said, still smiling. "I often wondered about you. The last I knew you were in an orphanage. What happened?"

I answered her by sharing parts of my history. I ended and said I could speak only a little German, and it would be helpful if she talked slowly.

"I am sorry, I don't speak English," Maria said looking genuinely sad. A noise from a back room interrupted our conversation. "Moment," she said and headed toward the noise. I heard a male voice talking and hers. A short time later she came back with her comforting smile. She had changed from bedtime attire to a nice blue cotton dress with matching belt and black low-heeled shoes. She looked like a model on the cover of a senior magazine. A man trailed behind, matching her years but lacking Maria's vitality. He walked with the slow, forced movements of age. He wore drab, gray dungarees, a dull, red flannel shirt, and sandals. Although slightly taller than Maria, her husband still had to look up to my face when she introduced us.

"This is Ilse's son—Peter," she said, looking at me with a sparkle in her blue eyes. "This is my husband, Hieronymus Kauer." We shook hands, and I sensed that he thought it was okay for me to be in his home.

Maria told us both to sit, and she walked into the kitchen to prepare breakfast. Hieronymus creaked into a burgundy armchair, and I sank into a matching sofa. He felt awkward being alone with a total stranger, and neither of us said a word. Only the ticking of a grandfather clock and Maria banging away in the kitchen broke the silence. I figured he didn't speak English though he occasionally gave a timid glance my way. My great-uncle picked up a newspaper resting at the foot of his chair and held it toward me as if asking if I wanted to read. I shook my head no and laughed, saying I couldn't read German. That broke the ice. I asked Hieronymus what he did for a living, and he gave a short chuckle saying he was a Pensionär, that he was retired. Pointing to a painting of a great cathedral hanging on the living room wall, I asked where the cathedral was located. He sat back in his chair, set the paper by his feet and told me about the cathedral. When he finished I asked about another painting and he gave its history. I kept pointing and Hieronymus kept explaining. I couldn't understand a lot of what he said, but our interaction made me feel welcomed.

Maria called from the dining area for us to come for breakfast. She had set the table with slices of dark bread, hard-boiled eggs, meat and cheeses, jam, butter, milk and coffee. In between bites, I took advantage of the opportunity to expand my German vocabulary. I asked the word for every item on the table I didn't already know. With the patience of a teacher, Maria answered each question and took the extra step of ensuring I correctly pronounced each word.

I held up a piece of cheese.

"Käse," Maria said.

"Käse," I repeated.

I picked up a spoon.

"Löffel," Maria instructed.

"Löffel," I repeated mispronouncing the word.

"Nein, Löffel," she said stretching her mouth outward to accentuate the difficult oi sound.

During breakfast my questions turned from basic German vocabulary to inquiries about my past. As before, Maria did the talking. She told me my mother now lived in Bad Nauheim. For the first time, I sensed Maria was uncomfortable, hesitating, as if unsure of her answers. She said my mother lived in a sanatarium, a group home. Maria said she'd call my mother after we ate but added she hadn't seen or talked to Ilse in five years.

After breakfast I helped Maria clear the table and wash the dishes while Hieronymus retired to the living room and read the paper. I was attracted to Maria, not only because she was my blood relative but also for her genuine warmth, intelligence and easy manner. Maria treated me as if I were a son who had returned from a long journey. She wasn't judgmental or overbearing and didn't seem to expect anything from me.

We finished washing dishes in the kitchen, then I followed Maria to the living room. She knelt in front of a large trunk and rummaged through a bottom cabinet. Hieronymus stopped reading and asked Maria what she was doing, a question he seemed not to expect answered. Maria kept quiet while inspecting the contents in the cabinet—boxes, photo albums, document folders—and stacked them in piles to her left and right. After emptying the cabinet, she asked me to help carry a pile to the dining room table.

I sat between Maria and Hieronymus as the education on my family history began. Maria opened a shoebox and pulled out a photo. She studied it and passed it to me while giving a brief explanation on the person. I looked at it and passed the picture to Hieronymus who adjusted his glasses and muttered a few sentiments. Maria said the photos were of their immediate and extended family. She had passed five or six photos when I interrupted and told my great-aunt and uncle that the pictures were of my family too. The intensity in my voice surprised even me. They paused and agreed that the people in the pictures were my relatives too, and that I was part of their family. Maria resumed digging through the shoebox with a smile on her face.

We finished reviewing the contents of the shoe box, and Maria opened the first photo album. The three of us scooted closer together to look. As with the contents of the shoebox, they were family photos. Maria flipped the pages and I looked for resemblances between myself and the people in the pictures, sometimes stretching my imagination to find them. The photographs were all black and white, page after page. Maria turned mid-way through the second album and stopped. She momentarily lost control of herself, staring at a single picture centered on the page—the portrait of a man. He looked distinguished and handsome, maybe in his fifties or sixties, wearing a dark suit and tie with a white shirt.

Maria leaned back in her chair. "That is my older brother," she said. "He died in the late 1950s and is buried in a cemetery at Mörfelden. He was Ilse's father."

She stopped looking at the portrait and turned her gaze toward me. "That is your grandfather—Peter Friedrich Sander. You were named after him."

I stared at the face in the photo.

Hieronymus finally joined in. "Your grandfather was a good and kind man. Family and friends respected him. He was an Oberlerher."

I didn't know the English equivalent for Oberlerher. Headmaster seemed to be the closest translation. I stared at the portrait of my grandfather and felt comfort in knowing how I got my name.

"My American parents kept my first two names," I said. "They changed Sander to Dodds."

Maria and Hieronymus tried to pronounce Dodds and after a few unsuccessful attempts returned their attention to the photo album. With each new page I soaked up the information, as if studying for a test. I tried to absorb everything about the people so I could learn my heritage. I gained a sense of history, where my family came from, and it helped explain the events that brought me into the world.

We finished the last album, but there hadn't been one picture of Ilse Sander. I asked Maria if she had a picture of my mother. She looked at me as if, "Oh yeah, I knew there was something I forgot," and returned to the trunk to look through the cabinets. "I'm sorry. I can't find a picture of your mother," Maria said, sitting back down at the table.

Hieronymus helped Maria unfold a large map of central Europe. "We are Sudetendeutsch," Maria said. "We are the Germans who for centuries had lived in western and central Czechoslovakia in the provinces of Bohemia and Moravia." She pointed her finger to the northern section of central Czechoslovakia, a town near the Polish border. "We lived here until coming to Germany. Kunzendorf isn't printed on the map because it's too small. That's the town where your grandparents and mother lived."

Another match. The adoption Consent of Release form listed Kunzendorf as my mother's birthplace. Further proof that I had found my true roots.

"At the end of the war the Sudetendeutschen were forced out of Czechoslovakia into Germany. We eventually arrived in Mörfelden and met the man and woman who helped you yesterday."

That's the connection, I thought. I silently vowed to one day visit Kunzendorf, Czechoslovakia.

"So what do you think?" Maria asked, standing up after putting the shoebox, map and albums back in the trunk.

"Thank you for telling me about my family. I always wanted to know where I came from and who my relatives were. You told me so much that I can't remember everything. You're very kind."

Maria showed her easy smile and sat in an armchair holding a small blue book, notepad and pencil. She told me to sit down, and picked up a telephone. I thought how lucky I was to meet a person as wonderful as Maria.

But the tone of her voice shifted from calm and soothing to powerful and authoritarian when she talked on the phone. She asked for Ilse Sander and listened while writing on the pad. She hung up with a professional, "Vielen Dank. Auf Wiedersehen."

I watched her dial a second number. Efficiency didn't allow her to give me the play by play. I sat listening and willed a connection between her and my mother.

Again she asked for Frau Ilse Sander. "Ja, ja, I can wait," she said twirling the pencil in her fingers.

More waiting. The grandfather clock ticked slowly. Moments dragged by.

I flinched when Maria resumed talking. The tone of her voice had changed back to a familiar one. She was talking to my mother. I knew it.

They exchanged courtesies. She asked Ilse to sit, saying she had something very important to tell her.

"I have news about your son. This morning Peter came here to try and find you. He's sitting with me right now." Maria became quiet and listened to Ilse's response.

I sat on the sofa, motionless. Maria's speech accelerated to a speed where I couldn't understand. She talked a few more minutes, lowered the phone and looked at me.

"Would you like to talk with your mother?"

I shook my head yes and went to her side. Maria handed me the telephone.

"Hello," I said.

On the other end I heard a raspy female voice speaking in German. "Peter, Peter is it you?"

"Yes," I answered, standing stiff as a board. My rigid body felt numb, as if the flow of blood had been cut off. Sweat turned the telephone slippery, as if it were covered with oil. I fought to control my emotions.

Ilse talked so fast I couldn't understand what she said. On the phone I didn't have the advantage of seeing body language and facial expressions. "I don't understand, slower please," I said, trying to put an image to the voice.

Ilse paused and started again. This time her words came forced. There were artificial pauses between each word as she tried to slow her rate of speech. She finished with, "Peter, Peter, come to me. Come to your mother."

I felt the last two sentences. They gave the same effect one has after downing a straight shot of whiskey. I had blackness around the edge of my vision, and a warm burst of energy erupting from the base of my stomach. Euphoric excitement spread throughout my body.

"Yes," was all I could say.

She returned to a normal rate of speech and I understood only her closing sentences. "Come to me Peterlein. Auf Wiedersehen." I handed the telephone to Maria without saying another word.

My great-aunt and mother talked a few more minutes as Maria reassured me with her smile. I had regained my composure by the time Maria hung up. Hieronymus stood in the dining room doorway wearing a grave face and clutching the folded newspaper. He and Maria disappeared into the kitchen and after a brief conversation, Maria said we were going to visit my mother. The three of us left Hofgeismar an hour later.

The First Key

I sat in the back seat of the Kauer's late-model two-door Audi as we pulled away from the apartment building. The car's red exterior glistened from a recent wash and wax. The interior was spotless and the engine sounded well-maintained. Before departing Hofgeismar, Hieronymus filled up at an Esso gas station and was seething when he got back inside the car. It was the first time I saw him display emotion.

"Gasoline is too expensive. We can't keep paying these prices," he told Maria. Hieronymus pulled out of the station gripping the steering wheel so hard his knuckles turned white.

"Calm down or you'll get us in an accident," Maria said. My great-aunt wasn't as patient with her husband as with me.

I offered to help pay for the gas, but they politely refused, and we left Hofgeismar heading south on an autobahn. Hieronymus drove about 60 miles per hour and stayed in the far right-hand lane as traffic whizzed by. I understood little of the conversation between my two relatives and turned my attention to the beauty of the passing farmlands and forests.

In one sense, the drive was boring compared to the exploits of the helicopter pilot who picked me up at the airport in Frankfurt. But on the final leg of my search I didn't want outside entertainment. The excitement of completing a life-long search fueled my emotions and thoughts. I tried to form a mental picture of the woman with the raspy voice but no image materialized. I'd have to wait until we arrived in Bad Nauheim to discover her appearance, and I kept my imagination in check to prevent expectations from ruining our reunion. I didn't prepare a script or list of questions as if I was headed to conduct a one-time interview. Time didn't seem to be a factor because, unlike 22 years ago when my mother abandoned me, she had welcomed me today. One brief sentence she said during our telephone conversation played over and over in my head, "Peter, Peter, come to me."

We exited the autobahn at Bad Nauheim and Maria gave directions as I leaned forward in the middle of the back seat with my fingers interlaced between my bent knees. The Audi wound its way through Bad Nauheim and I rotated my gaze like a radar dish, glancing left, right, and back to the front trying to pick up any signal of my mother. We turned off a main street and followed a road paralleling a park to our left. Maria glanced down at the directions resting on her lap and instructed Hieronymus to slow down. She said the name of a street where he should turn and the car slowed. Hieronymus flicked the blinker and we turned right onto a residential side street. Huge houses, more like mansions than ordinary homes, lined each side of the road. We drove two blocks further and Maria said to stop. An immense three-story, yellow house sat off to our left, with half-dozen lethargic men and women resting on its covered porch.

Maria looked at the huge house with the yellow stucco exterior so I looked at the house. That must be where my mother lived, and I sifted through the crowd on the porch trying to identify Ilse Sander. The group was busy doing nothing, so she certainly couldn't be one of them. The porch-sitters looked lifeless, too down and out for one of them to possibly be my mother. She must be inside, I thought.

Hieronymus parallel parked on the opposite side of the street. My eyes never left the sanatarium, not wanting to miss the moment when my mother walked out onto the porch. Maria got out of the car first and walked across the street. Hieronymus creaked his old bones out of the driver's seat and held his door open to let me out of the back. No one had joined the group of lifeless people while we parked.

Hieronymus and I crossed the street, and I saw Maria shaking hands with a woman on the porch. This was the moment I had thought of every day as far back as I could remember, and I had never wished that my mother have a certain physical appearance. But despite every conviction I had ever made, when the moment of truth came, I wanted my mother to be attractive, slender and tall. The woman I wanted wasn't on the porch.

Maria shook hands with a woman who had the hardened face of someone who had lived a tough life, a face like a bum. She was short and squat with huge bags puffing out from beneath her eyes. Even-cut greasy hair, thin and graying, just touched the base of her thick neck. Her clothes looked like they belonged in a Goodwill bin. She and Maria waited for me to reach the porch.

The woman with the face of having lived a hard life had tears in her eyes. "Peter come to me," she said in a raspy voice and Ilse Sander stretched both arms wide. Her figure transformed into the shape of the crucified Christ atoning for past sins as I moved forward to enter her embrace.

Our hug didn't last more than a second or two. As we parted and stepped back from each other, my mother fought for self-control with a ferocious inner strength. She stopped the flow of tears and used the back of her hands to wipe away those that had fallen. At the same time, I felt humiliating disgrace, a shame so deep that I withdrew into the safe confines of my interior castle where emotion and feeling could not follow. Out of the corner of my eye I saw my great-aunt and uncle watch the reunion with quiet respect and glimpsed the open-mouthed stares of others on the porch. No one's judgement or pity could harm me if I hid in my inner sanctuary. I felt absolutely nothing and sunk inward to a depth where I could watch the drama unfold like a disinterested third-party.

Ilse and Peter Sander, reunited mother and son, stood a few feet apart and stared at each other like boxers exhausted after the final round. After regaining her composure, the mother looked up at the man she had brought into the world. She stepped toward her creation as if spellbound and raised her hands to touch his face. Her son stood motionless while she pressed outstretched fingertips along the top of his forehead. Stubby fingers ran down the contours of the man's forehead, over dark eyebrows and onto his nose. His arms hung limp as she stroked his cheeks and pressed fingers against his jawline. Dropping her hands and retreating backward, she snapped out of her spell, satisfied by the touch of her own flesh and blood. Not once during his mother's inspection had Peter moved, and he felt no connection to the woman he had thought about every day for nearly his entire life.

"I thought about you every day since I had to put you in the orphanage," Ilse said. "I drank too much and couldn't take care of you. My father and mother took you from me because I was always drunk. They were too old to raise you and decided to put you in the orphanage. I didn't want them to. They made me sign the papers. After you were gone, I drank every day and always cried. I cried so much after losing you."

Peter knew little about alcoholism, only that it afflicted the dregs of society. Seeing alcoholism staring at him in the form of his mother frightened him. Hiding inside the castle was the only way he knew to cope with this fear.

"Everyday I thought about finding you," Peter said, substituting English words when he didn't know the German equivalent. "I wanted to know who you were and what you looked like. You have dimples when you smile, just like me." He placed his mother's hand on his cheek and smiled so Ilse could feel his dimple.

"Dimples?" she asked mispronouncing the English word. A faint smile graced Ilse's face as she rubbed her cheek.

"Yes, dimples. We have both have dimples." That and dark colored hair were their only two physical similarities. Ilse stood ten inches shorter than her son. Her face was round, Peter's angular. He had a Roman nose, his mother's small and pug-shaped. Ilse had thin hair, his was thick. His eyes were blue, her's hazel. She was squat, he was slender.

Have I found the right woman? Peter wondered. Is this Ilse Sander my mother? Yes, she had to be—every piece perfectly fits the puzzle.

"What happened to you? Do you have other parents?" Ilse asked with narrowed eyes and in a tone barbed with jealousy.

"American parents adopted me when I was nearly three. I grew up in the United States. Now I'm an American Army officer and am stationed at Mainz. I arrived in Germany three days ago and the first thing I wanted to do was find you."

"It only took you three days to find me? That was the first thing you did when you came back to Germany?" Ilse's face lit up as she looked at Maria

and Hieronymus. "Were your American parents good to you?" she asked
not really wanting to know.

"Yes, they treated me very well."

Ilse didn't want to know anything more about replacement parents and
switched the direction of the conversation. Her body tensed and in a
menacing voice she said, "You are German. Your father was German. You
have the blue eyes of a German. You should live here in Germany. Do you
have a wife and children?"

"No. I don't have any children and am not married."

"Good, you should marry a German woman!"

Her son nodded. "Do you know where my father is?"

Ilse's voice became increasingly bitter and fire blazed in her eyes. She
raised her arm and pointed a finger. "He was a bad man and died in the
1960s. He drank too much and died from alcoholism. He was from
Düsseldorf and was a very bad man."

Thick castle walls protected Peter from his mother's venom. "Do you
have other children? Do I have brothers or sisters?"

She dropped her arm and stopped pointing. "No. You are my only son
and my only child." The harsh voice turned melancholy and sorrow
replaced the fire in her eyes. Just as abruptly, her voice turned cheerful. "I
am so happy that you found me. I always hoped that you would come
back." Her only son stood, without emotion, as the castle protected him
from her drastic mood swings.

The Kauers stepped closer to join their niece and grand-nephew. Ilse led
them inside the group home—a sanatarium for the aged and chronically ill
with the atmosphere of a clean but shabby hotel. Faded furniture, frayed
rugs and bleak walls mirrored the resident's blank stares. The entrance way
opened to a large common area where nurses in crisp blue and white
uniforms tended residents who seemed to be waiting for death. Some sat
motionless in secondhand wheel chairs and stared into emptiness. Others,
with walkers parked by their sides, simply took up space. Ilse Sander
strutted like a proud dignitary and led her guests through the room. A
handful of residents gathered around a bare wooden table went through

the motions of playing a card game. They turned their heads and rendered hollow stares at Ilse and her guests. Visitors broke the routine of a monotonous existence.

The reunited family moved through the common area and arrived at a desk that served as a control point at the base of a set of stairs. A nurse behind the desk smiled politely while Ilse talked loud enough to be heard on the top floor. Ilse finished, and the nurse excused herself. Moments later, she returned with an administrator who looked proper and formal in his dark suit. Greeting the man like an old friend, Ilse introduced Maria and Hieronymus. Ilse tugged at his sleeve, and the administrator flinched as she led him to Peter.

"This is my son," Ilse said. She looked at Peter with a love known only by a mother for her child.

With reserved politeness the administrator shook hands with the three visitors. Ilse asked permission to bring her group upstairs. The man in the formal suit looked a bit hesitant and agreed only after getting an approving nod from the nurse at the desk.

Ilse did all the talking as she guided her visitors up the stairs and down a dormitory hallway. Halfway down the hall, Ilse opened the door to a room, leaving it ajar after her guests filed by. The furniture inside—a neatly made twin bed, trunk, small desk, matching chair and dresser—left little space for four people to stand. Ilse's personal living area also had a tiny private bath with a tub.

The visitors took in their meager surroundings and a new fear kept Peter locked inside his castle. Would he one day end up in a similar condition? His emotions reflected the depressing environment.

Their conversation stopped when a nurse ducked her head inside. Ilse looked at the floor, but Maria said everything was fine and the nurse continued her rounds. After the nurse departed Ilse resumed her boisterous talk and pointed to four shoddy watercolor paintings tacked to the walls. Proudly explaining that she had painted them herself, Ilse asked her son if he would like one. He graciously declined, knowing he would only throw it away. The rebuff didn't stop Ilse's desire to present a gift to her son. She stooped to search a trunk drawer and turned around holding a white candle. Guilt seemed to push her forward, and she thrust the candle toward her son, the wax a symbolic gift to make up for failed mothering. A sense of injustice in taking from the poor prevented Peter from accepting her second gift. He felt no connection, desired no connection, and a gift might force an artificial bond.

The group completed their tour of the room and headed back down the staircase where Ilse asked the nurse for permission to leave. Not sure how to respond, the nurse hesitated until Maria stepped in. "Ilse would like to take us for a walk and show us the area," Maria smiled. "She'll be sure to have us back within an hour." The nurse made a notation on her clipboard and permitted Ilse to leave.

Outside, on the porch, Ilse stopped and reached into her worn purse. She pulled out a wrinkled tin foil package containing tobacco and cigarette papers. Placing a single slip of paper on top of two fingers, she lined it with tobacco and expertly rolled a cigarette. She lit the cigarette and smoked while leading her relatives off the porch. That explained the yellow stains streaking the ends of Ilse's fingers.

They left the sanitarium and walked along the quiet sidewalks of Bad Nauheim, Maria and Hieronymus in front followed by Ilse and Peter. Ilse dominated the conversation and frequently glanced toward her son as if to make sure he wasn't a dream. She wanted him to be happy and tried through constant talk to make up for her years of lost motherhood.

Arriving at the Hofgeismar Hauptbahnhof, Maria asked her husband to bring the car to the station while they went inside to buy Peter a ticket for his return trip to Mainz. She offered to pay, but this time Peter didn't give in and bought his own ticket. The group reformed on the train station concourse and walked to a restaurant a block away.

They found an outdoor table beneath a red-and-white-striped umbrella that offered protection from the late afternoon sun. Ilse made a big show that she and her son sit side-by-side. A waiter approached and listened as the first three people ordered ice cream and Limonade, then turned to the squat woman with greasy hair. Maria's eyes drilled Ilse as she waited for her niece to order.

"Ice cream and a cola," she said, and the waiter departed. "I don't need alcohol anymore." Maria relaxed.

Italian ice cream melted in Peter's mouth, and despite the warm weather, they sipped drinks served without ice. Peter sat quietly at the table grasping bits and pieces of his family's dialogue but was unable to comprehend large segments of the conversation. Maria noticed his confusion and tried to draw him into the conversation.

"Do you remember your cousin Matthias? You saw a picture of him in one of the photo albums this morning. We were talking about him getting married in Hannover later this summer. Maybe you can come to his wedding. Would you like that?"

The man, stripped of his roots, nodded and said he'd like to attend if army duties didn't conflict. The Germans then slowly reverted back to a normally paced conversation, leaving Peter feeling like a foreigner.

The time came to pay the bill and leave the restaurant. Ilse put up a half-hearted effort to pay, although she didn't have any money. Brushing Ilse aside, Maria insisted on paying the entire bill. The family left the restaurant; Peter retrieved his suitcase from the Kauer's car, and they walked to the railroad station. The time had come to say good-bye.

Hieronymus and Peter shook hands while waiting for the train on the station concourse. Maria embraced her great-nephew and smiled, holding both his hands, "You are always welcome to visit us, Peter." Maria's touch warmed Peter's heart and for a brief instant he came out from behind the castle walls as he thanked his great aunt and uncle. But when he turned toward his mother he quickly retreated back inside. Politeness demanded that he hug his mother, but no tears filled either persons' eyes. Strain chiseled the lines of Ilse's hardened face deeper as she fought the memory of a good-bye long ago. She clutched her son's hands and begged him to visit again, not letting go until he promised to return.

When the train for Mainz screeched to a halt at the passenger dock Peter left the group and boarded a railway car. Inside a compartment he pulled down a window and leaned out to repeat last second good-byes. The train lurched forward, and he waved at his relatives who waved back in return. Soon after, the train station disappeared from his view and Peter ventured out of the castle.

The First Key is an Illusion

Lieutenant Charlie Alexander went to Airborne School after basic training and became a paratrooper. He skipped Ranger training and arrived in Mainz a month before me. Decent housing was scarce, but Charlie had a prospector's instincts and struck pay dirt, unearthing an apartment converted from the attic of a house. It was comfortable, removed from the American military presence and affordable. I didn't hesitate when he asked if I wanted to be his roommate.

Charlie Alexander had also lived across the hall from me at Fort Benning where we attended the Officer Basic Course together. He was from the bay area of California and had graduated from the University of San Francisco. He was a big man at 6'3" and 220 pounds. Charlie was a nice guy and one of the most compassionate men I'd ever meet. He kept a balanced life, dividing his time between the Army, reading best-sellers, buying and selling sports cars, and dabbling in a variety of investments. Charlie didn't consider the military the end-all in life, unlike many of his lieutenant brethren. I didn't understand his civilian pursuits. For me, there was the Army and little else. I told Charlie his outside activities were distractions from preparing for the ultimate reality—war. He said I was too intense and should broaden my horizons. Despite our different interests, we became good friends.

Duty in Germany was a vocation, a total life commitment that required many late nights and weekends. My first free Saturday came three months after arriving in Germany, and I decided to return to Bad Nauheim. I got out of bed, showered and walked into the living room, holding a cup of coffee. The freedom of a day off was exhilarating, like getting pulled over for speeding and hearing the cop say he'd issue a warning instead of a fine. I sat relaxing on the sofa with my eyes closed when I heard Charlie's bare feet shuffle by. Opening my eyes I saw my roommate dressed only in a pair of white cotton cabin-boy pants, rubbing his eyes as he looked out a window. In between yawns he mumbled something about "a great day," and scratched the dark morning stubble on his face.

It seemed late, although it was only a little past 8:00 a.m. I was accustomed to waking up at five to get on base by six. The 12 to 14 hour days started with physical conditioning calisthenics, followed by a two-mile run. A high level of physical fitness kept my mind clear, senses sharp and resulted in my needing little sleep.

Charlie turned toward me and asked with half-closed eyes, "What are you doing up so early?" His nostrils quivered. "Oh man, that coffee smells great. Hope you made enough for two."

"Yeah, there's plenty of coffee. Go grab yourself a cup, and how about filling mine up while you're at it?" I thrust an empty mug toward my roommate now busy rubbing his crotch. He yawned, took my mug and lumbered into the kitchen.

Charlie returned and handed me my coffee. He sipped his out of a black mug stenciled with white lettering—under "Airborne, Death From Above" was a human skull embossed at the base of a parachute.

He then slumped on the opposite end of the sofa and stared out the window as if hypnotized. "I thought I could sleep 'till noon but heard you in the shower and figured I may as well get up," and he took a big slurp of coffee. "You going somewhere?"

I froze. The adoption secret had lost much of its power when I told Karen Rice, but still, the dodge-ball affair lingered in my memory like a bad dream. Besides, it was different with Karen. I was drunk then, and Karen was a woman. It was easier to confide in women because they embodied the refined side of life—beauty, understanding, compassion and nurturing. Now I was stone-cold sober and my roommate was a big man, an infantry officer. If I told Charlie about my adoption and he ridiculed me I'd have to find another place to live and would be the laughing stock at the base. But my perspective about adoption had changed, and I knew living with a secret bred fear. I decided to tell Charlie about my adoption.

"I'm going to a town called Bad Nauheim to visit a very special woman," I said, aware of how my voice and body had involuntarily hardened.

"How'd you find a girl in Bad ...Bad ...oh Bad whatever?" Charlie asked running his hand through disheveled jet-black hair.

"Hey Charlie, I need to talk serious for a couple of minutes." Fear of his reaction started to choke me, but I controlled it in the same way I did before rappelling down a 60-foot cliff. I concentrated on breathing normally, keeping air flowing with a regular depth and rhythm.

"The woman in Bad Nauheim is my birth mother." I said, beginning to reveal the story of my childhood. Charlie leaned forward on the sofa and his eyes opened wide. I told him about the search, about Mörfelden and about Maria and Hieronymus. His hand holding the black and white coffee cup dropped from his mouth, until the death's skull and parachute disappeared beneath the sofa's edge. I ended my story with a few sentences about the reunion.

Charlie hadn't once interrupted and let out a soft exclamation when I finished. He slowly looked away, furrowed his brow and reflected on my story. He raised his cup to take a drink but instead the coffee cup hovered inches from his mouth. "Did she look like you?" he asked and returned his eyes to mine. "What about your father? Do you have brothers or sisters...?" There wasn't a trace of scorn or pity in his voice, only excitement and curiosity.

Charlie's positive reaction allowed a wave of relief to wash over me. I was uncomfortable, only because I wasn't used to talking openly about adoption. Now, any lingering insecurities I had about telling people I was adopted were swept away.

Then Charlie kept on asking questions. "Is your mom alright? Could she communicate? What was the sanatarium like...?"

I slowly answered them, like a fledgling learning to fly.

"That's really great you found her, uncovered your roots. You're 100 percent German by blood, aren't you?"

I nodded, and Charlie looked as if a light bulb went off in his head. He finally took a drink from the cup but nearly spat it out. "Damn, it's cold. I hate cold coffee." He slammed the cup to the floor, somehow not spilling a drop. He got off the sofa and walked back to the window. Golden rays of August morning sunshine gleamed on his olive skin as he pondered deep questions that he'd asked himself before.

He turned around and leaned against the windowsill. It was Charlie's turn to talk. "My mom's full-blooded Italian—Sicilian. When I found out I was going to be stationed in Germany, I wrote her and asked for information about relatives that live there. She mailed me the names and addresses of family members living in Sicily. Before I leave Germany, I'm going to visit them. I hope to have as much luck as you in finding my relatives."

I'd never before made the connections—his physical appearance, the fact he was Catholic, and that he cooked great Italian meals. Now it all came together. I asked about his heritage, what it meant for him to be half-Sicilian and what he knew about his father's background.

"My dad's a real mutt, a mix of so much that he can't trace his heritage back more than a generation. My mom never talked much about her family; that's part of the reason I want to go to Sicily. I feel like there's a void in me, and I need to connect to my past. Did you ever feel that way?"

We talked until the coffee pot was empty. On my way out of the apartment Charlie stuck his shaving-cream covered face out the bathroom door. "It's okay with me if you want to bring your mom here. We can barbecue steaks, or maybe she can cook something German. Have a great time, man. See you later."

"Later, man," and I closed the door.

Charlie had listened without judging. He didn't think I was a worse man or a better man simply because I was adopted. The lingering remnants of shame and embarrassment from having been adopted died that morning. I buried them in a mental cemetery alongside the graves of other childhood experiences. From then on I was able to talk freely about my adoption experience.

Since entering the Army I paid a price for allowing my time to blur into a streak of non-stop activity. My life became like stretched and unrecognizable lights on slow-shutter speed photos. The price I paid for this seemingly ceaseless action was that my introspective self became neglected, shriveled and nearly withered away. My internal gyroscope malfunctioned and orderly direction succumbed to a perpetual stream of restlessness. At 24 years of age, I was off course. A daily schedule that filled every waking hour had crushed my internal compass that pointed to balance in life. The army demanded 60 to 80 hours a week and 24 hours a day during field maneuvers. The one outside source that fed my self-awareness, Catholicism, had disappeared with the onslaught of college drinking. But I didn't care because I thought heaven was being an infantry platoon leader. Basketball and carousing with other lieutenants were my only other activities. I lived a narrow existence where my sole interests were the Army, sports and my army buddies.

A busy, non-stop life had a benefit though; I mistakenly thought my loneliness and other inadequacies had been resolved. But my insecurities weren't resolved; they lay hidden beneath a hurried life style and patiently waited for the right conditions to reemerge.

I returned to Bad Nauheim for more reasons than just a son's blind loyalty to his mother. I wanted to learn more about my family history. She didn't know I was coming. I forgot to get her telephone number during our first visit. I walked inside the yellow house that cloaked a sanatarium and moved past lifeless residents who seemed like cardboard props in a stage play. The sanatarium residents unwantingly lingered in my mind; I was afraid one day I might join their ranks.

"Is Frau Sander here?" I asked a middle-aged nurse stationed behind the counter at the bottom of the staircase. Her gaunt face mirrored the sanatarium's gloom.

"Who would like to know?" she asked looking up from papers spread across her desk.

"My name is Peter Friedrich Sander. I'm Ilse's, ah ... Frau Sander's son and would like to visit her."

Residents didn't have many guests, especially young men who came by themselves. The nurse carefully scrutinized me and her icy eyes held a questioning skepticism. She had the same look as the priest in Mörfelden. Keeping a watch on the stranger standing in front of the desk, she slowly picked up the telephone and dialed a series of numbers.

"Frau Sander? I'm sorry to disturb you, but there's a young man here. He says he's your son and wants you to come down." The nurse resumed her frown and picked up a pencil, bouncing the eraser up and down off the table. "Yes, I'll tell him," and she hung up. "Frau Sander will be right down.

You can wait over there." She pointed the pencil to a nebulous expanse on the opposite side of the staircase. I ignored the nurse while waiting in the designated area.

A whirlwind of noise coming from the second floor broke the uneasy silence. The noise swirled to the staircase and descended down the bare wooden steps. It was my mother, and she spotted me before reaching the bottom step.

"Peter, oh Peter," she exclaimed and pulled toward me like steel to a magnet. After a hasty embrace, she quickly backed away. "I thought you wouldn't come back. I thought I'd never see you again."

I didn't remember the roughness in her voice during our first encounter. And this time she had no tears.

"I'm here, mother. I'm sorry it took so long, but I had to find a place to live. The Army takes up a lot of time, and this is my first free Saturday. I came here to see you."

She responded without the slightest attempt to cover anger. "You should have come back sooner. I have waited for you every day since you came here with Aunt Maria and Uncle Hieronymus. I was afraid you wouldn't come back."

"I came as quickly as I could. These are for you." I handed her a brown paper bag. Inside she saw a box of chocolates and a carton of Marlboro cigarettes. Everyone enjoys chocolate, and I figured filtered cigarettes would help prevent yellow stains from forming on her fingertips.

A grin spread across her face as she took the presents out of the bag. "Are these really for me? You brought these for me? Thank you Peterlein, oh thank you!" and she cast glances at the work station to ensure the nurse knew about the presents. My mother looked as if she'd won the lottery and beamed at the nurse before putting the gifts back into the bag.

"I'll be right back. I want to put these in my room," and Ilse Sander trudged back up the stairs, grasping the guard rail for balance as her heavy footsteps echoed off the chipped wooden boards.

There was no whirlwind of energy the second time she came down the stairs. Only awkward sounds of an elderly person making a difficult descent. Reaching the bottom of the stairs was an achievement that earned her a few deep breaths before she gripped my waist to introduce the gloomy nurse. "This is my son, Peter Friedrich Sander. He is my only child." The nurse offered a smile so fake it looked as if she had put on a halloween mask. My mother didn't care and asked permission to leave, saying we wanted to take a walk.

"Ein moment." The nurse removed the smiling mask before picking up the phone. She stared into space while talking to someone with greater authority, nodded and put down the receiver. She finally gave the answer while making a note in her register. "Frau Sander, you can leave, but be back within an hour."

On the way out of the sanatarium my mother introduced me to her lifeless peers who did nothing but take up space. "This is Peter Friedrich Sander my son. I want you to meet my son." During the introductions, sparks momentarily flickered in the eyes of some of the undead. Perhaps they were happy for Ilse. Perhaps their eyes flickered because it was a diversion from the monotony of another day. Perhaps my coming signalled hope that the outside world hadn't totally forsaken people whom society otherwise wished would remain forever hidden.

I felt a strange sort of attachment to the residents of the sanatarium. It started as a vague awareness during my first visit, some kind of connection or relationship to the people who called the yellow house their home. The perception crystallized when my mother and I stepped out into the warm August sunshine. I realized only a thin membrane separated me from the residents. Our inner realities were much the same. We shared a common loneliness, both cut off from the world, living in isolation. The membrane preventing me from joining their ranks was my youth, a college education and a certain professional status. People with my credentials never fall to such desperate conditions that they have to live in a state-run institution. Still, I feared the possibility of one day sharing their fate.

My mother and I left the sanatarium and walked at a slow pace, exchanging small talk and an occasional glance. She dominated the conversation and never touched me. The only time she made physical contact was when saying hello, good-bye or making introductions.

We walked through neighborhoods of nice houses and fashionably dressed people. Expensive cars passed by on clean, well-maintained streets.

She told me people came to Bad Nauheim for health-vacations. They renewed their physical vitality while sitting in baths of hot mineral water piped up from beneath the town's surface. It seemed strange that a sanatarium was in the midst of wealth instead of being in a poorer neighborhood.

We made our way to a city park and walked along a gravel path flanked with rainbows of flowers. Manicured shrubs pointed the way to a blue lake dotted with swans that was not much larger than a football field. There were no clouds in the sky and the temperature was perfect for my short-sleeved shirt, jeans and tennis shoes.

My mother wore a loose-fitting brown knit sweater and a burgundy polyester skirt. Her wardrobe had a look of impoverishment. However, her clothes didn't create the distance I felt nor prevent a bond from developing. Clothes don't make a person. The woman wearing the clothes kept me away. She was not emotionally approachable.

I could have overlooked her crudeness and coarse, guttural language. I might have even been able to disregard her attempts to control me. What I couldn't overlook, what even a blind man could see, was that Ilse Sander didn't recognize me as a separate and independent human being. She made no attempt to know me. She never asked how I grew up or what I felt and thought. It seemed as if I didn't matter. To her, the past 23 years were a void. She tried to renew our relationship as if it was the day after she put me in the orphanage. Ilse Sander seemed to think we'd never really separated. She tried to relive bygone years by dragging me into her fantasy. I was her baby and she wanted to begin the mothering process.

But I was a grown man, responsible and independent, a lieutenant in the infantry used to giving orders and having men follow my commands. I wasn't going to get caught in her fantasy. I had my own life to live.

A picnic area rested along the bank of the lake. We settled into a pair of wrought iron chairs painted to match the white swans. The chairs faced the lake and I scanned the water, wondering how to bridge our growing gap. The water's mirrored surface reflected back a truth I'd been unwilling to accept: I didn't like the woman I'd dreamed about every single day for as long as I could remember.

She pulled a pack of Marlboro's from her purse, cut through the cellophane with her teeth, and slid the wrapper into her purse. I watched her light a cigarette. I was through talking; tired of having thoughts cut-off in mid-sentence, hearing disapproval of my every idea, that I had returned only to make up for her past failures. She took a few drags from the cigarette and started talking again. Her voice was flat, like a straight line on an operating room's monitor showing no pulse.

"When I was in my late teens I left Kunzendorf and moved to Prague where I found work as a secretary for a German firm. It wasn't much, but better than remaining in Kunzendorf. Hitler liberated Czechoslovakia a few years later and life became better for Sudeten Germans. I could hold my head high and for the first time was proud to be German. The Czechs hated us and became increasingly hostile as the war dragged on. Near the end of it the Russians advanced toward Prague and refugees flooded in from the East. They told terrible stories about the Red Army. They said the Bolsheviks raped every German woman in their path. Young or old, to them it didn't matter. They killed all the men and sent children into exile. It was scorched earth. I had no reason to doubt what the refugees said. I was terrified and fled to Germany before the Russians reached Prague."

Until then, my hate for the Russians was based on the American viewpoint that held the Soviet's as their great Cold War enemy. But hearing a first-hand account of the atrocities the Russians committed against my people amounted to throwing gasoline on a simmering fire. My mother's story doubled my commitment to serve in an army prepared to fight the savage Soviet hordes.

She continued on in the same monotone. "It was horrible in Germany. Wide-spread starvation. Cities in ruins. Disease everywhere. But it was better than facing the Russians. I ended up in Mörfelden. It was a gathering place for Sudeten Germans deported from Czechoslovakia."

She threw the cigarette onto the grass and crushed it under the heel of a ragged shoe.

"I couldn't find a job. There weren't any jobs after the war. So I drank. I liked to drink. Sometimes too much. My parents pushed me away. I didn't care. All my relatives rejected me. I didn't care. Then I got pregnant and named you after my father, Peter Friedrich Sander. I did it to try and mend our relationship.

"But there was another reason I gave you his name. I wanted you to grow up and be like him. With the same name, his spirit would live on in you. He was a man with principals. He worked hard and was intelligent. You had to be smart to be an Oberlerher. He was strict with his students, but they still admired him. People in Kunzendorf respected my father.

"He took you away from me saying I wasn't able to care for a baby, that I was a drunk. Afterwards, he wouldn't allow me to see you. I wanted to raise you, to give you good things. But I couldn't."

She lit another cigarette.

"My father was old when he took you from me. He didn't have much; everything was left behind in Kunzendorf except what he carried out on his back. Those were difficult times. I couldn't believe it when he told me he was going to put you in an orphanage. I begged and pleaded but he wouldn't change his mind. He told me I was unfit to be a mother." She lowered her head and clenched her hands at the sound of her own words.

"I was unfit to be a mother."

There was a long pause. The cigarette had turned to a cylinder of ash. She looked at the water. I looked at her.

"He was right. I couldn't take care of you."

Chronic alcoholism had killed Ilse's mothering instincts. The female mystique cannot blossom when life is a daily struggle for food, shelter and protection. Street life had sucked Ilse Sander's womanhood dry and not a trace of beauty remained. Compassion, understanding and nurturing were gouged away leaving only the ugly scars of an abandoned strip mine. The beaten women had nothing to give, nothing except years of chaos and misery.

All my years of searching had led me to this moment, but finding my birth mother didn't lead me to myself. I realized that she was the woman who gave me life and nothing more. The key to my happiness lay somewhere else.

Not to know who ones' birth parents are is to live on the doorstep of hell. Finding my mother was immeasurably better than the torment of not knowing. She provided answers to the most basic questions about my history, information that everyone has the right to know.

Though I was relieved when the time came to conclude our visit, Ilse Sander had a different response. She trembled and grasped both my hands, pleading for me to stay. I looked down at her and silently shook my head no. The woman devoid of feminine attributes looked like a wounded animal, pitifully dragging itself along the ground. Behind her lay the trail of a miserable past. There was only one way to end her suffering. I told her I'd return.

Only A Dream Away

The good life is only a dream away. At some point in time everyone has held hope of solving their problems in the blink of an eye. A sudden return to good health, an unexpected inheritance, a new job, a new wife. The heavens smile, troubles wash away and life finally becomes an unending stream of happiness. Doubters push these thoughts aside, others patiently wait and a third group searches for the dream. Doubters miss the gift when it arrives, the miracle never happens for those who wait, and it is often something different than expected for those who search. Miracles sometimes happen, but do we control miracles? Hope of healing the primal wound was part of my drive to find Ilse Sander, but she wasn't the miracle worker I had expected. But I still believed in a miraculous cure and turned my search in a new direction. Waiting was never my style and I was too much a dreamer to abandon hope. Like a father who endlessly searches for a cure to the mysterious disease afflicting his child, I continued seeking the miracle that would make me complete.

My new quest was to become German once again. What can be expected when one is torn from their country, language, culture, heritage and history? How would I have developed if I'd stayed in the orphanage or had been adopted by German parents? Would I feel such bitter emptiness? Deutschland gave birth to my parents, grandparents and great-grandparents. Germany was my ancestor's womb, and my lineage forever linked me to the Fatherland. I believed somewhere within the blurry existence of Germany was the key to my happiness. I wanted to feel a connectedness to my past, so I turned my energy from looking for my mother to bonding with a nation.

A bell curve shows a distribution pattern of a population. The sum total of U.S. servicemens' perceptions about Germany while stationed in that country could be pictured as a bell curve. The majority of soldiers, pictured as the bell of the curve, had neutral perceptions. My roommate, Charlie, was in the middle of the continuum and belonged to the group who enjoyed some things about Germany and disliked others.

On opposite sides of the bell curve are extremes. At one end were soldiers who boasted they had never eaten in a German restaurant. They went to the Post Exchange, commissary or American-run snack bars to eat and shop. A mix of revulsion and terror kept them confined at the military bases and housing complexes. To them, Germany was a foreign country and a miserable tour of duty. They counted the days until they would return to the United States.

I was the extreme opposite. Germany wasn't a foreign country but my home, a home I'd only briefly known. It wouldn't be enough simply to live in Germany, that was only the beginning. I wanted to be melted into liquid, poured into a cast-iron mold and reshaped into the original German form. My new search was for communion with the Fatherland. Through becoming totally German, I felt I would find what I had always wanted: acceptance, belonging and love. I was on a pilgrimage to find where I belonged and Germany presented the new hope.

This search was going to be a process, much more than a simple matter of regaining German citizenship. I needed more than a piece of paper. That doesn't change a person even as adoption paperwork doesn't eliminate the adopted child's birth parents. I needed a vital, real connection to my past. I wanted to speak my mother tongue fluently, absorb the mentality and embrace the culture. The journey had already begun. I knew German history and a little of the language. A complete metamorphosis would be the key that would open my castle door.

But it wasn't an easy quest. The enormous time demands required by the Army limited my transformation to weekends. I avoided restaurants and discotheques frequented by the thousands of Americans stationed in the area. However, places free of GIs were usually off-limits to American troops. Some German owners, who prided themselves on proper etiquette and manners, barred Americans from entering because of their rowdy and sometimes violent behavior. So I went to the outlying areas, removed from the military presence, to commune with my people.

During the summer I took my platoon on a training exercise to the
Taunus Mountains north of Wiesbaden. While setting up checkpoints for a
land navigation course I drove through a small town with a *Discotheque-
Tanzen* sign hanging on the side of a building. Making a mental note of the
location, I planned to visit the discotheque in the future. Months later I
returned as a civilian on a snowy December night.

As I stomped my feet, snow fell off my penny loafers inside a barren concourse past the outer entryway door. The discotheque was 30 miles from
Wiesbaden so there shouldn't be any Americans. Would the trip have been worth
the drive? The only thing certain was that it was a place to dance. Worst case
scenario would be to open the inner door and have the place filled with geriatrics
dancing to German oompah music. No risk, no gain, and I pushed open a second
door as snow from my shoes melted into clear pools on the outer stone floor.

A thin blue carpet stretched along the floor and the faint smell of beer greeted
me as I stepped inside. Young people in their twenties, dressed in solid winter
colors, nearly filled the interior which had a capacity of no more than 100. Thick
coats were thrown over the backs of chairs behind tables that surrounded a
rectangular hardwood dance floor. Overhead light, built into the white tiled
ceiling, filtered through a haze of cigarette smoke and provided dusk-like illumina-
tion. The clear sounds of Euro-tech Pop, heavy on the synthesizers, blasted out of
strategically placed speakers providing 360-degree sound. I stopped at a long
wooden bar separated from the dance floor by a row of tables and ordered a Pils.

I surveyed the room and didn't see any other American soldiers. No other
man had the telltale cropped haircut. Mostly women danced on the floor, some
alone while others danced in pairs. German guys weren't much for dancing,
and girls together here had none of the lesbian overtones like in the States. A
disc jockey with wire-rimmed circular sunglasses and a goatee sat tucked away
in a corner. His long dark hair swished from side to side as he jerked his head
to keep beat with the music. The solid chatter of my mother tongue provided a
carpet of background noise broken only by shouts of laughter erupting in
geyser-like bursts. The discotheque seemed the essence of German culture, at
least to this 24-year-old man and I was thrilled to be in the midst of it.

The waiter set the Pils on the counter. Saturday nights allowed me to
relax and enjoy myself knowing I wouldn't hear the sound of an alarm
blaring at 5:00 a.m. the next morning. I took a couple of gulps of the

delicious beer and set the glass mug on a cardboard coaster stenciled with the emblem of the local brewery.

Upbeat Euro-tech songs, sprinkled with British and American rock and roll, poured out of the speakers. Thankfully, the disc jockey didn't play any of the polyester disco-crap that was the rage in America. Songs by Euro-tech bands whose names I didn't know played along with The Cars, Cheap Trick, Pat Benetar, Aerosmith, Van Halen and Loverboy.

Unlike most German guys I loved to dance. Dancing was like playing basketball—moving to a rhythm, sliding into a constant flow of energy, body separating from mind while drifting to a different level of consciousness. I got off the stool and leaned against the bar. Moving to the music, I unzipped my brown leather jacket and stuffed a hand in the front pocket of my faded jeans. Still leaning against the bar, I picked up my beer, moved to the sounds of the music and looked for unattached females.

I danced my way to a table with two women sitting by themselves and asked a blonde with straight hair to the middle of her back if she'd like to dance. "Ja" was all she said. Her hair was platinum, parted in the middle, and she wore little, if any, makeup. She had to be 5'10" and her beauty struck me as a very different beauty from the glamorous women of the deep South. To my great disappointment she paid me little attention and after a few songs I returned to my roost leaning against the bar.

I looked toward the entry door and saw it open. A slender woman with brown, shoulder-length permed hair walked in. A man and another woman trailed behind, and they scanned the room looking for a place to sit. The threesome strolled to empty seats by my side at the bar. The brown-haired woman, the apparent leader of the group, radiated energy and sat in a chair at my side. Her friends piled into the other seats. It's surprising how even a small, pleasant distraction can completely take away one's focus. Losing sight of everything in the room, I watched the leader. She flashed a beautiful smile at the bartender and joked with him as she ordered drinks for her entourage. The bartender turned to fill the order while she took off her coat, laid it over the back of the chair and lit a cigarette. Did everyone in Germany smoke? She turned to her friends and left me staring at her thick, permed hair and narrow shoulders. Her friends didn't seem as outgoing. They held affectionate stares and exchanged short kisses, obviously a couple. I returned my gaze to the dance floor and focused again on the activity in the discotheque.

Another guy sat at the table with the tall blonde, so the pool of unattached women grew alarmingly small. I pivoted in my stool to order another beer. The woman next to me had turned to look at the dance floor, and her hazel eyes sparkled in the light. I leaned toward her and asked in German, "How are you doing?"

She flinched backward and closed her mouth tight, surprised a complete stranger would initiate a conversation. Studying me, her questioning eyes searched mine and traveled over my face, returning to rest on my eyes. She probably wondered what kind of man would violate an unwritten German code: No matter what, maintain a reserved disposition. Carefully weighing options, she decided to respond and slowly bent my way until our eyes were inches apart. She pressed a little closer and asked the most profound question, "Do I know you?" She sat back in her chair and waited for my response.

Now I leaned toward her. "I don't think so; this is my first time here. I live in Mainz and came to listen to music, dance and have a good time. The music is really good." A song by Sniff'n In the Tears, *Driver's Seat*, started playing.

"Yes, we came here to have a good time too," she said. "I'm glad to be inside, away from all the snow. So you like to dance?" and the corners of her mouth slightly rose.

"You bet. How about this one?" I asked. She didn't immediately respond but kept her eyes on me, deciding if I looked trustworthy. I asked her to dance a second time.

"Sure," she said. "I'm glad there's an American here. German guys never want to dance." She grabbed her female friend's arm, whispering in her ear she was going to the dance floor.

"What makes you think I'm American?" I asked getting up off the stool.

"Well, for one thing your hair is short, and your accent is a dead giveaway. But you look like a nice cowboy," and she smiled as we moved to the crowded dance floor.

So much for trying to pass as a German. On the dance floor she moved easily to the music, her body in tune with the rhythm of the song. We danced to three more songs, and she smiled at my maneuvers that were so unlike the stiff movements of German men.

"I'm Petti, and these are my friends Petra and Berndt," she said when we returned to our seats.

"My name is Peter," I said extending my hand.

"Oh good, you have a German name," she laughed while I shook hands with each of them. They exchanged glances and gestures, close friends, able to communicate without words. Petti called the bartender to order drinks. Almost as an afterthought she turned to me and asked, "Would you like to join us in a toast?"

"Sure," I answered, not having the faintest idea of what it was I was being asked to toast to.

The bartender put four drinks not much bigger than shot glasses on the counter. Petti made sure everyone had a drink in their hand, then raised her glass, "To my friends, Petra and Berndt, who will soon be married." We stretched to clink our glasses then downed our drinks.

I shook my head and made a face as the liquor burned its way down into my stomach. "What's wrong, can't handle the Schnaps?" Petti asked.

"Not really," I said, shaking my head side to side and blowing out my mouth. "I'm not much for hard liquor. I like to drink beer. Do you want one?"

"No, but I'll take a cola with a slice of lemon."

"Sure," I said and ordered her drink plus a beer for myself.

Petti went back to talking with her friends. When the bartender came back I nudged her arm. "Here's your cola," I said sliding the glass toward her.

"Thanks," she said, and took it.

"Would you like to toast again?" I asked.

"Okay. Here's to meeting a cowboy." She smiled, raised her glass, and we interlocked arms to drink. We finished, and she leaned back against her chair.

"Where's my kiss?" I asked. I'd been in Germany long enough to learn it was a custom that when a couple toasted with arms interlocked, the woman always kissed the man.

"Sorry, I'm not going to kiss you if that's what you're looking for."

"Well, yeah that's what I was looking for," and I let a sad expression cover my face.

She waved a hand no and shook her head no to emphasize the point. I kept on my sad face. "Oh cheer up, I'm sure you're going to live!" she laughed.

"What's a cowboy?" I asked.

"That's what we call Americans. All your western movies, you know. So tell me, did you drive a car or ride your horse here tonight?"

Here I was in a room full of Germans. What would it take for them to realize I was not a foreigner? It was a case of mistaken identity, made more painful by the wrong label being attached by one of my own. I didn't say anything, knowing it would be a long, slow road back to my roots.

Petti lived in a nearby town and worked in Wiesbaden as a secretary for a large firm. Petra and Berndt lived in the same town and were her life-long friends. In between her jokes she asked me thought-provoking questions. When I had difficulty answering in German, Petti encouraged me to speak English. "The German language is difficult," she said, speaking for the first time in English with absolutely no trace of a German accent.

"I'm sorry I can't speak better German," I told her. "I want to learn to speak it perfectly."

"Really?" she stared in surprise. "That's very unusual. Most Americans are so lazy they don't want to learn another language, even when they're living in someone else's country," and a frown extended across her face.

"I agree with you. When one is in Rome, one should do as the Romans do," I said, raising both hands to my front like a politician giving a speech. "When one is in Germany, one should speak German."

"Bravo! Bravo!" Petti stood up, applauded and blew a kiss from the palm of her hand. "So let me guess, you're the American goodwill ambassador to Germany? May I have your autograph?"

"No I'm not an ambassador but if you're lucky maybe you'll get my autograph! I'm a lieutenant in the American Army, an Airborne Ranger who parachutes out of jets, climbs mountains with his bare hands and slithers along jungle floors like a snake." A flood of male braggadocio crashed through my dam of self-restraint and the momentum was unstoppable. "I drive my car like a rocket, slam dunk basketballs, and women find me irresistible. There's nothing I can't do except have babies and fly!"

She paused and looked at me with curious delight. "Well you're quite a guy, aren't you?" Petti said with good-natured sarcasm. "I don't know how I survived this long without you. If only there were more men like you the world would be a much better place. Now Herr Peter, are we going to dance to this song, or are you going to make me wait until you sweep me off my feet?"

It was the first and only slow song played that night, *Babe* by the group Styx. Petti grabbed Petra and Berndt and finally got them out on to the dance floor. As Petti and I danced together the wonderful aroma of her faint perfume drifted into my senses. The only makeup she wore was a touch of mascara and I found her wonderfully feminine and attractive. I liked her energy, the way she made me laugh and the fact she wasn't a helpless pushover.

I wasn't sure why Petti talked to me so much that night. Maybe she was interested in me, but my insecurities fought that idea. More likely she had no one else to talk to since Petra and Berndt were engrossed with each other.

Later that night Petti and her friends got up to leave. I stood and helped her with her coat. "Hey, I'd like to see you again. Can I get your telephone number?"

"No, I won't give you my telephone number. If you give me yours, I'll call."

Sure, I thought, but wrote my number on a piece of paper anyway. Petti looked at it and tucked it inside her wallet-sized brown leather purse. I watched her walk out of the discotheque, certain I'd never hear from her. I stayed for a couple of more songs and left. Outside it had quit snowing but an icy wind bit against my face.

Over breakfast the next morning, I told Charlie about my evening in the discotheque.

"You went all the way to the Taunus Mountains to go dancing?" he mumbled stuffing a poached egg into his mouth.

"Yeah, you know I don't like going to places where there's lot's of GIs. I met this interesting woman, lots of fun and smart too. Her name's Petti. I gave her our number, so if she calls and I'm gone, let me know."

"Sure thing. Hey man I bet she'll call." He folded a piece of toast in half and crammed it into his mouth. "Last night I went over to Sam and Cathy's house. They invited me for dinner, and afterwards we played Risk until two in the morning. I really like them; they're a great couple."

Charlie left later that morning to look at sports cars. I stayed in the apartment, studying an army manual about how to breach a Russian trench system. The telephone rang. I walked across the room and picked up the phone. It was Petti.

Trust and Intimacy

"What are you doing later tonight?" Petti asked in German over the telephone. "Petra, Berndt and I are coming to Mainz and were hoping you could join us for a few games of bowling." I held the phone as if in shock but eagerly accepted the invitation. We agreed to meet at seven o'clock.

I got a late start and walked into the bowling alley 15 minutes after seven and saw them changing into shoes at a settee. Petti looked up and saw me standing just inside the entrance. She left the settee and limped toward me with one foot in a bowling shoe and the other in a sock. "So, where have you been Herr Peter? We thought we might miss you this evening," Petti sarcastically joked and folded her arms across her waist.

"Sorry I'm late," I replied, looking like a boy caught with his hand inside a cookie jar. The apology didn't include the obligatory excuse because I didn't have a reason for being late.

"When people say they are going to meet at a certain time they should arrive at the time agreed. It's okay this time Peter, but don't make it a habit. Now, let's get ready for tonight's games." I followed Petti to the main counter and heard her words loud and clear.

American women are notorious for being "fashionably" late. My idea that it was some kind of universal female trait came to an abrupt end with Petti's clear signal. Punctuality, or lack of it, was not about gender characteristics but a matter of cultural upbringing. Germans prided themselves on timeliness, both in their personal lives and the way in which their society functioned.

Berndt and I bowled as if our lives depended on our scores. He wanted to win because he was competitive. I wanted to win to gain acceptance. We'd swoop down the lane like big cats closing in on their prey and launch a bowling ball with a final surge of energy. As it rolled down the alley we strained our necks and gyrated our shoulders to coax the ball to knock over pins.

Petti and Petra bowled for entertainment. They didn't care how many pins they knocked down, only how much fun they had doing it. They broke out in hysterics every time a ball ended up in the gutter or when their foot accidently skidded crossed the foul line. Petra threw a ball that slipped out of her hand during the second game. The errant ball veered sideways across her lane, bounced over one gutter, then the next and travelled down the adjacent lane knocking down a few pins. Petra and Petti jumped up and down and grabbed each other laughing so hard they cried. I couldn't help laughing, and even Berndt, violating the German code of somberness, cracked a smile.

Berndt won two out of three games and I tried to mask my disappointment. I wouldn't have made a good poker player, and Petti picked up on my frustration. On the way out of the bowling alley she stopped and said, "You take yourself too seriously." I took a step backward and bit my upper lip as my shoulder muscles tightened. I liked Petti and was afraid that my feelings of discontent might lead to rejection.

"Bowling is only a game." She smiled, inching into the empty space between us. "It's something to have fun at. You don't have to be perfect. I like you for who you are and want to see you again. I'll give you a call later this week. Tschüss," and she went outside to where Petra and Berndt waited in their car.

Our next date came on a weekday night, after New Year's. Petti extended an invitation no single man can refuse—a home-cooked meal. Supper would be at Petra and Berndts' apartment, and Petti volunteered to pick me up after work. "The drive will allow us to spend more time together," she said. "You live a long way from Mainz, so bring a change of clothes. I have a comfortable sofa, and you can spend the night at my apartment. In the morning I'll bring you back to Mainz. I'll pick you up at the main gate at six o'clock, sharp," she said before hanging up the phone.

A few minutes before six on the designated evening I stood waiting in my uniform outside the front gate of Lee Barracks, returning the salutes of passing soldiers. It had been dark for an hour, and a wet cold hung in the January air like morning mist over a swamp. At exactly six an off-white VW Bug pulled along the sidewalk. The driver kept the engine running and stretched a slender arm across the passenger seat to roll down a frosted window. "I'm here to pick up my dinner date. If you're hungry, lieutenant, you'd better hurry up and climb aboard."

I laughed and trotted toward the car. I pulled open the passenger door and threw a gym bag stuffed with civilian clothes into the backseat. "Hi Petti. I'm glad to see you," I said, settling into the passenger seat kept warm with a gray sheepskin cover.

"I'm glad to see you too, Peter. I thought about you all day." Her eyes stroked my face as I stared out the front window. She lifted her gaze and shifted the car into first, easing the Bug into traffic. Chit-chat gave way to laughs, two people with a magical chemistry that turned a forty-five minute drive into ten.

A heavy snowfall waited in the mountains. Petti drove skillfully; the car never swerved or skidded on the icy roads. Towns and villages sprinkled the German countryside, urban islands in a sea of forests and fields. On the outer streets of each town, buildings clung to the roadway like berries on a vine and formed a clear line separating civilization from nature. Concrete and steel on one side, forests and fields on the other. It was a country with a high population density whose people cherished nature and utilized every available acre for agriculture, farming or forestry. No ugly strip malls polluted the pristine countryside outside of urban boundaries.

We drove through miles of forested hills until Petti slowed the car after rounding a curve. The town where she lived had a distinct boundary. Reflected in the car headlights was a massive stone wall that surrounded the town.

Walled cities started replacing castles during the Middle Ages. Mammoth walls constructed around urban areas protected civilian populations from marauding military forces. Over the centuries Germany had fought more than its share of foreign armies.

Yellow light escaped from tiny windows in a tower built over the archway. The tower was not a museum piece or historical site. The glowing lights were needed by the people who lived inside. The road narrowed to one lane and we drove under the archway, built in a time when transportation came only on foot, horse or carriage. The car passed through the hole in the walls and took me another step closer to my roots.

On the opposite side of the archway the road widened, but not by much. Narrow winding streets made centuries-old buildings appear taller than their three or four stories. Traffic lights at street corners seemed out of place. The town was empty of fast food slop houses serving cardboard meals loaded with cholesterol. No billboards papered with sly advertising gimmicks, someone's prayer of making a quick buck, polluted the town environment. No neon lights in store window-fronts blinked the latest fad. The plastic flesh of American culture was no where to be seen. In its void rang tranquil bells of quiet simplicity. I looked at the medieval town where Petti lived as if viewing a painting, and I stepped onto its canvas when getting out of the car.

"Don't worry about locking it," Petti said, seeing me fumble with the door lock. "No one ever steals anything. Bring your bag, and you can change clothes at Berndt and Petra's. I live over in that building." She pointed a leather-gloved finger down the street's darkened tunnel. "We'll go to my place after dinner."

Snow crunched under foot as we crossed the dimly lit street. I'd never been in a place as old. Pensacola, Florida, the City of Five Flags, traced its history to five nations. The United States defeated the Confederacy on land bought from the French, preceded by the British who had expelled the Spanish. Pensacola's history spanned three centuries. I walked with Petti in a town that might have origins to when Germanic tribes first settled on the Rhine River. The town was a symbol, a link to my ancestors, extending over two millennia.

From the street we entered an unheated stairwell. Our breaths formed frozen white clouds as we climbed a circular staircase, and our shoes left imprints of snow on the staircase's bare wooden boards. Petti rang a buzzer on the third floor. The door opened, and Petra appeared, along with a tidal wave of the cooking smells of meat and vegetables. She waved us inside and gave Petti a small kiss. I closed the door and Petra, seeing me dressed in my uniform, good humordly tried to stand at attention before rendering a salute. She wouldn't have made a good soldier. Berndt came around a corner holding a bottle of beer and walked toward Petti, wrapping her in his arm. He looked at me and said in English marked with a heavy German accent, "Peter, welcome. Do you want a beer?" I never again heard him speak English.

Berndt gave me a tour of their modest apartment and let me change in the bedroom. I joined him in the living room and heard the women busily chatting in the kitchen as they completed final preparations for dinner. The living room had one lamp with a low wattage bulb. Two candles in an opposite corner added light and warmth and helped create an environment of bygone days. The only place warm was the kitchen. "Electricity is expensive," Berndt said as we sat in the living room. Classical music played from a stereo, and our conversation wasn't interrupted by the non-stop blaring of a television.

"Is this a radio station?" I asked Berndt, pointing to the Blaupunkt stereo system.

"No it's a cassette. Sometimes I like to listen to classical music. It mellows me out after a hard day."

"Can you pick up a rock and roll station? I'd like to hear some German rock."

"We don't have any stations that only play rock and roll," he answered.

"In America there are radio stations that play only one kind of music. You can listen to rock, classical, country, anything you want, 24 hours a day."

Berndt's eyes lit up. "That's unbelievable. German radio stations play a variety of music. If I want to listen to rock I have to tune in during the time that program is played. That's why I buy lots of cassette tapes, so I can hear my favorite music whenever I want." Petra called for help from the kitchen.

"Moment," Berndt answered, and journeyed to the kitchen to see what his fiancee needed.

He came back a few minutes later and took a sip of beer before sitting down. "Petra needed help getting a pot out of a cupboard. I love her so much. We went to school together, and she's been my best friend since I was a boy. After school I did my compulsory service in a hospital. I didn't want to go into the army. Besides, working in a hospital gave me freedom to come home on weekends so I could see her. I couldn't have done that if I were in the Bundeswehr."

"You mean you had a choice?"

"Yes. After graduation every man has to serve Germany for 15 months. There is general conscription but we have a choice between the army or civilian service. I chose civilian service. I object to war and did my time working in a hospital. Were you drafted?"

"No. I volunteered for the Army. The draft in America ended a few years ago." Petra called us to dinner before I could explain the "All Volunteer Army."

Four candles on the center of the dining room table illuminated our meal: Jagerschnitzel, veal covered with a tangy mushroom gravy; Spätzle, a kind of dumpling; and Rotkraut or red cabbage cooked in garlic and red vinegar. A glass of white wine stood by each plate. I wanted to toast and raised my glass before saying, "Thank you to my new friends. Prost."

They all laughed. "No Peter," Petti said. "You only say prost when you drink beer. With wine we say Zum Wohl."

"Then Zum Wohl, but the rest of the toast stands."

"Zum Wohl," the others chimed as we clinked glasses.

My new friends helped improve my German. I had no choice because Petra and Berndt didn't speak English. Petti mostly talked in German and said to learn German I would have to practice. They'd help when I was stuck in a sentence and corrected my grammar when it was particularly poor. It was a similar situation as at the outdoor cafe in Bad Nauheim where I'd eaten dessert with my mother, Maria and Hieronymus. Except now my German had improved considerably.

After dinner Petra started clearing the table and Berndt went to the living room. I would have felt guilty not helping and interrupted Petra, saying she should take a break. She didn't bother to look up. Only after Petti's urging did she stop wiping the table and join Berndt in the living room. Petti and I finished cleaning the dining room table and went to the kitchen to wash dishes. Petti washed and I dried.

"Nice of you to help," Petti said, dipping a frying pan coated with dried gravy into soapy water. "It's not often a man will help do dishes. Berndt may not like it though. Petra will want him to start helping in the kitchen," she laughed.

"It's not right that Petra should have to do everything. She put a lot of effort into preparing that great dinner, and besides, I've got two arms and know how to use them. It's the least I can do to repay their hospitality."

Petti looked at me and grinned. "I was right," she said handing me the wet frying pan.

"How's that?"

"The night we met, remember. I said you were quite a guy. I was right."

A tingle spread up from my stomach. I used my achievements as a way to get people to like me because I thought I had little else to offer. Petti was interested in my qualities rather than my accomplishments. She saw me in a different light compared to how I viewed myself. Status, education and money weren't as important to her as the manner in which people treated one another. She saw the good side of me, one I rarely noticed.

Petti and I started dating, in between my busy military schedule. I had spent over six months away from the garrison, conducting maneuvers, by the end of my first year in Germany. It wasn't a solid six months but instead was broken into shorter chunks of time. The officers spent a week at Fulda, reconnoitering the ground we'd defend if the Russians attacked. Then back to Mainz to prepare for the entire battalion to go to Baumholder for two weeks to fire machine guns, rifles, anti-tank missiles, detonate mines and practice maneuvers. We returned to Mainz, and three weeks later the officers left for a month to act as controllers for a large-scale exercise in central Germany.

Germany didn't have enough open space to set up miles and miles of sprawling, military training centers like back in the States. We maneuvered through the local countryside and trained in a way that never would have worked in America. Americans wouldn't put up with tanks and armored personnel carriers rumbling through their towns or with having thousands of armed men camped in public forests. But in a country that had known war since the times of Roman legions, it was business as usual.

During large war games, opposing forces tied blue or red canvas recognition signals to the sides of their vehicles. The different colors enabled everyone to know who was on each side. The red side simulated a Soviet force; blue was always NATO. Mock battles went on for days and fast-paced events often resulted in confusion. The biggest problem was not knowing the location of friendly and opposing forces. My knowledge of the German language came in handy during these exercises. I'd stop my armored personnel carrier when I saw a farmer and get out to ask him questions. Depending on what side I was on, I'd ask if he'd seen any blue or red tanks in the area.

The farmer answered saying blue tanks were in a field across a river or that he'd seen a column of soldiers with red armbands marching north six hours earlier. The older men always wanted to talk. They'd tell me stories of how they'd fought the Russians in World War II. Then they'd offer advice on how to sneak up and attack the blue or red tanks across the river. A certain comradery exists between all combat arms soldiers, no matter which army they serve. The farmers asked where I learned to speak German and then reached inside a coat pocket to give a cigar or offer some other fraternal gesture. Even though I wanted to, I couldn't talk long. I had a war to fight. Thanking them for the information, I'd get back in my armored carrier after I gave them a gift of C-rations or a piece of insignia from my uniform. The men in my platoon watched in amazement, and I always helped American soldiers who also wanted to learn German.

Petti moved to Wiesbaden at the end of the winter. She wanted to be closer to work and rented a studio in the downtown area. It now meant we were separated by only a fifteen-minute drive and were able to spend more time together. Petti and my roommate Charlie met after she moved, and he liked her for the same reasons I did—high energy, intelligence, no-nonsense manner, good looks and a sense of humor. Petti spoke English when Charlie was around. He was learning German at a snail's pace, and she wanted to include him in our conversations rather than have him feel like an outsider.

Petti Stöcker took me to my heart's desire. She introduced German friends, showed me the customs, was a guide to out-of-the-way places and taught me the language. She helped me become German once again. On a group afternoon outing, one of her friends said, "If I saw you on the street and didn't know who you were, I'd think you were German by the way you look." Her friend's statement showed I was on my way to where I belonged, and I was overjoyed.

One day after work, in the spring of my first year in Germany, I returned to the apartment and found my second love putting finishing touches on dinner. We ate and cleaned up, then left the apartment to take an early evening walk. Past the edge of town we followed a tractor path through fields with orderly rows of emerald shoots blanketing the musty soil. We walked, laughed and played beneath the day's final rays of sun.

Petti stooped to pick up a few rocks and threw them. "Do you think I'd make a good American baseball player?" she asked, after tossing the last stone.

"Well, you only missed that mound of dirt you were aiming at by fifteen feet. Maybe with a little practice though." We laughed and she threw a pebble at my feet.

As a child, I saw everyone leading happy and content lives. Everyone except me. This perception widened the barrier between me and the outside world. In addition to the damage caused from having been adopted, I thought I had more defects because I wasn't always happy. To make up for my imperfection I strove to perform extraordinary feats to win respect, friendship, and love. But it never seemed enough. My parents wanted excellence. Being the best was the goal of sports. Fraternity life was geared toward building future success. The materialistic culture of America signalled that happiness was achievable only through the acquisition of possessions and money. The culture of the Army officer corps also demanded constant perfection and left no room for weakness.

Then came Petti. She didn't expect me to be perfect and accepted my positive attributes as well as my faults. I had never before heard anyone tell me, "Just be yourself." I didn't know how because I thought I had to be perfect just to be on equal footing with everyone else. I didn't think anyone else had emotional troubles.

Continuing our walk, we came to an orchard full of trees clouded in pink and white blossoms. Petti bolted to a tree. She had snapped off a small branch before I caught up. "Here smell," she said handing me the broken branch.

"Smells good," I said.

I returned the branch and she raised it to her nose, closed her eyes and inhaled. A smile arched across her lips. Gently setting the branch on the ground, she slid slender hands behind her back and turned toward the sun's golden ball touching the horizon. I walked to her side and joined her to look at the western sky.

"When I was a little girl I always thought I'd be like a tree that grows up and has perfect form and symmetry. I never knew life isn't perfect, that sometimes I'd suffer broken branches. When I was nine, my parents divorced and my father moved away. He never visited after that. It broke my heart that he didn't want to see me anymore. It was like a large branch had broken off the tree of my life. I continued to grow but wasn't the same tree I'd have been if my father had stayed. I was disfigured and grew in a different shape. I lost my perfect form." Then she stopped talking and lost herself in the sunset.

It was the first time someone told me about an experience that troubled them. In revealing the truth, Petti gave me a part of her self, a part shared with few others. I realized I wasn't alone, that I wasn't the only person in the world who was lonely, sad or angry about the way life unfolded. It was my first encounter with intimacy, where another person shared with me their deepest feelings. Petti taught me intimacy and love are two separate commodities.

I told Petti about my adoption soon after we met but stopped short of expressing any weakness. I wanted her to believe that I was a fearless man who could do anything except fly and have babies. But I began to trust her after she shared the experience of her father. Trust allowed me to reveal my emotions. What I said to her wasn't much because I had never been taught how to express emotion or talk about feelings. It amounted to saying that being adopted and taken from Germany really bothered me. Still, it was the first time I shared my true feelings.

Petti did not abandon or reject me after I admitted insecurity. She listened without passing judgment and didn't say that I shouldn't feel the way I did. With the onset of trust I took my first steps of intimacy and it vaulted our relationship to a higher dimension.

A few weekends later Petti went to visit her mother. That Friday night I got home and at eight o'clock collapsed in bed exhausted from the week. Saturday I cleaned the apartment, played basketball and started reading another war book. Night came and with it restlessness. I put the book down and decided to go drink beer at a local Gasthaus.

I'd never before been to the Gasthaus located only a couple of blocks away. I stepped inside the working man's joint packed with burly and rough-looking farmers, construction workers and mechanics. The spartan interior had no frills, only curtainless windows and a concrete floor. No music played. Men drank and smoked over bare wooden tables. Their jokes brought heavy laughs and they pounded tables and slapped each other on the back. It seemed a good place to be without Petti.

I spotted an empty seat at a table with five men. Nothing else looked better and per the German custom I asked the group, "Ist hier frei?"

"Nein. Sitzen Sie, junger Mann," came the surly voice of one of the occupants who stared me down into the seat.

The only woman in the place, a husky blonde with hair pinned in a bun, came and hurriedly wiped the table. She emptied the ash trays and sped away after taking my order.

Long hair, beards and goatees signaled I was the only American in the place. Great I thought. It would be another opportunity to connect with my countrymen.

The waitress returned with a tray full of bottles and mugs. She placed two coasters, one for the empty ceramic mug and the other for a bottle of beer, in front of me and left without bothering to pour.

The men at the table watched as I emptied the bottle into the mug. "I love to drink Sonnen Pils," I said, complimenting a beer brewed in Mainz. "Prost," I nodded, and we all raised mugs and drank. Some went back to talking, drinking and smoking. Others watched me. Finally, a man about 10 years older who sported two days growth across his broad face asked, "You speak German. How'd you learn to speak German?"

My German brothers still didn't get it. So I told them about studying German at Auburn and wanting to learn the language perfectly. That seemed to warm them up and sparked a conversation. I had drunk half my beer when they asked me my name.

"Peter Friedrich Dodds. But my real last name is Sander," and I went into a brief bit about my past.

Before I finished, the man with two days' facial growth laughed and elbowed his buddy. His companion cocked his head to listen, and I watched as a sneer spread across his face. The two finished and the second man rang a metal key against his mug to get the attention of the entire table. He paraphrased my story and the entire table broke into hysterics pounding the table so hard that the ashtrays and mugs jumped. Their responses flew in between hoots and howls, in no particular order, but in short, random bursts. "You aren't German. Go back to America. Your mother's a whore. They don't let bastards in here. You will never be German."

I stood up and tried to look strong to hide my fear, like a cat arching its back, and hurriedly left before they decided to beat the hell out of me. I escaped unscathed and walked aimlessly in the night, their words ricocheting like loose ball bearings pinging inside an empty steel drum. I drew only one conclusion from the men at the table. They confirmed how I truly felt about myself.

Gifts of Eternal Love

Petti invited me to her studio for dinner on a Saturday night during my second summer in Germany. Her natural beauty sparkled as she scampered about the kitchen in a sleeveless blue cotton dress and light tan sandals. Now that the weather had turned warm she shaved her legs and under her arms. "Why should I shave in the winter when my body is covered?" she answered when I first questioned her body hair. It seemed a practical answer and another cultural barrier fell. After dinner we went for a walk and returned to her flat just as darkness enveloped Wiesbaden. Petti flicked on a table lamp and asked me to sit on the sofa that doubled as her bed.

"Wait there, I'll be right back." She smiled and left the room to rummage through a hallway closet. She found what she looked for and I heard the closet door close. Her footsteps stopped just outside the room.

"Are you still on the sofa?" she asked giggling behind the wall. "I've got something for you."

"Yes ma'am. Sitting here and waiting further instructions," I replied, sitting comfortably and leaning against the back of the sofa.

Peeking around the corner, Petti slowly tiptoed into the room with an angelic smile that matched the glow in her sparkling eyes. Happiness radiated from her face, the happiness of a beaming little girl running across a sun-drenched meadow in pure, innocent joy. Behind her back she held a surprise for her best friend.

Petti stopped at my feet. Her energy cascaded like a waterfall and the misty spray coated my face with a smile. I sat up straight and put my hands on her hips while stretching my neck trying to glimpse the secret behind her back. "What have you got there?" I asked my best friend.

She didn't reply and used a knee to spread my legs, then crept closer. She breathed heavily with excitement, her breasts inches from my face. A package appeared from behind her back. "This is for you," she said and took a step back.

"Wow, thanks Petti. What is it?" I asked, taking the soft package and squeezing it to the rustling sounds of rose-colored paper. Despite my excitement, I remained completely at ease.

"You'll have to open it and find out," she smiled.

I slowly removed the wrapping paper, alternating glances between her and the package. Inside were three t-shirts; white, light blue and dark blue.

"I thought you could use them with summer coming up," she said.

"These are great, Petti. Thanks a lot! Let me try them on." I stood and modelled each t-shirt for her. "What's the occasion?"

"Nothing special. I just wanted to let you know that I care about you. I like the dark blue t-shirt best. It matches your eyes. Leave that one on."

"Okay."

For the first time in my life I received a gift when it wasn't my birthday, Easter, Christmas or a graduation. Petti's gifts came without strings; she wanted nothing in return. This was a new experience for me, receiving something given purely out of love and generosity. It made me tingle with emotion.

I didn't like it when my adopted parents gave me gifts. It was as if they tried to fulfill a requirement and satisfy some sort of parental obligation. They carefully watched me open their gifts and I was uncomfortable under their gaze. They pulled strings and expected me to perform. The toys and clothes were their strings and they hoped I would love them in return for their gifts. But I didn't love them and couldn't pretend. I was always a terrible liar. Instead, I responded as taught by saying thank you and quickly left before forced to respond to the pulling of strings.

Unfortunately, gift giving can sometimes become a marionette show with the person receiving the gift acting as the wooden puppet and the giver as the puppeteer pulling strings. A supposed celebration then crumples into an obscene theatrical performance where gifts are only manipulative strings exploiting the recipient.

To give a material object and expect something in return is not giving. True gifts seldom receive wide spread attention. Hidden in anonymity, the selfless giver desires only to demonstrate affection or lend help where it is needed and seeks nothing in return: a loving husband who comes home every night and remains faithful to his wife, a woman who spends one night each week at a food bank helping feed the hungry, Catholic nuns and priests caring for helpless and abandoned children.

Petti had kept one hand behind her back the entire time. When I finished refolding the t-shirts she slid a second package into my hand. "Here's a little something for us."

I removed the wrapping paper and saw inside an album by the group Styx. "Do you remember the song *Babe*?" Petti asked.

"Yeah, I hear it all the time," I said looking at the album cover. I set it on an end table, stood up and put my hands on her shoulders. "So what's the deal?"

She looked up and lightly kissed my lips. "The song *Babe* is on that album. It played the night we met and was the first slow song we danced to. It's our song, Peter. *Babe* is our song," and she backed away, taking the record off the table. On the way to the turntable she stopped and turned around. "Light the candles," Petti whispered.

I lit four candles that transformed the room into a flickering romantic paradise. Petti lowered the turntable needle until it rested on the album and *Babe* started to play. From across the room she looked me straight in the eyes, "Are you going to ask me to dance, Herr Peter?"

"There's nothing I want more in the whole world. Will you dance with me my sweet, beautiful Petti?" I walked across the room and slid into her waiting arms.

We danced slowly and let the music do the talking. Our bodies pressed closely together; her head rested against my shoulder and our eyes shut tight. The song ended and Petti drifted back to the turntable and moved the needle to play *Babe* again. Then she returned and we danced a second time. The tiny studio became a grand ballroom and I felt immersed in her warm body and intoxicating perfume. The soft music and flickering candle light added their magic and I wanted that night to stretch into eternity.

Later that summer I crossed another item off the list of activities I thought I'd never do. I visited an art museum on my way home from playing basketball on a rainy Saturday afternoon. It wasn't because I really wanted to but I needed to kill a few hours until that evening when I'd join three lieutenants for an evening of beer drinking and bar hopping in Frankfurt. Walking up the museum concourse, I found myself searching for reasons to go inside. I lived in Germany, a country many Americans paid thousands of dollars to visit. I wanted to take advantage of the opportunities afforded and thought I should at least once take a look at masterpieces, no matter how boring they might be. The same curiosity that led me to the German Alps to snow-ski for the first time pushed me through the art museum doors. Still, it was with a great deal of reluctance. I was a gung-ho Airborne Ranger and believed art was for sissies.

The surroundings in the lobby didn't alleviate my reluctance. Stuffy and snobbish looking groups of well dressed people milled about in the rotunda. The book shop and information office pointed toward petrifying boredom and I seriously second-guessed my decision. I didn't want to take part in a group tour. I could do this myself, and I hurriedly left the rotunda and jogged up a small flight of stairs. I planned to take a quick look at a few paintings and then leave. Reaching the top of the stairs, I rounded a corner and stood beneath a wide entrance way that opened into a huge viewing area. The scene stopped me dead in my tracks.

Striking colors jumped out from the myriad of paintings displayed on the walls, like a rainbow had shattered and splashed magnificent shades of blue, gold, green, and red on canvases throughout the room. Some of the paintings took up an entire wall. People in the scenes were life-sized and looked real, as if only moments before they had dressed in medieval clothes and stepped into the painting. Many of the scenes portrayed events from earlier centuries and appealed to my interest in history. Painted angels looked down at me from the ceiling, cherubs smiling from their celestial posts at the grandeur in the room below. Visitors moved slowly across the white marble floor in hushed reverence. The viewing area had a sense of sacredness, and I quietly entered the room, not wanting to disturb the atmosphere. Stopping at the edge of a red velvet rope that separated paintings from visitors, I stared at a masterpiece created 400 years earlier.

The painting grabbed me and I was temporarily lost to everything but the scene to my front. Then I side-stepped along the rope and stopped at the next painting. I continued around the room and viewed every piece. The paintings sparked my imagination and appealed to my emotional attraction to the heroic, adventurous, remote, mysterious and idealized. Wanting more, I walked into a second viewing room to drink in the mood-creating grandeur. Nearly every piece flourished with astonishing beauty. Some depicted great moments in history, others biblical events, nature's majesty, or Greek and Roman mythology. Ordinary people were captured in extraordinary events that depicted love, sorrow, joy and awe. The characters' passions silently reached from the paintings and touched me. They allowed me to escape my limited perceptions and sense of isolation.

The timeless gifts of the masters invited me to join in the wonder of human experience. The paintings formed a bridge where I crossed over the abyss of loneliness and connected to other human beings. The scenes caused me to feel, and I did so without shame. No one in the art museum told me that what I experienced was wrong. There were no adopted parents to tell me I shouldn't be sad, no Army officers to say that strength is all that matters, no cultural taboos saying that real men don't feel pain. Art opened a door to a hidden part of me. The gifts of the masters helped lead me to my true self.

As I continued exploring the museum I felt a sense of comfort and inner peace. Art's beauty imparted a wonderful calmness that evaporated my insecurities. The sensation was vaguely familiar. One never forgets moments of overwhelming contentment. Standing in the midst of master-pieces, I stared into my past and flipped back through the pages of my life. I wanted to find the other time when I'd known the same inner peace. When I had back-tracked to the sixth grade, I stopped mentally turning pages. Then I remembered. The presence of love that I knew when I had wanted to become a priest was the same force I was experiencing when surrounded by works of art. My human mind couldn't comprehend a love so great.

The great calm disappeared when I stepped outside the museum. No matter how hard I wished for the feeling to return, it wouldn't, and that love was outside my ability to control. But the seed of art had been planted, and during my European travels to Paris, London, Munich, Barcelona, Athens, Brussels and Amsterdam, my first stop was always the great museums and cathedrals.

A desire to learn more about my origins drove me to continue exploring the history of my German family. Knowledge wasn't enough. I wanted to see and walk the ground where they had lived, so I put in a leave request to travel to Kunzendorf, Czechoslovakia. The Army denied my request. My security clearance had been upgraded to Top Secret, with a Background Investigation. The Cold War raged and Army policy prohibited soldiers with Top Secret security clearances from travelling behind the Iron Curtain. But my vow to travel to Kunzendorf remained, and it was only a question of when I would visit.

I had never forgotten one sentence Great-Aunt Maria told me, "Your grandfather is buried in the cemetery at Mörfelden." I'm not really sure why I went; it was only a grave, but Petti and I traveled to the cemetery during my second summer in Germany.

We arrived in Mörfelden on a warm and muggy afternoon. Parking the car on a side street, we walked along a red brick walkway toward the cemetery. It wasn't a large cemetery. I saw the stone walls forming its boundaries from the entry gate. Inside the gate, shade from towering evergreens offered a refreshing coolness. Sun rays slivered through the overhead branches, filtering light into geometric patterns of weightless sheets. A peaceful and serene atmosphere enveloped the cemetery, and even the birds muted their cries while flying from tree to tree. Silent gravestones arranged in parade-ground precision guarded the resting places of the dead. A scattering of visitors solemnly paid homage to loved ones whose final home lay in darkness beneath the ground. Stooping to place flowers beside a grave, mourners paid symbolic reverence to those in eternal sleep.

At a small cement shed we asked a caretaker for the location of my grandfather's grave. He went inside the shed to look at a map and told us the man I was named after lay buried on the opposite side of the cemetery.

We left the caretaker to his chores and walked to the grave along a dirt path. I grew quiet and let go of Petti's hand, not wanting to talk while uncovering another fragment of my past. A tombstone, somewhat larger than the rest and made of gray mortar, lay directly ahead. As if mesmerized I glided toward my destination. Etched into the mortar were the words "Peter Friedrich Sander" and beneath the name, another word, "Oberlerher." I couldn't pull my eyes from the grave marked with my name.

Though numb, a tidal wave of love, more powerful than the feeling of tranquility at the art museum, washed over me. I couldn't fathom the depth of such love and closed my eyes in surrender. Petti faded to a dream and the outside world ceased to exist. Time stopped while I sat alone in a small room deep in the interior of my castle.

My secret self was slumped in a chair with eyes half-closed. Three white candles dripped wax onto a coarse wooden table at the side of the chair. With the sudden gust of a warm wind I opened my eyes as the candle flames flickered. Looking ahead, what I saw caused me to bolt upright in the chair. My eyes flashed wide open. An intruder stood a few steps in front of me. Someone had penetrated the walls of my castle.

A radiant light emanated from around the head and body of the intruder, a light so dazzling that I could make out no more than a silhouette. Squinting to make out who had invaded my sanctuary, I cupped a hand over my brow. The brilliance of the light slowly paled to a bluish-white aureole that allowed me to see the form. It was a man, tall, distinguished and handsome. I had seen him before, in a photograph glued to a page in one of Maria Kauer's photo albums. The man was my grandfather, Peter Friedrich Sander, Oberlerher.

He didn't say a word, and the aureole ringing him fluctuated in intensity like flames dancing in a campfire. I stared at him until the energy of his aureole increased and radiant light again engulfed his body. Only his silhouette remained visible. The intensity of his love increased, so powerfully that my eyes filled with tears of joy. Everything in the castle room faded, the table, the chair, my troubles and fears, every physical thing and emotion disappeared except my grandfather, bathed in love's light. His love took root in my soul and seeped outward to my heart before emptying into my mind. I could never have conceived of anything so great—pure love, freely given.

Then his light and silhouette began to fade. I didn't want my grandfather to leave; I wanted him to stay with me forever. "Please don't go," I begged. "Don't leave me. Take me with you." But when I reached out to touch him my hands grasped empty air. Once again I sat alone in my castle.

But I felt someone else touch me and looked to see a slender feminine hand wrapped around mine. "Are you all right?" Petti asked." I took a walk because you stood motionless in front of your grandfather's grave with your head bowed. I thought you needed some time."

"Thanks Petti, I'm okay. I was just thinking about my grandfather."

We stood silently at the grave a little while longer. Then she pulled me away.

"C'mon, we have to go. It's getting dark, and the cemetery is going to close."

One with Nature

The United States Army in Germany participated in a huge annual war game each autumn named Reforger. My second autumn in Germany I took part in Reforger, along with a large group of officers from my battalion. We were responsible for helping control and evaluate another American unit that fought in the exercise.

We loaded jeeps onto a train at Mainz and railed to central Germany. Unloading the vehicles at a small town near Kassel, we convoyed to a huge forest and set up camp for four days until the start of Reforger. We spent the days before H-Hour reconnoitering the future battlefield and learning the rules of engagement required to control the war game.

The camp had a relaxed atmosphere at night. Junior officers mixed with enlisted men and spent evenings joking and laughing around campfires. Field grade officers retired early, too old for the nonsense of youth.

After the first two nights, boredom descended on the campsite, along with darkness. There was little to do and I hated routine. Without challenges, I quickly became restless and grew eager for the start of Reforger.

On the third night I joined a small group that walked to a nearby village hoping to find a place to eat and drink beer. We discovered a Gasthaus and stayed until the proprietor closed. Beer bottles stuffed in the pockets of our field trousers clinked with each faltering step as we staggered out the door and stumbled back to camp. The pitch black forest rang with songs of drunken soldiers who frequently stopped to open another beer and toast to bravery, courage and intelligence. The scene would have made the Keystone Cops and Three Stooges blush. Our ruckus woke the field grade officers who promptly put the village off-limits. Except for carrying out official duties, we were now restricted to the encampment.

I felt like a caged animal trapped in the camp the last afternoon before the start of Reforger. I decided to sneak away and go for a joy-ride. Before leaving, I studied a topographic map and planned a circular route that would get me back before dark. My buddies covered for me and I rode away in a 4-wheel-drive jeep to relieve claustrophobia.

I travelled across fields bursting with crops ready for the autumn harvest and bounced in my seat as I drove along a dirt trail through ancient forests with huge evergreen trees. Following the pre-planned route, I paralleled a lazy flowing river and entered a narrow valley. Leaving the river's hollow I pushed the jeep into second gear and drove up to pasture lands, then scaled the valley's eastern hills. Near the top I turned the jeep to face the valley and shut off the engine. I climbed out and leaned against the hood to watch the sun set. The sun hovered barely above the western hills, and from my vantage point I could see the entire valley which dozed quiet and peaceful, with not a building or other human in sight.

I stripped to my waist and created a makeshift cushion from my olive-green t-shirt and field jacket. Propping muddy boots on a dirty bumper, I sat on the jeep's hood enjoying the sun's lingering rays warming my skin. No signs of civilization broke nature's perfect beauty. Tracts of forests and fields reflected different shades of green, like a patchwork quilt. A hawk effortlessly soared overhead, riding currents of air with outstretched wings, circling the valley in search of an evening meal. A breeze carried crisp, sharp smells: fresh cut hay, manure, my own skin—an aroma shifting between fragrant cleanliness and barnyard stench.

The sun continued its descent and touched treetops on the opposite hills. I had time to think and reflect. Solitude freed my thoughts, and I didn't have to concentrate on pressing Army duties. Free of mental clutter, a new understanding about my relationship to the earth began to emerge.

For over two years I had been living close to the earth. Beginning with officers basic training, I had spent more time in the woods than in civilization. Life in the infantry required knowing how to blend with nature; camouflage and stealth were needed to conceal movement. Many months outdoors, in all weather conditions, allowed me to regain primal senses that had been lost from living in suburbs and cities.

At first, the return to nature was difficult. Ranger School taught me that. But at some point I crossed the line to where living in the wilderness became second nature. I knew from changes in the air and rustling of the wind when rain was coming, 24 hours before the first drops fell. Markings of topographic maps rose off paper and spiralled in my imagination. They formed pictures so clear it was as if I were looking at the countryside. That ability worked backwards and I could gaze at terrain and visualize what it would look like on a map. At night I glided through woods seeing like a cat and never stumbled on uneven ground or tripped over fallen logs. To keep body heat from draining into the earth when sleeping outdoors in freezing weather, I learned to layer straw and leaves between myself and the ground. The touch, smell and feel of moist dirt from freshly dug foxholes awakened my dormant senses. I had stepped back to the time when man and nature were one.

I knew sunrise would soon arrive when birds awakened, chattering in the pre-dawn darkness. They gave the first signal that night would soon leak a kaleidoscope of purple and gray before the morning sun appeared. Smells in the forest constantly changed during the spring, summer and fall. Mornings were more powerful than midday, but sunset carried the strongest odors—a honeyed sweetness trapped beneath overhead branches. Steely German winter skies brought blankets of silent falling snow, unlike the noisy clatter of pouring rain. It yielded a peaceful white countryside with the only sounds my boots crunching snow across barren fields.

Still sitting on the hood, I understood that I was connected to nature but would never master it. I was only a part of the earth; Mother Nature was infinitely more powerful than I.

Daylight had turned to dusk and washed the valley in a light gray. I took in the surrounding beauty as if viewing a painting hung on an art gallery wall. Nature's canvas stretched and groaned, and then absorbed me into the masterpiece. A great and tranquil calm flowed into me. The serene valley sunset brought another experience of complete and absolute peace. I now encountered the identical sensation of serenity and tranquility as in the art gallery and when wanting to become a priest in the sixth grade. Mother Nature wrapped her arms around me and gave me another piece of my true self.

◆◆◆

At the end of Reforger we established a new campsite along the edge of a small town. We waited there for three days until the time came to board trains and return to Mainz. Like evenings before the start of Reforger, there was little to do. It took one full day to clean our equipment and personal gear. Afterwards we waited. Somebody had brought a football and I joined in the game. Others played poker, wrote letters, read or slept.

The football game broke up and I walked back to my pup tent. I took my topographic map out of its plastic case and spread it on the ground. Kneeling behind the map, I reviewed the 11-day Reforger war game and reevaluated what had gone well and where deadly mistakes were made. I traced a finger along the map to the town where we first unloaded the jeeps which was near Kassel. This sparked an idea. Hofgeismar wasn't far from Kassel and the next day would bring another day of petrifying boredom. I decided to visit Maria and Hieronymus.

Using the excuse I needed to conduct a recon I received permission to leave the camp. I said it would be helpful in writing the after action-reports. It was a stretch, but the officer in charge bought it. I called my driver, an 18-year-old mechanical wizard from Kansas, and told him to prepare the jeep. The next day we left camp immediately after lunch. An hour later a U.S. army jeep with two American soldiers in full-field uniform pulled up outside 1600 Hemminger Strasse.

"I'm going inside to visit some relatives and will be an hour or so. Keep an eye on this," I said to the driver handing him my M-16 rifle. "You got something to read?"

"Don't worry about me, sir, I just like being away from the campsite."

"Well, all right. Feel free to walk around, but make sure you lock the vehicle. And make damn sure you keep the rifles secured."

"You bet. I'm going to stay right here, sir. Maybe get out and stretch my legs a little."

I left the driver in the jeep, listening to the sounds of my boots thumping the sidewalk leading up to the doorway. Wooden boxes filled with red and white flowers lined the bottom of the Kauer's windows. I didn't remember them from my first visit.

A part of me loved the United States. During parades, I'd stand in front of my platoon and feel goosebumps as a military brass band played the national anthem. But as I headed up the walkway to rejoin my German relatives a totally different sensation overwhelmed me. I felt like a traitor dressed in the American uniform. The United States had killed millions of Germans, civilians as well as soldiers during World War II. My birth father had most certainly been in the German army. Did he fight against the Americans? The only thing I knew for certain about my German family's history during the war was that an uncle had been killed on the Russian front during the battle of Stalingrad. I felt embarrassed, ashamed and guilty to be visiting my relatives while dressed in the uniform of a former enemy. I rationalized my service in the American Army by making the excuse that I was really defending Germany from its long standing enemy—Russia.

Standing on the porch and cradling a steel helmet in one arm, I rang the Kauer's buzzer. "Ja?" a female voice questioned through the intercom system.

I bent over to speak into the intercom. "This is Peter Friedrich Sander. Is this Maria?"

"Aacch Peter! Moment, moment, I'll be right there." Within seconds great-aunt Maria hugged me on the doorstep, a warm and caring embrace. Nothing artificial in the way she held me, no puppeteer seeking control.

Like the first time we met, Maria dropped whatever she had been doing and welcomed me with an open heart and arms. She invited me inside, asking that I leave my boots outside the door. Great-uncle Hieronymus greeted me, still formal and quiet, and his movements had slowed since I last saw him.

Maria's everyday solid gray dress was pleasing to the eye. She brushed her silver hair straight back and it just touched her shoulders. Her twinkling blue eyes gave way to rosy cheeks and a refined jawline. She flashed the same caring smile, and radiated energy. Maria was beautiful.

Just as before, Maria did the talking for her and her husband. "You must be on maneuvers. We saw the jeep pull up on the street. We were wondering what happened to you. How are you? You should have the driver come in."

"No, he's okay where he is."

I had become nearly fluent with the German language and had no difficulty talking to or understanding Maria. At this point, I even regularly dreamed in German. Sometimes my dreams were bilingual, part English and part German. Rarely did I dream only in English anymore.

"Are you hungry? I'll make us all something to eat," she said walking to the kitchen, not waiting for my reply.

I followed right behind, leaving Hieronymus in the living room. I helped partly out of politeness, but mostly because I wanted to be near Maria. She kept me busy cutting cheeses and meats while she prepared the rest of the mid-afternoon snack.

Hieronymus shuffled to the dining room and eased himself into a chair to watch Maria and me in the kitchen. He said he was happy to see me again and asked a few questions about the army. My great-uncle couldn't have been a puppeteer if he tried.

"Are you sure you don't want the driver to come in?" Maria asked above the clatter of dishes being removed from kitchen shelves. "There's plenty of food."

"No, he's all right in the jeep."

Maria's smile disappeared when I answered her last question. "If you're sure. Let's go to the dining room and eat."

At the dining room table Maria asked once more if the driver could join us. It wasn't so much a question as a pleasant directive. I left their apartment and walked to the jeep. Her smile reappeared when I returned with the driver. Maria Kauer was a saint.

The four of us sat down to eat, and the driver lost his infantry swagger being surrounded by people who spoke a foreign language. I acted as translator and saw myself in him, a scared foreigner, only a few years earlier.

"So, have you gone back to visit Ilse?" Maria asked, pouring the driver a cup of coffee. It was a sincere question and reminded me that my adopted parents rarely asked questions that were more than conversational pieces. And my birth mother didn't bother to ask any questions.

I told them about my second trip to Bad Nauheim concluding it wasn't a good idea to visit regularly. Farewells gravely upset Ilse Sander.

"I noticed that at the train station in Bad Nauheim when you left to go back to Mainz," Maria said. "Perhaps you've made a good decision." Her response contained no judgment or manipulation to force her ideas on me.

We talked as equals, communicating as one adult to another.

I wasn't used to hearing someone talk openly about life's realities. In the home where I grew up we never discussed serious problems and instead let them simmer in darkness until they eventually blew up. Petti was the first person who talked openly about her life with me, Maria the second.

Maria again shifted the conversation as Hieronymus continued to listen. The driver sat quietly eating and listening. He cocked his head as if that might help him understand German.

"When I was a little girl my grandfather used to put me on his knee when sitting in his rocking chair by the fireplace. He'd smoke his pipe, and I loved the smell—as long as the smoke didn't go up my nose. He'd tell me stories with one hand wrapped around my waist and the other holding his pipe. One of my favorites was about his father. That would be your great-great-grandfather, Peter. His name was Josef Sander."

I sat staring at Maria. She was going to tell a family story that had been passed from generation to generation. Hieronymus had finished eating and sat with both hands on his lap, leaning back in his chair. The driver asked me to translate as he worked on a second helping of food.

Maria told the story about my great-great-grandfather, Josef Sander. "French soldiers came to Kunzendorf one winter, and all the villagers had to quarter officers in their houses. Josef was just a boy then. Two French lieutenants stayed with his family. They were surprisingly nice and helped with chores around the farm. Sometimes the lieutenants played with Josef and let him ride one of their horses. They wrapped him in an army coat before lifting him up to a horse. Then they put one of their French army hats on his head, after first stuffing it with straw to keep it from falling down over his face. Josef made believe he was a calvary officer galloping toward the enemy and shook a stick over his head, pretending it was a sword. Of course he never got out of the corral. The lieutenants walked in a circle, leading the horse by the bridle and let Josef make believe he was in the army. When spring came and melted the snow the French officers left and headed to the East. He was sad to see his two lieutenant friends leave. Josef never forgot them."

Maria had shared more than just a story because it firmly placed my family in the drama of history. My great-great-grandfather would have been a boy in the early 1800's. Only once in history have French soldiers occupied the lands around Kunzendorf. The two French lieutenants in Josef Sander's story were part of Napoleon's *Grand Armée* on its way into Russia in the year 1812. Although the tale took place four generations earlier, with Maria's passing along a family story, the days of Napoleon didn't seem that long ago.

"Did your American parents raise you with a religious upbringing?" she asked, after I translated the story to the driver. He asked me who Napoleon was.

"Yes, Catholic," I said, wiping the corners of my mouth with a cloth napkin. "We went to mass every Sunday, and I was an altar boy. When I was growing up we moved a lot, but they always sent me to Catholic schools whenever one was close. There was even a time when I wanted to become a priest." But I skipped the part about not having been to mass on a regular basis since college.

She listened attentively, looking me in the eyes as I spoke. When she was sure I had finished she joined in. "The entire Sander family is also Catholic, as are most southern Germans. Martin Luther's Reformation took place in northern Germany, and the march of Protestantism stopped at the borders of the former Austrian Empire."

"My family is also Catholic," Hieronymus chimed in, then retreated into another period of silence.

We talked a little more about Catholicism, and then I said that I'd visited my grandfather's grave. They looked surprised, and said they hadn't been in many years. Maria nudged her husband, saying they should visit the grave again, and he nodded and mumbled something.

We talked at the dining room table until the driver and I had to leave. I asked, but Maria wouldn't let us help clear the table or wash dishes. The driver and I put on our boots at the doorway and Maria and Hieronymus accompanied us to the jeep. They shook hands with the driver and hugged me. My great-aunt and uncle extended another invitation for me to visit, and I thanked them over and over again as I got in the jeep. The driver started the engine and slowly pulled onto the street. I hung out the side and looked back until my great-aunt and uncle disappeared as the jeep turned a corner.

The Tragic Flaw Strikes a Second Time

Petti and I had been together for over a year the day we returned to her apartment after hiking in the Taunus Mountains. She drove, and I sat in the Volkswagen's passenger seat happily chatting to my second great love. We rounded curve after curve, and darkness enveloped the Bug as we descended into Wiesbaden. Feeling as happy as I'd ever been I reached over and put a hand on her thigh. Petti had grown closer to me than I imagined possible.

The love I had for Petti steamed like milk boiling in a pot. The words "I love you" bubbled inside, at any moment ready to overflow. But before the words could pour out I froze. I had never told her that I loved her. I couldn't find the courage. Fear strangled the words. I trusted Petti, but only to a point. Revealing my love would make me vulnerable and I still refused to face the possibility of rejection. My worst fear was to be abandoned by someone I loved. I couldn't overcome a little boy's fear of rejection even though I'd long since become a man.

As the Bug rounded one last curve we crested a hill and the lights of Wiesbaden appeared. The best this little boy covered with a man's body could say was, "I'm glad I'm with you, Petti."

She glanced at me and slid one hand off the steering wheel and covered mine. "I know, Peter. I'm glad I'm with you too."

I had a powerful dream soon afterward. Filled with grief, I walked alone in an empty cemetery and headed toward my destination. I stopped at the grave I had come to visit and bent down to look at the name carved into the tombstone. In the dream, I visited the grave of Petti Stöcker. The fear of people leaving was firmly planted in my psyche.

We met at her apartment on a Sunday afternoon after I played a couple
of pick-up basketball games at the base gym. I hurried to Wiesbaden, not
bothering to change clothes and greeted Petti dressed in full basketball
regalia—sweats, tennis shoes and a baseball cap. We left her flat and
walked downtown to find a place to eat. Petti didn't mind my clothes, but
other people did. They stared and frowned whispering amongst themselves
while passing by.

"Why are people giving me nasty stares?" I asked.

She put her slender hand in mine and whispered in my ear. "Haven't you
noticed? Germans always dress nicely when they're in public."

"Well, in America it doesn't matter what you wear," I answered. "You can
wear a Bozo the Clown outfit and it doesn't matter. Those people are so
snobbish. Why do they care what I wear? I dress appropriately when we're
going somewhere nice." I had just referred to Germans as "those people"
and stepped over to side with American culture. It marked the first time I
recognized an aspect of German culture I didn't appreciate. Until then I
had thought I would embrace every piece of German culture easily.

The next weekend we went dancing at a discotheque in downtown
Wiesbaden. I never had a problem getting into German establishments
when I was with Petti. If owners thought I was American, they let me in
anyway. They probably figured an American with a German date wouldn't
cause any trouble. Petti and I danced and laughed long into the night, until
we finally left around 4:00 in the morning. Outside, we walked arm-in-arm
and didn't see any people or cars as we strolled the eight blocks back to her
apartment. A hushed silence engulfed the city, and only the sounds of our
voices and footsteps broke the early-morning quiet. We stopped along the
sidewalk in front of a four-lane intersection. I looked left and right before
stepping down the curb but my arm didn't budge and I lurched to a stop.
Petti hadn't moved, and she pulled me back up the sidewalk.

"Hey, what's going on?" I asked.

"We can't cross," she answered. "The man is red," and Petti pointed
across the street to the pedestrian signal beside the traffic light. They both
glowed red.

"What?" I asked. "C'mon, let's go, Petti," and I stepped back down the curb.

She still wouldn't budge. I took her hand and leaned forward, trying get her to cross the street. "No! We have to wait until the light changes."

I let go of her. "Petti. There are no cars. Do you see any cars?" I said walking to the middle of the street. "There are no cars; there are no people. Now would you please come over here?" I asked, walking backward and reaching the other side of the street. She remained on the opposite sidewalk and stared at me as if I were a stranger. When the light changed and the little man in the traffic signal turned green, she crossed the street. Germans obeyed rules, even when no one checked on them. Another obstacle stood before me and my desire to become German once again.

We argued the rest of the way home. I said it was stupid to stay on the sidewalk when there weren't any cars.

"You're undisciplined," she countered.

"Wait a minute. I'm in the Army. I'm more than in the Army. I'm an officer in the infantry. My middle name is discipline."

"You're not considerate of German culture, and don't raise your voice when talking to me. You can't become a German if you don't act like a German. You have to do more than simply wish." We were outside her apartment, and she took a deep breath, "Are you coming in?"

"No. I'm going back to Mainz." I walked away without giving her a goodnight kiss.

I thought my insecurities stemming from adoption had been put to rest when I found my birth mother. I was wrong. My inability to interact with people in close personal relationships became an increasing problem in my relationship with Petti. Life-long insecurities had been concealed inside a cardboard box since being commissioned a second lieutenant. I had buried them deep beneath a busy lifestyle and covered them up with Army pride. My insecurities never went away because I'd done nothing to resolve them. Time didn't heal my emotional trauma. It was as if a bottle had spilled and liquid gradually seeped downward through the box. At the end of my relationship with Petti, the liquid had trickled out the bottom and revealed an ugly mess. Inside was an even bigger mess. I didn't have any tools that could help reconcile the problem—no ability to search my heart to try and understand what was behind the emotions causing such rotten behavior. I had only one solution: withdraw inside the castle. Behind castle walls my problems with Petti went away because I felt no emotion.

I thought relationships were supposed to be constantly happy affairs. When I became uncomfortable with Petti, I believed something was wrong with our relationship and suspected Petti didn't really love me. This confirmed what I had always known, that I was unworthy of being loved. It didn't matter that I had a college degree, was an infantry lieutenant or an Airborne-Ranger. It wouldn't have mattered if I were Mozart or Frederick the Great. Achievement by itself wasn't going to overcome my feelings of inadequacy. The damaged little boy inside me screamed out that if she knew what I truly felt she wouldn't like me and I'd be abandoned. So I secreted the parts of me I didn't like and she knew only a shadow, not the man casting it. It was impossible for me to receive Petti's love when the insecurities I had from adoption still festered.

Life for me was black and white with no shades of gray. I didn't know how to express my feelings and wouldn't admit emotional problems. When I became uncomfortable in our relationship I had only two choices: stay in an uncomfortable relationship without hope it could ever improve, or end it. I couldn't discuss what was troubling me because I was too afraid. Petti was too close to discovering the truth, and I started pushing her out of my life.

"If war broke out and I was horribly wounded, would you stay with me, Petti?" I asked. If she said no, it would be an excuse to end the relationship.

"I'll stay with you forever, no matter what happens," Petti answered, but her words couldn't penetrate my walls, so I continued pushing her away. I wouldn't call or make plans and hoped she'd simply go away. When Petti came to visit I ignored her. She was confused and wanted to know what was happening. Petti asked if there was anything she could do. What could I tell her? Take my insecurities away? Impossible. I wouldn't even admit them.

Charlie shook his head at my behavior and called me an iceman. I ignored him and changed the subject whenever he talked about Petti. After work one night I came home and found her in my apartment.

"Who asked you over?" I sneered, watching Petti carrying a plate of food into the dining room. She set the plate on the table and walked toward me forcing a smile. "When you gave me a key to your apartment you said I could come over whenever I wanted. I thought you'd like a nice dinner and company tonight." She hesitantly stretched out her arms to give a hug.

I pushed her away. "I don't want you here. I'm tired and need to get some sleep. I've got to get up at five. I want you to leave. Get out!" and I escorted her to the door. I slammed it shut and walked past the dining room table where two plates of food grew cold.

I only withdrew deeper when Petti tried to talk about healing our broken relationship. I didn't believe our relationship could improve, and my damaged emotions blocked out her appeals to my sense of reason. Nothing could save it; not pleading, not threatening, not crying, not begging. She eventually gave up, and our relationship came to an end. I would regret it the rest of my life.

Afterwards, I dated a lot of women, always German women. It never amounted to much, a few dates and then on to someone new. I also thought sex would fill the void, but it never did. There weren't enough women in the world to heal my emotional insecurity.

Those who were unfortunate enough to get close, Petti Stöcker and Jean Daems, went away hurt, confused and questioning their own sanity. I made sure that no one else came near. My friendships with other officers were based on Army brotherhood that didn't require me to reveal my inner self.

Adoption is an unnatural act. It's like a surgical pin holding a fractured bone, a painful attempt to repair separation. As a metal pin replaces the natural order of the body, adoption replaces the natural order of the family. Both become permanent attachments.

Charlie flew to San Francisco to be with his family my second Christmas in Germany. My car was in the shop that holiday period, and I took public transportation to work on the 24th of December. The Strassenbahn, a streetcar, ran near our apartment and dropped me off by the base. Work that day ended at three in the afternoon. My boss and a couple of married friends asked me to join them for Christmas Eve dinner, but I declined their invitations. I didn't want to be pitied. Christmas was for families, and I didn't believe I had one. I didn't want to see my birth mother, and it never occurred to me to make arrangements to visit Maria. A warped sense of my place in the world prevented me from thinking anyone would want me as their guest on Christmas Eve.

I got on the Strassenbahn after work and headed home. It stopped at the Mainz Hauptbahnhof where the driver got up from his seat and walked back through the streetcar. "Time to go home and enjoy Christmas Eve with your family." He had the look of a kind grandfather. "Public transportation is finished because of the holiday."

I got off and walked into a specialty shop at the Hauptbahnhof where I bought two bottles of wine. A clerk put them in a white plastic bag. "Merry Christmas," he beamed handing me the bag.

"Merry Christmas," I said in a voice that matched my blank stare.

Snow fell outside. I barely noticed a cold wind cutting through my field jacket as I walked the last two miles to my place. An occasional car passed, headlights on. Wiperblades brushing snow off a windshield. Only one set of footprints in the snow.

There were no Christmas tree or decorations in my empty apartment, only a card and unopened presents from adopted parents. I put a record on the stereo and listened to Neil Young sing *The Loner* as I drank both bottles of wine. The wine numbed me, but emptiness would return in the morning. I staggered to bed. It was ten o'clock on Christmas Eve.

A Product of the Cold War

I grew up under the shadow of the Cold War. The conflict between the United States and the Soviet Union was the second most powerful force influencing my life. Only adoption had a greater effect.

The failure at the end of the Second World War of an East-West agreement over the future of Germany was a crucially important reason for the start of the Cold War. It began in Europe in the aftermath of World War II when the Soviet Union extended its control into Eastern and central Europe by imposing communist regimes on Poland, Hungary, Bulgaria, Romania, Czechoslovakia and East Germany.

Post-war Germany was divided into four occupation zones governed by the Soviet Union, the United States, Britain and France. The Soviet Union was assigned the eastern section of Germany, the United States the south, Britain the north and France the west. Berlin sat in the center of the Soviet zone but each of the four occupation countries were given a sector to govern in the former German capital. In 1948 the allies decided to permit the three western zones to unite as a semi-independent German state. This infuriated the Russians who responded by blockading all overland transport to the three western sectors of Berlin. The Allies broke the blockade by supplying West Berlin by air. One year later the Allies terminated their occupation governments of the western zones and created the Federal Republic of Germany. The Russians responded by announcing their zone had become the German Democratic Republic. This created the Iron Curtain.

To stop the expansion of communism into western Europe the United States initiated the North Atlantic Treaty Organization. The 12 members of NATO agreed that an attack on one was an attack on all. The Russians reciprocated and formed the Warsaw Pact, a military alliance of the Soviet Union and East and central European countries under their control.

The orthodoxy in Stalin's day, after WWII, held that the capitalist West would never tolerate communism. Communist Russia believed a clash between the two worlds inevitable. Stalin and his advisers were haunted by the nightmare of new German armies in a capitalist coalition. The Truman Doctrine and Marshall Plan were seen as evidence of steadfast Western hostility, a grand design to revivify former enemies and undermine the hold an economically weakened Soviet Union held over her satellites. Britain and the United States would not share their atomic secrets and the Soviet Union viewed the West's stockpile of atomic bombs as the gravest threat to their existence. The Soviets stressed a hostile world beyond their frontiers and colored the West in the darkest colors.

America had its own fears about the Soviets. The United States accused Julius and Ethel Rosenberg of conspiring to commit espionage for the Soviet Union. The government executed the Rosenbergs for allegedly giving top secret information about the atomic bomb to the Soviet Union. Fear of the Russians translated into general hysteria about communism and Senator Joseph McCarthy instigated Senate hearings before the sub-committee on Un-American Activities. Simply being accused of being un-American at that time cost many people their jobs in government, education and entertainment.

As the West German economy surged and stagnation took hold in the East, large numbers of people fled the German Democratic Republic. From 1949 to 1961, one-sixth of the population of the German Democratic Republic crossed the border into the West. To stop the exodus, Russian troops and East German police closed all rail and road crossings between East and West Berlin. They sealed the border with trenches and barbed wire and went on to construct the Berlin Wall. The communists said the wall was constructed to prevent the insertion of Western agents into the Eastern Bloc. All movement by Germans, east or west, between the sectors was forbidden. Hundreds of East Germans were shot and killed trying to cross the Berlin Wall. At the same time the Wall was being constructed the communists constructed a second barricade that wound through a divided

Germany and continued along the Czechoslovakian border. The Iron Curtain divided Europe physically, morally and ideologically.

The Soviet Army crushed popular uprisings in Hungary and East Germany to maintain their hold on the Eastern Block. They continued their plans for world domination, trying to expand their influence by delivering nuclear missiles to Cuba. President John F. Kennedy gave the Russians the ultimatum of removing their missiles or face American intervention. The Soviets backed down, withdrew their missiles, and the Cuban Missile Crisis ended. The world breathed a sigh of relief.

The Cold War went on. When the United States was bogged down in the jungles of Vietnam, Russian tanks rolled into Prague, crushing Czechoslovakia's first steps toward democracy. The Russians then got bogged down in their own war in Afghanistan. Jimmy Carter wanted to send his message of disapproval and had the United States boycott the 1980 Summer Olympic games held in Moscow. Carter shattered dreams for hundreds of American athletes, and a world sadly shook its head about America's political leadership.

My family history reinforced what I had been taught about the Soviet Union. Ilse Sander's story of Russian atrocities committed during World War II added to my image of a despicable Soviet Union.

I grew up along with millions of confused and frightened American school children who placed their right hand over their heart and pledged allegiance to the flag every morning. After reciting the pledge we crawled beneath our desks practicing atomic war drills. Teachers told us we'd be safe hiding under our desks if the Russians launched an attack. At the same time children hid under school desks, grown-ups built bomb shelters in their backyards hoping it would spare them from a Soviet attack. Firmly planted in the American psyche was Premier Nikita Khrushchev's infamous declaration, "We will bury you." The Americans countered with their own slogan, "Better Dead than Red."

My child's mind was sculpted by Cold War propaganda as two superpowers engaged in an unending competition for supremacy. The United States battled the Russians in the space-race, the arms-race and the race to win hearts and minds. The U.S. government painted Russia in the bleakest terms, and I grew up listening to *Voice of America* and *Radio Free Europe* broadcasts of anti-Russian propaganda. At Sunday mass I joined Catholic congregations reciting prayers for the conversion of atheist Russia. I was required to take a course titled *Americanism verses Communism* during my junior year in high school. The course portrayed the virtues of democracy against the immoralities of the Soviet Union's system.

My life's path led toward confronting the Russian Bear, and I took my place in the Cold War as an officer in Germany. I wore the army uniform proudly and each morning put on a pair of freshly starched olive-green fatigues. A lieutenant's bar was meticulously centered on the crown of my hat with the brim perfectly curved like a baseball player's cap. I shaved each morning, never grew a moustache or sideburns and got a haircut each week. My "gig line"—buttons running down my fatigue shirt, the left edge of my black polished belt buckle and the flap covering the zipper on my trousers— was always perfectly aligned. I carefully tucked creased fatigue legs inside my spit-shined black boots whose tips and heels reflected like mirrors.

Never once did I go home for breakfast or lunch during the work week while stationed in Germany. Instead, I ate in the mess hall along with the troops. When soldiers in my platoon worked late nights repairing their armored vehicles I got dirty alongside them. I spent weekends checking on their morale and welfare, ensured they attended schools needed for professional development and wrote letters of recommendation for those leaving the service. I was the epitome of a loyal, protective American Army officer and field duty was the part of the Army I enjoyed most.

Field duty was practice for war, the ultimate athletic competition. We had an opponent, trained hard and developed a game plan. I made certain soldiers in my platoon had the skills required to survive and win a war. We drilled on tactics adapted from Ranger School until they could satisfactorily do them at night and when they were exhausted. I pushed my soldiers hard but pushed myself harder. If they were cold and tired, I was cold and tired. In the field I made sure every one of them ate before I did, checked them at night, woke up before they did. Soldiers who excelled were rewarded, those who struggled were encouraged and troopers who got out of line were disciplined. I had dreams of fighting the Russians and wondered how good I was, how well I had trained my platoon. Part of me wanted to find out.

I was promoted from second to first lieutenant during my second year in Germany. Along with the promotion I was assigned to lead one of the special platoons in the battalion, the heavy mortar platoon. I returned to Fort Benning to attend a six-week mortar platoon leaders' course in preparation for the assignment. After returning to my unit, I took charge of the battalion commander's personal artillery: four 4.2 inch mortars, each mounted in an armored personnel carrier that could hurl a twelve pound projectile nearly five miles.

Ronald Reagan became president of the United States during my time in Germany. America once again came to believe in itself under Reagan's leadership. His characterization of the Soviet Union as the "Evil Empire" focused American energy and attention on a foreign enemy. He never flinched from confrontation and spent whatever was necessary to ensure military dominance. The public held the military in high regard with Reagan as Commander-in-Chief, a far cry from Vietnam era bitterness.

My unit received new and better equipment every month after Reagan became president. We never lacked resources like equipment, ammunition or fuel. With Reagan the volunteer Army drew better soldiers, and we learned new and improved tactics and doctrine. We were part of America's spear protecting a world from the Russian menace.

The Army offered responsibility, team work, world travel, adventure, fun, danger and challenge. It brought the best friends I'd ever known, and I felt like I belonged. My world was black and white, me against the Russians in a desperate battle to determine whose system would prevail. The Cold War completely absorbed me and I lived the Army officer lifestyle once described by my battalion commander, "An Army officer is one who has entered a vocation, similar to that of a priest. It demands selfless sacrifice and a total life commitment."

The Army was something to believe in. Military service was the sole activity providing meaning and purpose. My search for contentment had failed everywhere else. I had believed finding my birth mother would lead to happiness. But it didn't. The Catholic Church's promise of joy never materialized. Alcohol's euphoria ended the morning after a night of drinking. Searching for satisfaction through women left me feeling empty. And I couldn't seem to cross the cultural barrier that would lead to fulfillment by rejoining my heritage. So I put my faith in the Army and became the uniform.

My newest search for well-being was based on the Russians. I needed them. They were the enemy and the reason my military service was important. The Russians now gave meaning to my life and I waited for the day when the satisfaction I found in the Army would spill over into the rest of my life. I hoped the Army would be the key that finally opened my castle door.

The Wooden Guardhouse

Lieutenant Guy Leeks formed another link in the chain of Army brotherhood. Guy, Charlie and I met at the Infantry Officer Basic Course, and Guy and I graduated together from Ranger School. The Army assigned him to Berlin and for two-and-a-half years he pleasantly badgered Charlie and me to visit. We finally took him up on his offer and made plans to go to Berlin during our last Thanksgiving weekend in Germany.

Getting to Berlin located, 100 miles beyond the East-West German border, meant traveling through East Germany. We had three options: fly, take the military "duty train," or go by car. It was an easy decision; Charlie had just bought a brand new 911 Porsche.

Allied officers followed rigid procedures when travelling by car to Berlin. We needed military travel orders because the route included driving through the territory of a Cold War enemy. Three weeks before Thanksgiving Charlie and I filled out paperwork that needed approval from two generals. I worried that I wouldn't get to go because of my top-secret security clearance, but the paperwork came back approved. We'd cross East Germany on the Helmstedt Autobahn, the only highway the Russians permitted Allied soldiers to use when traveling through the German Democratic Republic. The route included Allied and Warsaw Pact checkpoints at the East-West German borders. We had to travel in the Class A uniform—black shoes, dark green pants with black piping on the side of each leg, jacket with brass buttons, khaki shirt, black tie and saucer hat.

On the Wednesday before Thanksgiving day Charlie and I changed to Class As immediately after lunch and left Mainz for Berlin. We were excited to be seeing an old friend and to explore a new city. I punched a rock and roll cassette into the tape player while Charlie cruised the autobahn in excess of 120 miles per hour. Speed fueled our excitement, another example of my living with thrills and on the edge of danger. But on the autobahn we weren't the fastest. A 928 Porsche, 700 series BMW and even a BMW motorcycle whizzed by as we roared along. We stopped once for gas and arrived in Helmstedt, 220 miles from Mainz, in a little less than three hours.

The border crossing awaited a few miles east of the city of Helmstedt. Charlie slowed the Porsche and I turned off the music. A series of highway signs warned motorists of the approaching international border. I leaned forward as the seatbelt cut into my shoulder, reading highway signs in three languages: German, French and English. Words on the signs grew larger as we closed in on the border dividing Germany. "WARNING: Border Five Kilometers" "DANGER: End of Allied Controlled Zone" Signs signalling the end of the world—the end of the Western world.

We were directed to park to the side of an Allied administrative building. Three flagpoles flew the standards of Britain, France and the United States and stood like sentries guarding the entrance to the building. No West German flag flew; there was no German control at a border ruled by post-World War II agreements. I spotted the Allied checkpoint, a solitary concrete bunker wedged into dark earth a football field's length beyond the administrative building. Somewhere past the checkpoint's concrete wall lurked the Iron Curtain.

Charlie parked and we walked inside. A well-lit and spacious lobby had wall placards pointing to the Berlin Travel Office. We followed the signs and entered a large rectangular room the size of a modest one-bedroom house, separated by a long brown counter. Having grown accustomed to harsh infantry life, it looked like the most sanitary and efficient office in the world. A waxed floor glistened beneath spotless desks behind the counter. Uniformed clerks typed or talked on telephones. A British sergeant with a rock-solid build that bulged against his brown woolen uniform sat behind the desk closest to the counter. He sprang out of his chair when we entered and marched to the counter as if drilling on a parade ground. The sergeant took our paperwork and examined it as if he were a robot; his head jerked from side to side like a scanner. He completed the inspection and set both hands on the counter still holding our papers. "Reason for travel to Berlin, sir?" the British machine asked.

"To visit a friend," we answered.

"I'll be right back. Please help yourself to a cup of coffee," and in one smooth motion he executed a 180-turn and marched to the back of the room and transferred our paperwork to a second British soldier behind a desk. The soldier carried out a second examination of the documents, made a telephone call and then stamped our travel orders. The machine marched back to the counter and returned our paperwork. He issued instructions for travelling through East Germany giving contingencies for every possible situation: what to do at the Warsaw Pact checkpoint, if stopped by East German police, if the car broke down, if we had an accident, warned us not to get off the autobahn for any reason and explained what to do when entering Berlin. The machine finished his instructions and handed us a sheet of paper that repeated the information. He asked if we had questions and then escorted us to another room for a briefing and film on the political nature of East Germany. Viewing the film was our last requirement to travel through East Germany, and we left the building under a twilight sky.

Back in the Porsche we filled up at an adjacent service station then slowly followed the car's headlights 100 meters to the Allied checkpoint. We didn't have long to wait; Charlie's Porsche was the only car at the bunker's gate. We stayed in the car as a sentry examined our orders. He disappeared inside the bunker, came out a moment later and returned the papers. Finally, the sentry raised the gate and waved us through.

While the gate closed in the rearview mirror we entered no-man's land. Ninety-degree turns along the narrow road forced our speed to five miles per hour as we headed to the Warsaw Pact checkpoint. The radio was off and we didn't talk. The soft throbbing of the Porsche's engine was the only sound as we inched our way through this eerie landscape. Lights mounted atop wooden telephone poles illuminated shadowy death traps. Rows of concertina wire were spaced between iron obstacles and cement barriers. We passed over a deep trench flanked on each side by a 10-feet-high concrete wall. Open areas contained buried mines. Mid-way through no-man's land the design and construction of obstacles, barriers and trenches suddenly changed. We had entered East Germany. Why did I feel a knot in my stomach and feeling of an impending gloom instead of excitement fueled by an adrenaline rush? Of my own free will I had entered the enemy's land. A knot spread from my stomach into my chest. I had to concentrate to breath normally and block out fear that yelled at me to grab the steering wheel and turn the car around.

I prepared to confront Russian soldiers, the soldiers who gave me my life's purpose. The British machine had stated during his political briefing that only Russian soldiers manned the border checkpoints, Russian soldiers specially picked for border duty because of their outstanding military abilities and political reliability. I was certain they would be at least six feet six, two hundred and fifty pounds and the most sinister-looking men imaginable.

Charlie alternated between first and second gears, driving through the strip of land that was the Cold War's border. Ten minutes after leaving the Allied checkpoint the car crawled past a final wall and we emptied out of no-man's land, halting in front of a red and white barber-pole which blocked the road. A wooden guardhouse stood to our immediate left. We had arrived at the Warsaw Pact checkpoint. One of us now had to go inside the guardhouse to have our orders stamped by Russian border guards.

My roommate shut off the engine and we sat listening to the deafening quiet. I turned to Charlie who sat with both hands clutching the steering wheel. He turned to me, grim faced with eyes wide open. "Want me to go inside?" he asked.

"Naw man, I'll do it. Give me your orders." He didn't hesitate and reached behind the seat to retrieve them, and I stuffed them in my brief-case before pushing the car door open. An icy blast of air smacked my face. Twilight had turned to night and a light snow fell. I slid out of the seat and shoved the door shut. Thousands of hours of army training paid off as I willed my fear to become energy and prepared to accomplish a mission. Standing outside the car, I put my hat on and looked down, making sure my uniform was straight. Polished first lieutenant bars were precisely pinned on the epaulet of each shoulder, a black and gold Ranger tab was sewn a perfect half inch below the left shoulder, silver jump wings glistened above the left breast pocket. I took a deep, cold breath and looked around the checkpoint. No one was in sight. Only empty farmland and forests, and a barren early-winter countryside disappeared into darkness behind the red and white barber-pole. No cars were in front, no cars came from behind.

Two floodlamps erected on telephone poles at each side of the horizontal barber-pole illuminated the Porsche, a small stretch of road and the wooden guardhouse ten yards off the road. The guardhouse was small, the size of a trailer at a construction sight. Two windows with yellowish light escaping from behind drawn shades watched me take slow, careful steps across the pavement dusted with snow. I carried my briefcase in an ungloved hand and glanced from side to side, probing the darkness for the slightest movement. Snow crunched under my patent leather black shoes and I felt a distant, piercing cold. My heart pounded; every nerve was on edge as I advanced toward an enemy I'd been taught to hate since childhood.

Reaching the solid door of the guardhouse I knocked as instructed by the machine. I knocked so hard that my knuckles hurt, then waited for a buzzer sound that would signal the door was open. The seconds dragged by. Snowflakes clung to the shoulders of my uniform. Finally the buzzer sounded. I raised a bare hand to grasp an icy doorknob, slowly turned the knob and with one quick motion pushed the door open. I stepped inside prepared to meet soldiers of the "Evil Empire."

A single room the opposite of the well-lit, clean administrative building on the Allied side was before me. No one was inside. My shiny black shoes stepped onto dirty, gray peeled linoleum. Walls, once white, had yellowed. Naked light bulbs hung from the ceiling, yielding sharp contrasts of light and dark. A disgusting smell of inferior tobacco smoke lingered in the stale air forcing me to breathe through my mouth. Lenin, scowling with his bald head and goatee, eyed me from a picture mounted on a wall. A red cloth flag clung to a dark pole next to the picture of the Soviet Union's first premier. A dirty ashtray and magazines covered a plastic table, centered between two red chairs against a wall. A radiator gurgled hot water, filling the room with musty warmth. That was it. Nothing else was in the room.

I searched the interior a second time. A drywall partitioned the guardhouse. Built into its side was a thick, discolored sliding glass window positioned over a counter. I couldn't see past the drywall or through the discolored glass. The flimsy wall muffled sounds of boots stomping and voices. There were words in a language I'd never heard before—Russian.

The British machine said to knock on the sliding glass window. I rapped the window with my knuckles and stepped back. The window slowly opened from the bottom up. It stopped, leaving a gap the size of an outstretched hand. I couldn't see anyone through the opening, but a heavy masculine voice with a thick accent demanded, "Papers." I instantly propped the briefcase against the counter, removed the travel orders and set them on the counter beneath the opening. A hand on the opposite side grabbed the paperwork and the glass divider slammed shut. I tried to stare through the window but it was useless. On the other side papers ruffled and Russians talked. More waiting. I eased over to the plastic table, keeping one eye on the partition and picked up a magazine. A couple of quick glances revealed words written with Cyrillic characters, the Russian alphabet.

The partition had a door. It opened. I dropped the magazine onto the table at the same time turning to face the door. I froze, staring at two Russian soldiers.

Only my eyes moved. Their uniforms jumped out at me—Soviet greenish-brown field uniforms embellished with red ornamentation. Their heavy, knee-high brown boots were polished to match waist and shoulder belts. Black pistols hung from holsters along their waists. Their jackets were impeccably pressed, with two rows of polished brass buttons running from the neck to the waist. Their uniforms could have passed my closest inspection.

I remained motionless. Eyes narrowed, teeth clenched, jaw muscles tight.

The Russian soldiers stood just past the door, shoulder to shoulder, hands at their sides, feet slightly apart. I shifted my attention to their faces. They were young, even compared to my 26 years. Maybe 19, 20, 21. They stared at me with lips pressed shut, and their faces betrayed no emotion. They were two professionals doing their duty, clean-shaven, with short groomed hair and shining eyes, the look of athletes. I stood a few inches taller but gave up 20 pounds to each of them.

Where were the gorillas, the evil monsters? The two Russians on the opposite side of the room looked like they could have been the guys I grew up with. In civilian clothes they could be anyone I played basketball with, drank beer or chased women with. My brain registered what I had never expected: two humans stood inside the Russian uniforms.

They continued standing just past the door. One of them held out the travel orders. He gestured with a hand and seemed to ask a question. I couldn't understand the language, so I stood by the table returning their stares. The second soldier waved a hand over his brass belt buckle adorned with a red star at its center. He wanted to trade the belt buckle for something on my uniform. I shook my head no.

He forced a smile. They slowly walked toward me. Side-by-side the Russians advanced, heavy boots thumping against the floor. I fought an urge to step back. They stopped an arm's length from me. One of the soldiers extended his hand holding the travel orders.

I reached out and took the paperwork. "Everything okay?" I asked in English, using an icy voice and not bothering to look at the documents.

They didn't answer but continued staring at my uniform.

"Can I go?" I asked in German keeping the icy voice.

One of them raised an eyebrow as he stared at me. "Yes," he replied in German. "You may go."

I immediately returned to Charlie waiting in the Porsche. He started the engine, the barber-pole raised, and we began our journey through East Germany.

I grew up in a culture that portrayed Russia as a vicious country filled with wicked people. I had never doubted Cold War indoctrination. Not ever, even for an instant, did I consider Russians to be human. But in the guardhouse I came face to face with the object of Western propaganda. I met two men whom I had been taught to fear and hate. I was shocked to find they looked like me instead of like creatures out of a science fiction or horror film. The reality of the Russians in the guardhouse didn't match the illusion produced by capitalist sensationalism. I asked myself questions about who the Russians really were. Accompanying the questions was a sliver of doubt about Cold War teachings, and a tiny crack appeared in the foundation of another one of my beliefs.

Berlin

Charlie and I drove through East Germany without incident and entered West Berlin late Wednesday night. We called Guy from the U.S. Army Headquarters building and asked for directions to his apartment. He told us to wait and that he'd come and pick us up. Charlie hung up the phone, unbuttoned the brass buttons of his dark green military jacket and collapsed into a chair at the entrance foyer. I kept my jacket buttoned and sat in a chair next to him waiting for Guy to arrive. Fatigue set in from the long day. We small-talked to keep from falling asleep but didn't have a long wait. The double glass entryway doors to the headquarters flew open and Guy appeared. He jogged toward us wearing a gray sweat shirt covered by a brown leather winter coat, blue jeans and tennis shoes. Our exhaustion disappeared as soon as we saw him. Charlie and I erupted in shouts of joy and laughter and swaggered toward our friend. I wanted to give a high-five, but we shook hands instead. My friends weren't basketball players, and men in the infantry didn't hug one another. But we whooped and hollered so loud that alarmed night duty soldiers emptied out of their offices to investigate the commotion. Their fears melted to grins as the soldiers watched our reunion. They returned to their posts laughing and shaking their heads. It was Army life—make best friends in a short time, endure a prolonged separation and pick back up again as if never having parted. We quieted down, fearing our boisterous behavior might cause an incident and followed Guy to his apartment.

Guy Leeks grew up in New York City and stood five feet ten inches tall. He had a medium build and his blonde hair was kept shorter than Army regulation. The wire-rimmed glasses he sometimes wore on his hawk-like nose added intensity to his dark brown eyes. Our friendship had almost never gotten off the ground. I had difficulty understanding his northeast nasal dialect and shied away from him after we first met at basic training. But once I got past his accent we developed a close friendship. He was a history buff, a devout Catholic and well read. He loved to play the piano and enjoyed classical as well as rock and roll music. Guy wasn't particularly interested in sports, but what he lacked in athletic ability he made up for in cultural sophistication. Besides playing the piano he had expert knowledge regarding literature, music, art and architecture. And Guy was a kind man. Even the most gracious Southern gentleman would have been pleased with his manners and the politeness with which he treated people. Unlike my narrow black and white perspective, Guy saw many shades of gray in the world.

Lieutenant Leeks lived in housing provided by the military—the Bachelor Officer's Quarters. The three of us entered his small one-bedroom apartment, a shrine to the chaos of abstract art. We stepped over discarded newspapers, magazines and dirty clothes that carpeted the floor as Guy gave an obligatory tour. His bedroom looked as if it had been taken from the epicenter of a major earthquake. Dirty socks and underwear resembled Christmas ornaments, hanging over jumbled dresser drawers. Sheets and blankets swirled into a single mound on the bed. Uniforms lay scattered throughout the apartment as if replacing the green of houseplants. A thick grime ringed his bathtub and sink, the toilet bowl cried to be cleaned and toothpaste oozed onto a filthy counter. Sanitation didn't improve in the kitchen. The sink contained a stack of dirty dishes and our shoes made sucking sounds on the floor every time we moved. A half-dozen bottles of German beer in the refrigerator provided Guy's only redemption from poor housekeeping.

"How do you live like this?" I laughed, taking three beers out of the refrigerator. I asserted an outgoing and good-natured temperament, the mood I always had whenever surrounded by Army buddies.

He returned the laugh, "There's too much to experience in life and it keeps me from keeping my quarters spotless."

"Spotless? More like a pig sty," Charlie grinned. "Smells like one too," he said waving a hand in front of his face as the aroma from inside the refrigerator hit him full-force.

Guy apologized and shrugged his shoulders as he led us into the living
room. An upright piano, pushed against a wall, dominated the surroundings. A
white linen cloth spread neatly across the piano headboard contrasted with the
rest of his apartment. It had been ironed and painstakingly folded so that not a
wrinkle showed. Guy displayed the most important influences in his life—an
array of icons—across the linen. A silver crucifix with a rosary at its base stood
at one end. Three-by-five pictures of friends gave way to displays of military
insignia from Guy's brief Army career. Two white candles flanked a golden
picture frame at the opposite end of the cloth. His mother and father, arm in
arm, smiled from inside the frame. I moved to the edge of the piano and leaned
forward to get a closer look at Guy's parents. I noticed a faint outline of lip
imprints where Guy had kissed the glass in front of his parents' picture.

The remainder of the living room's decor was less personal. A row of albums
stacked knee-high took up one wall and a bookshelf filled with classics covered
another. Well-used furniture completed the furnishings. A small American flag,
a calendar and a couple of prints kept the walls from being bare.

Charlie and I cleared wreckage from the couch and looked for places to
sit as Guy lowered himself onto the piano bench. Over two beers' time we
talked, laughed, exchanged stories and caught up with each other. We
hadn't missed a beat in two-and-a-half years.

"So what's the weekend game plan?" Charlie yawned.

Guy leaned back against the piano, bit his upper lip and squinted. He
looked as if ready to announce his candidacy for president before telling us
the itinerary. "Tomorrow we'll have Thanksgiving dinner at the mess hall,
and afterwards I'll show you some of West Berlin. You know, art museums,
historical sites, the downtown area. Tomorrow night we'll go dancing, I
know a couple of hot discotheques with lots of babes. Friday I want to take
you guys to East Berlin, and Saturday is open. Sound all right?"

"Sounds good to me," I nodded and stretched my arms upward before
finishing my bottle of beer.

Charlie slowly got off the couch and yawned again. "You're our guide so
I'll trust your judgement. Now I gotta go piss, if I can find the bathroom
that is," he said, sidestepping debris down the hall.

Charlie crashed on the couch; I curled up in a sleeping bag spread on the living room floor, and Guy fought his way into the mound of entangled sheets and blankets on his bed. I considered any place dry and warm a luxury and instantly fell into a deep sleep.

Guy woke us up at 10:00 o'clock the next morning. We dressed in civilian clothes and ate a traditional Thanksgiving meal at his unit's mess hall. Then we drove to the downtown area to see the sights of West Berlin, walking along the Kurfürstendamm. I found it hard to believe that Berlin had been destroyed during the Second World War. Glitzy stores overflowed with fashionable merchandise along West Berlin's main shopping boulevard. By nightfall we ended up at a discotheque filled with Germans, American and British soldiers. I spent the night drinking beer and joking with my two friends, exchanging war stories with the Brits and chasing the best looking German women in the discotheque.

Friday morning we rose at 7:00 and dressed in Class As as required for U.S. Army personnel visiting East Berlin. The three of us piled into Charlie's Porsche and drove to Check Point Charlie, the U.S. controlled passageway to East Berlin. The economic disparity between the two halves of the city became apparent after only a few minutes driving inside East Berlin. We bumped along on roads full of potholes and passed many buildings that still needed repair from damages suffered in World War II. The few cars in East Berlin looked small and shoddy, cardboard boxes compared to Charlie's Porsche. I didn't see advertisements or billboards littering the city. None were needed. There was no competition in a society where the government controlled all the means of production.

Guy had been to East Berlin many times and directed us to Alexander Platz, a huge cobblestoned square surrounded by government offices and stores. It was East Berlin's answer to the Kurfürstendamm in West Berlin. We had no trouble finding a parking place, and it didn't cost anything.

We left the car and walked across Alexander Platz toward a nameless three-story department store. Guy said he wanted to give us a feel for how East Berliners lived. Sparsely stocked department store shelves contained products of an inferior quality. Bland-colored clothing felt papery to touch and didn't bear brandname trademarks. Display counters lacked accompanying corporate logos, and there weren't any pictures of smiling models luring customers into choosing one product over another. Radios, televisions and other electronic equipment looked like pieces out of a museum dedicated to the 1950's. Glum salespeople mirrored their dreary surroundings as they labored through another monotonous work day.

Small groups of Russian soldiers, in uniform but off duty, picked through merchandise while shopping in the store. I spent more time watching them than looking at anything else. The Russians behaved well; I admired their manners. They took clothes off the shelves and refolded them before putting them back. The soldiers of the "Evil Empire" treated store clerks with courtesy unlike some American soldiers who were rude and inconsiderate when taking part in West German society. I looked at the enemy soldiers in the department store and tried to hate them; a lifetime of learned behavior doesn't easily go away. But I found I couldn't. Instead, I saw the Russians as real people, laughing with one another while looking for a gift to send a loved one back home. As in the guardhouse, I asked myself where the monsters were. I stared at the Russians with such intensity that I lost track of my surroundings until feeling a sharp pain against my arm as Charlie elbowed me. "C'mon man, let's go," Guy and Charlie snapped. "There's lot's more to see." I shook my head to empty thoughts of the Russians and followed my friends to another section of the store.

Other Americans were shopping, recognized as easily by the huge packages they carried as by their uniforms. And not all East German goods were shoddy. The store contained some of the world's finest porcelain and crystal, and one dollar in East Berlin had 10-15 times the purchasing power as in the West. Americans carted away the best products at disgustingly low prices. This disturbed me. East Germans made the porcelain and crystal but couldn't afford to buy their own goods. Ever since the dodge-ball incident, I hated seeing anyone bullied. It didn't seem fair that East Germans couldn't enjoy the fruits of their labor. The workers weren't responsible for the communist system. They silently watched in despair as another American carried five crystal platters to a cash register. Did they know that greed was the West's tragic flaw?

We left the store along a wide sidewalk lined with bare winter trees, skeletons stretching into the lifeless gray winter sky. At a kiosk, a stand selling magazines, snacks and beverages, we stopped for a short break. After buying drinks, sausages and rolls, we sat down to eat on a nearby bench. The temperature couldn't have been warmer than 20 degrees but, thankfully, no breeze blew. The warm food felt good pressed against my cold hands and the three of us ate and talked.

We watched a young mother and her son slowly approach the kiosk along the sidewalk. The boy's head barely came even to his mother's waist as they walked hand-in-hand, the mother patient with her son's small steps. They shared similar physical characteristics, both bone thin with hollow cheeks stretched against pale white skin. They walked by us in silence. A patched, dark wool coat covered the woman's slender frame. The irregular patches didn't quite match the color of her knee-length coat. She wore a maroon glove on one hand and a dark red one on the other. The boy had outgrown his blue coat but fading yellow mittens protected his wrists from the cold. Socks poked out of holes on the fronts of his worn-out shoes. After they passed Guy set down his food and quickly stepped to the kiosk to buy a chocolate bar. "Wait right there," he yelled to Charlie and me. Guy ran off holding his hat on top of his head with one hand and a chocolate bar in the other.

Guy ran toward the mother and child and caught up with them fifteen yards from our bench. He stopped in front of the pair and the woman froze while wrapping a protective arm around her child. She stared with wide-open eyes at the enemy soldier, her lips sealed tight and every muscle taunt as she pulled her son closer to her tattered coat. "Excuse me Ma'am," Guy said in German. He smiled and extended the candy bar, trying to ease her fear. "The chocolate is for your child," Guy said, shifting his smile to the boy.

God only knows what she thought. The woman should have been terrified if she'd grown up exposed to as much propaganda about the United States as I'd learned about the Eastern Block. She didn't respond to Guy's offer and tightened her grip around her son. The boy stared up at Guy, his eyes huge and mouth wide open, innocence tangled with confusion. He remained silent as did his mother.

Charlie and I gawked from the bench. I couldn't believe Guy was fraternizing with people belonging to a system that promised to "bury us." I felt he was aiding and comforting the enemy.

Guy lowered the candy to his side but kept the smile, trying to reassure the scrawny, pale woman. "It's okay," he continued in German. "I'm not going to hurt you or your child. I bought the chocolate for your son. It's a gift. All children love candy and I thought he might like a little treat," and Guy extended the chocolate bar a second time.

The young mother slowly raised a hand, keeping the other clutched around her child, and took the bar. "Thank you. You're very kind," she said, looking down at the sidewalk instead of at the lieutenant from an enemy country. She put the chocolate in her tattered coat pocket and led the boy away. Guy returned to the bench.

"What were you doing?" I scowled. "You just gave two East Germans, two of the enemy, a candy bar."

"Why not?" he answered. "Think how hard it must be for her to raise a child under the communist system. Didn't you see the way they looked and dressed? You could tell they didn't have much. The boy will enjoy the candy, at least he'll have a little something to be happy about."

I shook my head in disgust but Guy went on.

"That chocolate bar was my offer of friendship, and the woman will be happy to have something to give to her son. The Cold War isn't her fault and certainly the child isn't to blame. Maybe my gift will help change their perceptions about people in the West. East Germans love their children too."

We finished eating and returned to the car. A class of elementary school children on a day's outing surrounded the Porsche. Boys ran around the sparkling automobile shouting "vroom, vroom" to power their make believe-cars while turning invisible steering wheels. Girls giggled, watching the make-believe race car drivers. Their teacher stood on the sidewalk and glanced at us, then called her pupils forward. But curiosity and imagination proved stronger than their caretaker's beckoning. We walked to within 15 steps of the car before the children spotted us. They came to a standstill. The boys and girls in the second or third grade stared with enormous eyes at three foreign soldiers. Two of the girls stood a few feet from the car and offered shy smiles as Charlie unlocked his door. I looked at their blue eyes, rosy cheeks and blonde hair tied in pig tails silhouetted against a blackened, jagged building gutted by war. They continued staring and smiling as their teacher frantically called them to join the group. The girls' eyes, eyes filled with naive curiosity, grabbed me. I had one foot in the backseat but stopped to return their smiles. I wished I had something to give them. At that moment a question exploded like lightning striking a tree. For a split second I wondered if the girls' fathers were East German soldiers, soldiers I was trained to kill. Who would care for them if I killed their fathers? Was military service an exercise in orphan creation? Maybe the real enemy was war.

I shoved myself into the back of the Porsche. Guy and Charlie closed the doors and we left the shepherd to tend her flock. The longer I spent behind the Iron Curtain, the greater the distance became between Cold War propaganda and reality. The people I saw caused me to question what I believed. Doubts nagged me about my role as a gung-ho Airborne Ranger.

We left Alexander Platz and drove to another part of the city. "What's next?" Charlie asked, as we walked toward an ashen building taking up a quarter of a city block. The building's facade looked like the exterior of a museum with its roof supported by stately Greek columns.

"It's the East German Tomb of the Unknown Soldier," Guy answered.

"They pay tribute to their dead?" I asked in astonishment. There was only one Tomb of the Unknown Soldier in my narrow black and white world and that was located in Arlington, Virginia.

"C'mon, you'll see," Guy said, leading us up the marble front steps.

Two statue-like East German soldiers guarded the entrance to their monument for warriors killed in battle. The helmeted East Germans presented a striking appearance that spoke to my love of military grandeur. They dressed in impeccable knee-length gray overcoats, white shoulder and waist belts, polished black leather boots; they clutched rifles at their sides. We fell silent in respect for their dead and walked past the guards to enter the shrine. A gas-fed, golden-blue flame swayed from a copper base in the center of the room. I stopped at the edge of a black iron chain encircling the flame and paused to reflect on the meaning of the memorial. I knew from personal experience that life in the infantry was hard. It demanded physical and mental sacrifice. I was expected to fight during war and, if required, make the ultimate sacrifice. The golden-blue flame swayed back and forth as a tribute to soldiers who had paid the ultimate sacrifice. I understood from my experience why the memorial stood and felt a kinship for my enemies through the brotherhood of arms.

We departed the tomb and Guy led us to an art gallery. Beautiful paintings and sculptures adorned the interior, and I realized art is universal, not the singular possession of any one culture. Another question surfaced. Why would an "Evil Empire" exhibit beautiful works of art?

We left the museum and drove to a Gasthaus. Shaking off the cold once inside the restaurant, we looked for a table. An elderly man and woman sat in the middle of the rectangular-shaped dining room containing three rows of four tables each. Three uniformed East German soldiers, all about our age, and an older man dressed in civilian clothes ate and talked in a corner table to our right. The soldiers alarmed me. I didn't expect to eat alongside the enemy and wanted to leave. Guy and Charlie didn't share my concern and said Allied soldiers could eat at any public facility in East Berlin. My friends out-voted me and we settled at a table on the opposite side of the room from the Warsaw Pact soldiers. I made sure to sit with my back to them.

A stockily built waitress in her forties with muscular arms and brown hair pulled back in a bun sullenly took our orders. The she-male didn't change her irritable disposition even though we all spoke German. She offered no suggestions and answered our questions with curt one or two word replies as if we were morons. But the food tasted delicious—fresh salad, fried potatoes, carrots and roast covered with gravy. We finished, and the waitress cleared our table without saying a word, wanting to make sure we knew her displeasure in having had to serve us. We asked for three mugs of beer and she threw her head to one side and marched to the kitchen, plates and silverware clinking on her tray. She returned with three beers and three crystal glasses of what looked to be cognac. The disgruntled waitress slammed down the beer mugs somehow not spilling a drop and might have done the same with the cognac except it would have broken the delicate crystal.

"We didn't order cognac," I interrupted, thinking she had misunderstood our order.

She cast a cold look my way and set the last glass by Charlie's beer mug. "The cognac is from the gentlemen sitting at the table in the corner," she said, referring to the table across the room. I looked over my shoulder and saw the three uniformed East German soldiers and older man in civilian clothes. They smiled at us and held cognac in crystal glasses high in toast.

The waitress stomped back to the kitchen. I threw a questioning look at Guy. "Those guys bought the cognac? I don't want it. Can we take it?" Charlie turned to Guy, waiting for the answer. The table of East Germans held their smiles and their glasses.

"Why not?" Guy answered. "They're extending a gesture of friendship. Take your cognac and raise it," he said.

Charlie followed orders and picked up his drink. I did so reluctantly and turned around to face my Cold War enemy. Guy continued giving instructions. "On the count of three, drink, say thanks and give them a cheer. Ready? One-two-three!" I tipped my head back and threw down the cognac, keeping my eyes peeled on the East German soldiers, fearful they might attack. "Thanks for the drinks. To the brotherhood of soldiers," we shouted after emptying our glasses. They nodded, returned our toast and downed their drinks. I couldn't believe I had yielded a smile and turned back to the table seeing Charlie and Guy doing the same.

"It would be polite to return their gesture and buy them a drink," Guy said, using a cloth napkin to wipe the corners of his mouth.

"No way, man," I answered and leaned back in my chair. "Enough is enough."

My roommate had caught the atmosphere of collaboration and sided with Guy. "C'mon, what's wrong, Peter? They're not going to shoot us."

"Go ahead, but I'm not buying them a damn thing!" I insisted. Guy ignored my remark and called the waitress. He ordered a second round of cognac for both tables. The muscular brunette scowled at Guy and left. A few minutes later she appeared on the other side of the room cheerfully serving cognac to the East Germans. The scowl returned as the she-male stomped over to serve our drinks. She left and the East Germans rendered their Cold War enemies a toast. Both tables emptied their glasses and the East Germans broke out in a German drinking song that included stomping their feet and clapping their hands. They finished with a shout and pounded their hands on the table. We mirrored them and pounded our hands on the table. They stopped pounding and we stopped pounding. They broke out in laughter and we did the same. I laughed so hard I grabbed my sides, and my stomach hurt.

"Hey man," Charlie said, when things had quieted down. "Let's sing a German drinking song for them. How about Ein Prosit, Ein Prosit?"

"You bet," Guy exclaimed. "You know that one?" he asked, grinning at me.

"Of course I do, but after the song I want to get the hell out of here." So I joined in singing a beer drinking song to Warsaw Pact soldiers I was trained to kill. Our enemies joined in after the opening line and it could have been a scene from any military bar on the Western side if it weren't for the different uniforms.

We finished the song and paid the bill, making sure to leave an extra large tip for the waitress. We got up from the table and walked past the East Germans on our way out the door. Guy and Charlie stopped to thank them for the drinks and to wish them well. I stood watching with my arms crossed until the older man in civilian clothes turned in his chair and looked at me. "What part of the United States are you from?" he asked in German.

"I'm from Florida, that's in the southern part of America," I answered in German with a neutral voice, looking at him with neither ill-will nor cheer.

"Oh yes, lots of water and sun. That's the state where you launch your astronauts," he said. "I have read many books about the United States and someday want to visit your country."

I glanced up from the man and noticed my friends had sat down at the table to talk with the East German soldiers.

"Yeah, that's where the astronauts take off. Florida is a beautiful state," I said, feeling a smile spread across my face. "And it's a lot hotter than Germany." The civilian took an empty chair from an adjoining table and asked me to join the group. I hesitated and weighed my options. He seemed pleasant enough and my friends didn't look as if they were leaving anytime soon. I sat down.

"My son is the soldier sitting next to me," the older German said, glancing with a smile at the young man sitting in a gray uniform at his side. The East German man had the exact same look as my father the day he pinned jump wings on my uniform at Airborne School graduation.

He continued. "My son completes his military service tomorrow, and I came to Berlin to watch the farewell ceremony. He's in the same unit I served in when I was in the army. My son's an army engineer, just like me." He reminisced about his days in the army just as my father had done when I visited Florida after completing Ranger School. The East German father's perception of his son uncannily mirrored that of my father. Francis Dodds was proud when I decided to become an Army officer and prouder still when I chose to follow in his footsteps and serve in the infantry.

The man took his son's arm and introduced us. The East German soldier looked a bit awkward but extended his hand. He was no puppeteer; there was no hidden motive behind the handsome face, no manipulative posturing by offering his hand. I took his hand firmly, looked him straight in the eye and shook while respectfully nodding my head.

The pair asked me questions about the United States and wanted to know if every American owned a car, if people carried guns at all times and if Americans could travel without first obtaining permission from their government. Then they shared fragments of their own lives. The son told me about his fiancee, saying they planned to marry after he returned home. A job as a civil engineer waited for him after the service. I asked them questions about life in East Germany but kept the conversation superficial, shying away from discussing the military. They could be spies and the entire scene an elaborate set-up to gather information about the United States Army. However, I didn't pick up the slightest trace of being interrogated.

We left the Gasthaus after fifteen minutes of exchanging stories. They wanted us to stay and even offered to buy another round of drinks. Guy wanted to stay, but this time Charlie and I out-voted him. On the drive back to West Berlin I reflected on the day's events. The people I encountered were like anyone else I knew. They had needs and wants, hopes and fears. The crack at the foundation of my belief had enlarged to a gaping hole.

All three of us had to get out of the car before passing through the Russian-controlled checkpoint at the Berlin border. Guards inspected our paperwork. They directed us to put our hands over our heads while they patted us down. German Shepherds sniffed the car inside and out, hunting for escapees. Guards with loaded submachine guns ordered Charlie to open the trunk and engine compartments so they could look inside. Then they rolled mirrors under the car in another effort to detect escapees or contraband. Their system left much to be desired, but I'd already learned that individual people were not the system.

We spent Saturday touring more of West Berlin and that night walked along the Kurfürstendamm. A skinny man with black, greasy hair and beady eyes handed us a business card on a street corner. I read the card, "Nice girls wait for you in a pleasant atmosphere." Prostitution was legal in West Berlin as it was in many parts of western Europe. I threw the card away and we continued down the Kurfürstendamm. Wealthy people draped in gold, diamonds and furs window shopped along storefronts. Obese people gorged themselves in expensive restaurants. As I looked at them, images of shabbily dressed people in a sanatarium entered my mind. I saw the specters of elderly people whose wretched lives never included a diamond or a fur. I watched a spoiled West Berlin boy scream at his parents for not buying him toys displayed in a window. The parents ignored his temper tantrum and walked to the next storefront. The figure of a bone thin mother walking silently, holding her young boy's hand appeared in my mind. Why did this boy scream and cry for a toy? He didn't have any holes in the tips of his shoes. Would he even appreciate a chocolate candy bar? How could some live in extravagant wealth when across the border people struggled every day just to live? Others existed in hopelessness inside a sanatarium in Bad Nauheim. How could life be so unfair?

The Soviets characterized the culture I grew up in as the "Decadent West." I never understood the term "Decadent West" until my perceptions broadened while walking along the Kurfürstendamm my last night in Berlin. That night I glimpsed what the Russians meant. Ingrained beliefs crumbled. My search for contentment and meaning through service as an Army officer had ended in failure.

Return to the Land of Adoption

In May of 1982 I completed my tour of duty in Germany and returned to the United States. I flew into Dover Air Force Base and took a cab to the Philadelphia airport. The morning sky held billowing white clouds and a mild spring breeze. It felt good to be back in the States after three years abroad. I looked out from the cab at the Delaware countryside as if it were my first time in America. Garbage littering the sides of the road surprised me because Germany didn't have trash along its highways. The cab driver liked my curiosity and talked non-stop about America's state of affairs. He helped unload my luggage and wished me well on my return to America. I told him I appreciated the conversation, left a tip and walked inside to catch a plane to Pensacola, Florida. I had a couple of weeks vacation and I'd never found a better place for fun and relaxation than northwest Florida's Gulf Coast.

I noticed America's rampant commercialism for the first time and how it infested every aspect of American culture. Advertisements constantly bombarded me through television and radio commercials, billboards, magazines and newspapers. Even bathrooms had advertisements on the walls. I couldn't escape annoying sales pitches. The guy standing in line next to me at the airport even wore a shirt and shorts marked with a corporate name and logo. He looked more like a sandwich board than a fashionably dressed man in designer clothes. No West European would have paid money for "designer clothes." It amounted to paying a corporation for the privilege of advertising them.

No other country I had visited came close to equalling the consumer plague I saw slowly destroying America's moral fiber. Art and nature's beauty allowed me to touch deeper parts of myself. American culture had the opposite effect. I shut down emotionally to avoid the incessant commercials.

An unparalleled sense of freedom was the second most striking realization I had when returning to the States. It wasn't any one occurrence, but a combination of events that imparted an awareness that in America I had a greater degree of freedom than in any democratic country in western Europe. Military guards and police officers didn't ask me where I was going here after I cleared customs. I wasn't required to carry identification and didn't have to report to anyone or any organization. Americans walked around the airport dressed in outfits ranging from three piece suits to sweats, and no one cared. Intellectual freedom flourished. I read a newspaper editorial criticizing my favorite president, Ronald Reagan. Only after stepping outside the United States and returning three years later did I understand that America offers more freedom than any other country in the world.

I felt I was truly back home when I reached the Atlanta Airport. My last two years of high school in northern Florida, coupled with four years in Auburn, Alabama, was the longest I'd ever lived in one region. Outside of Germany I considered the Deep South home. I'd always appreciated the charm and beauty of southern culture and in the Atlanta airport saw men opening doors for women, took in the soothing sounds of southern accents and heard children addressing their parents using "sir" and "ma'am." Glamorous women adorned the airport hallways, and the scene looked like an art gallery with beautiful paintings. Southerners treated strangers in a warm and friendly manner unlike the cold and unsociable Germans.

My parents met me at the Pensacola airport on a sunny afternoon, waving and smiling from the concourse as I stepped off the plane. I shook their hands, surprised at how they'd aged in just three short years. My father insisted on helping carry my luggage, and my mother made me sit in the front seat on the drive home. We turned into their driveway flanked by a manicured lawn that held the imprints of lawnmower wheels from a recent mowing. The house didn't have a speck of dust, hardwood floors shone from a recent waxing, and I saw my face reflecting from the dining room table smelling of lemon polish. They had prepared my old bedroom for my visit, and I pulled back the bed covers to the wonderful aroma of freshly washed sheets. My parents had left the dresser drawers open, so I unpacked my belongings. I'd forgotten much about the environment where I grew up. The cleanliness and orderliness, a ceiling fan slowly spinning to cool the living room, statutes of Saint Francis and the Blessed Virgin in the garden all rekindled memories of the safe and comfortable surroundings I'd known as a boy. My mother prepared my favorite meal that night—roast beef, corn and mashed potatoes followed with homemade angel food cake. She waited on me hand and foot. It felt strange to be taken care of, but the former nurse, housewife, and mother found happiness when caring for others. My sister was taking final exams at Saint Leo's College in Orlando and couldn't come home.

I woke up with my parents the next morning. Jet lag, the seven hour time difference between Germany and Pensacola, didn't phase me because of my irregular sleeping patterns in the Army. My father took the day off saying we'd go and play golf at the Navy air base where he worked. Before our golf game he took me to his office in a huge hangar and introduced me to his coworkers. My father paraded me from colleague to colleague and always began introductions with, "This is my son Peter who's an infantry lieutenant and just returned from three years of duty in Germany." He reminded me of the East German father in East Berlin.

I wasn't home long before I remembered why I'd never bonded with my parents. We never talked. Sure, we engaged in superficial discussions about their neighbors, the weather, the Army, their garden, but we never really talked. We never discussed emotions, feelings or problems. I had buried my emotions as a boy, and things hadn't changed when I visited them as an adult.

Although I'd often written about Petti, she never came up in any of our discussions. I hadn't explained why we went our separate ways, and their absence of questions about Petti signalled a lack of interest or an inability to discuss something that might trouble me. My adopted parents never asked if I had searched for my birth parents and I never told them about Ilse Sander. I also didn't discuss the change that occurred in me as a result of events in the Russian guardhouse or East Berlin.

The television added to our communication barrier. It blared from the time they woke up until they went to bed. Besides being annoying, constant noise spewing from the TV acted as a distraction, preventing meaningful conversation. I could have asked that they sit down and engage in purposeful talk, but I still didn't know how to confront someone when it might lead to conflict. I didn't know how to tell my parents that their actions upset me, so my solution was to pretend that I lived a perfect life. My parents and I lacked communication skills, and I continued to feel like a stranger in their midst.

Charlie came to visit the last week before we would start the Infantry Officer Advance Course at Fort Benning, Georgia, and my parents took him in like an old friend. Charlie and I had a blast drinking beer all day on the beach and dancing all night. It felt great for a while to be free of the responsibilities of leading men in the pursuit of war. I needed the time in Florida to readjust to American life. Everyone spoke English, but I missed speaking German.

In Florida, drinks always came served with ice, beer was carbonated, dollars the only currency needed, and the weather was hot and humid. I double-checked with my parents the first few times I made phone calls to make sure I remembered how to use the American telephone system. Then I had to readjust my driving. Police cited me for speeding three times in my first two months back in the States. Fifty-five miles per hour was slow-motion compared to driving in a country with no speed limits.

I didn't know the direction of my military career but knew I wouldn't fight the Russians or the Warsaw Pact, and I never desired to wage war in a Third World country. Third World countries didn't threaten the United States, and I didn't want to be part of a bullying campaign. Intervening in another country's civil war held no attraction. I had reached a point where I no longer supported the goals of the Army and as an officer knew my days in the military were numbered. My pattern when confronted with the need for obvious change, this time a career change, was to do nothing. But instead of submitting my resignation and pursuing a new career, I continued in the Army and attended the six month Infantry Officer Advance Course.

Still, my perception of the Army continued to drastically change. The Advanced Course was a regular 8-5 Monday through Friday routine with no weekend duty. We spent the entire six months in classrooms, and I hated being stuck behind a desk eight hours a day. The schedule was relaxed, but the challenge was gone. I missed not being in charge of soldiers and conducting intricate operations. The Army no longer offered excitement or adventure.

Most of the curriculum focused on the European theater. We studied fighting a "limited nuclear war" against the Warsaw Pact on maps of Germany. Entire sections of Germany were obliterated under mushroom clouds during these exercises. What would a "limited nuclear war" mean for a bone thin mother and her son, for two girls with blue eyes, rosy cheeks and blonde pig tails? What would it mean for my birth mother and Maria and Hieronymus? The thought sickened me. Army mentality dictated that it was necessary to destroy my homeland in order to save it from the Soviets. Americans didn't mind obliterating Germany as long as their country wasn't harmed.

My circle of friends gradually narrowed. Many of my buddies from basic training left the service after their first tour. Most of those who stayed had married, and their wives put single men off-limits. The Advance Course didn't offer intense comradery, and I now viewed the Army as just a job. I quit reading war books in my free time. On drives through the country I no longer imagined fighting on the surrounding hills, valleys and forests.

I was promoted from first lieutenant to captain and filled out another dream sheet for the location of my next assignment. I wanted to return to Germany, but Army policy prevented officers from serving back-to-back overseas assignments. But I did receive my first choice, Fort Lewis, located 40 miles south of Seattle.

A regular schedule now allowed me to pursue outside activities. I had always wanted brothers when growing up but didn't find them until the Army. Figuring other boys wanted male companionship, I signed up for the Big Brother program. I was designated the Big Brother to a 12 year old kid without a dad who lived in poverty with his mother and sister. Each week my Little Brother and I spent a couple of hours together, fishing, visiting the Fort Benning museum or working out in the gym. We always finished our activities with a delicious ice cream cone. He was a good kid and only wanted to spend time with an older guy. I hoped I made a good role model. My Little Brother gave me a sense of responsibility in my personal life and showed me how fortunate I was to grow up in a two parent household.

Being a Big Brother was the closest I'd ever come to wanting children; otherwise, I never thought about having them. The desire to raise children never rooted in me because my childhood had been painful, and I didn't want to recreate that same experience for other children. Family bonds didn't exist for me, and my concept of family was merely a group of people living together in the same house. From a practical standpoint, I saw children as a loss to my personal freedom, as a financial drain and as a frequent pain in the butt. I couldn't fathom why people wanted kids.

It never occurred to me to use free time to develop my inner life, and I still paid no attention to my emotional or spiritual development. The only connection to my interior world had been through the Catholic Church, but that ended when I quit going to mass during college. While visiting my parents I attended mass but only to keep my mother happy. I believed I hadn't learned anything useful from my Catholic upbringing, I thought that upon reaching adulthood, my thoughts, personality and behaviors were permanently formed. I didn't think they could be changed. Not having learned to pinpoint my inner troubles, I didn't know what actions to take to resolve them. Loneliness and inadequacy still plagued me, but I didn't see the Catholic Church offering a solution.

Christ's message of joy hadn't materialized for me and I had become agnostic. I didn't deny the existence of God but believed knowing Him was unattainable. God had no influence in my life I believed, except to punish me one day for my sins. There was no God of love because if there was, then I wouldn't have been so miserable.

And the Army environment was not the sort of culture that placed emphasis on a man's inner journey. Discussions relating to mercy, forgiveness, guilt, charity, hope, faith, good and evil had never been part of the curriculum of any military training I attended. The Army had a Code of Ethics—standards that governed the professional conduct of officers; but not a Code of Morals—standards to govern the human goodness of an officer's character and behavior. Officers with morals were a liability by their questioning of orders. Was it right to kill another man? Was a "limited nuclear war" moral, since the Army's sole purpose was to fight and win a war? Professional development for officers emphasized leadership, and

Army culture discouraged any notions I might have had for an inner journey. To philosophize on war would lead to questions. And the Army didn't want officers with questioning minds when it came to leading soldiers in killing other human beings.

Even though I was emotionally disturbed, I never succumbed to the American myth that money equals happiness. I never thought that material wealth might open the castle door and instead looked toward ideals or another person to quiet my insecurities. Yet these had all led to dead-ends: military service, finding my birth mother, romantic relationships, alcohol. But I still longed to reconnect to my German heritage, which had been my latest hope for finding happiness.

In Germany I met Petti, and after two years my love for her had never dwindled. We broke up because I didn't know how to handle feelings of inadequacy and, as with Jean Dames, ended the relationship when I became uncomfortable. Before leaving Germany I met with her, hoping she might consider visiting me in the United States. My dream died when she told me she was engaged to a German man. I wished her well and promised myself I wouldn't make the same mistake twice.

Halfway through the Advanced Course I went to the Officer's Club one evening and met a platinum blonde from Georgia. The woman reminded me of Petti — the shape of her face, her body build, and she shared a few of Petti's mannerisms. We dated a few times and I was convinced she would turn out to be just like Petti. I thought I'd grow to love her just as I had grown to love Petti. But I was soon leaving for Fort Lewis, Washington and we didn't have time to develop a deep relationship. I didn't want to make the same mistake as with Petti, so the platinum blonde and I were married in a simple ceremony at a base chapel. Our honeymoon was the drive from Georgia to Washington.

That was Army life. No stability and no time to develop long-term relationships. Constant moving prevented me from gaining a sense of community. The ongoing uprootedness of military life added to my lack of connectedness, so I still felt I didn't belong to anything or anyone.

At the age of 27 I was an emotional and spiritual midget. I didn't have a clue as to who I was or how to find my key to happiness. I lacked the ability to engage in healthy, meaningful relationships and made poor choices. I married a woman, hoping she would be like Petti—clearly a poor choice.

Stumbling before Falling

My wife and I drove cross country and arrived at Fort Lewis in the spring of 1983. Within two weeks we bought a house and had our household goods delivered. A new beginning. Then I left to join my unit at the Yakima Firing Range in central Washington for two straight months. When I returned I quickly discovered the platinum blonde from Georgia wasn't Petti Stöcker.

Like a man drowning in quicksand, my world continued to shrink as my small circle of friends in the Advanced Course dwindled to a few casual acquaintances at Fort Lewis. But they too were married couples and the days of merrymaking in bars with other single officers came to an end. As the realization grew that my wife wasn't at all like Petti, I rarely talked with her and we seldom engaged in activities. My life consisted of working at Fort Lewis and drinking beer in my free time. I blamed my unhappiness on Mrs. Dodds and vented my frustrations on her. Something ailed me, and I believed she was the cause.

Alcohol had now grown to be major a problem. Every night after work I'd buy a six pack of beer and drink most of it on the twenty-minute drive home. I'd finish the beer after dinner, and if not in a state of oblivion, I would leave to buy more so I could pass out and escape. My evenings usually ended with me lying comatose on the living room couch. The next morning I'd go to work, buy beer on the way home and spend another night drinking to avoid emotional problems. One six pack quickly turned to two, so I wouldn't have to leave the house and buy more beer to drink myself unconscious. Weekends streaked by in an alcoholic blur. My wife was a light drinker, and because I wouldn't talk to her she couldn't understand my torment. This pattern continued for a year, and I became increasingly sick of life and the woman I had married. I moved to an apartment and filed for a separation fourteen months after we'd been married.

My wife did everything humanly possible to mend our relationship. She wanted to work things out, tried to talk, asked what troubled me and if she could do anything to help. She tried to get me interested in outside activities, but I wouldn't try any of her suggestions. The same scenario played out as with Jean Daems and Petti except for one big difference—I didn't love my wife. This time I didn't bother to run away. Alcohol proved easier and gave the same feeling of escape. I had no other solutions for handling my problems.

My wife called my apartment a week after I'd moved out. "Would you go to marriage therapy with me?" she asked over the phone. "It might help us."

"Go to marriage therapy? Are you crazy? I'm not some spineless worm who has to rely on other people to my fix problems. I'm a captain in the Army and get paid to solve problems. My only problem is you. I wish I'd never met you. Now leave me alone," and I slammed down the phone.

She called again a few nights later. "What do you want?" I asked.

"Peter, I know deep down you're really a good man, but you have a drinking problem and need help."

Listening to someone say I had a drinking problem was like an electric shock. Deep inside I'd known it for years, but to hear I had a problem from another person terrified me. God, I didn't want turn out like my mother and father. "I don't have a drinking problem!" I screamed. "I'm a captain in the Army and don't have any problems except you," Anger swept over my fear like ocean waves slamming against a rocky beach, and I stopped to finish my fifth beer of the night.

She didn't immediately respond, and I waited, hoping to hear her ask for a divorce. After a long pause, my wife spoke again, and I could hear her trying to remain calm. Like a rope groaning as it lifts a heavy crate she mustered enough courage to continue. "I want you to get help. You need it, if not to save our marriage, then to save your life. If you don't get help for your alcoholism I'm going to blow the whistle on you and tell your commander how you spend your free time."

A second period of silence followed as I recoiled from her threat like a boxer reels after an opponent's best punch. I couldn't believe what she said. The Army was the only thing I had going for me, and I couldn't tell them I needed help for a drinking problem. It would be disastrous to my career. She had me in a corner and I grasped for straws. "You don't mean what you're saying. You're just upset. Now think things through. Don't you think a divorce is the only option to end our unhappy affair?"

"No, you need help. I'll give you a week. Goodbye," and the line went dead.

Two days later I stood in front of the major I worked for. He sat behind a desk in his office thumbing through a stack of paperwork and finally looked up when I didn't say anything. I stuttered and stammered, trying to find words to satisfy my wife's demand. The major put down the paperwork and wrinkled his forehead as his lips drooped in a frown. "Sir. I-I-I think. I think, I think I might have a dr-dr-drink, a drinking problem."

"What do you mean?" he asked, looking as if I'd said I wanted to defect to the Russians. I'd never been late or missed a day of work. I kept my drinking hidden from everyone. The army provided the only symbol of success that said I was okay and provided income to pay for my drinking. My career had to be protected at all costs. The major's reaction indicated I had done a good job of secreting my drinking.

"Once I start drinking I can't stop, and it's beginning to bother me," I answered.

"Why don't you just stop drinking if you think you have a problem?"

I didn't know how to answer his question. I had tried to quit countless times but after a day or two of gritting my teeth while constantly thinking about a beer, I started drinking again. The compulsion to drink possessed me, and despite an inner voice yelling "Stop!" I'd again find myself at a convenience store counter buying a half case of beer.

The Army sent me to William Beaumont Hospital located at Fort Bliss in El Paso for a six-week in-patient alcoholism treatment program. The entire program was an exercise in humiliation. My life hit a new low at meetings filled with alcoholics trying to help each other. I hated the meetings and fought the idea that I was alcoholic like a man denies a medical diagnosis indicating he's terminally ill. I had a long list of reasons why I couldn't be an alcoholic: I was too young, I never drank in the morning, had a college degree, was raised in a non-alcoholic family, was a captain in the Army, I never drank at work... The humiliation continued when instructors demanded that I call my parents and tell them where I was and why I was hospitalized. I begged the instructors to let me off the hook, but they said openness about alcoholism helps prevent drinking relapses. My continued pleading resulted in a threat that I'd be discharged from the Army.

That evening I sat alone in the hospital cafeteria and pecked at dinner while pondering different ways of breaking the news to my parents. Unable to eat I dumped the food in a garbage can. Then I slipped away to find a phone. Finding my way to a deserted ward I wound through a labyrinth of empty passageways before turning a final corner. At the end of a long, gloomy hallway stood a phone booth, waiting like an eerie stranger in the night. I slinked forward, listening to the sounds of my hollow footsteps moving across a linoleum floor like slow tickings of a clock. I stopped in front of the phone. My nervous oil-slick shadow wavered on the floor as I shifted my weight back and forth in one last desperate search for a way out of the predicament. I had no choice.

Off the receiver, the phone slowly bounced up and down in the palm of my sweaty hand. Apprehension cut through my consciousness, revealing layers of fear.

My adopted parents' reaction stood as the first fear. The phone call would destroy them. Although emotionally distant, I still felt a certain loyalty. I wished it wasn't so, that they'd left me in the orphanage and let me grow up in Germany. But that's not how my life unfolded, and part of me felt I owed them. I realized I'd lost in this puppet game, as if I hung suspended in mid-air and dangled from the ends of strings, swaying back and forth in front of the phone. What they wanted from me was confirmation that they had succeeded as parents. This required my being a perfect son. My accomplishments were symbols of their success. Having to admit I was in a hospital for alcohol rehabilitation marked the end of my perfection and would shatter their illusion of good parenting. Despite not loving, bonding and sometimes not even liking them, I didn't want to hurt my adopted parents.

I couldn't gather the courage to call. More than only a fear of hurting my adopted parents made me replace the phone. I would have to reveal a second and deeper fear during the call—that I wasn't good enough, and no matter what I did it would never be enough to put me on equal footing with others. Masking my fear for years with accomplishments and trying to fit into groups never had taken away the belief that I was different, inferior and an outcast. Having also to admit a weakness for alcohol confirmed the shame and guilt I'd known since I was a boy.

I stared at the phone and a third fear appeared—my deepest, oldest and most powerful one—abandonment. It originated when my birth mother gave me away, a terror so frightful that I'd buried it and hoped to forget its existence. But this monster couldn't be forgotten; it had a life of its own and reared its ugly head only when I became involved in close personal relationships. The monster again crawled out of its crypt now that I had to admit personal failure to people close to me. As it slithered out of its burial ground beads of sweat formed on my face and body, my hands shook, and a twisted knot gripped my stomach. The idea that my adopted parents might reject and abandon me put me in a near state of panic.

Finally, I pressed the receiver against my ear, determined to confront these three monsters. A cat-like screech broke the monotonous dial tone each time I pressed a digit of my parents' number. I hit the last number and slammed the phone back on the receiver. Stepping backward out of the phone booth, I looked up and down the still empty hallway. With clammy palms pressed against my sweat-drenched face I slowly ran shaking fingers back through my moist hair, over the back of my head and down my neck. I took a deep breath and slowly exhaled, trying to think of anything to get out of making that call. Then a sudden surge of adrenaline swept through me, and I quickly picked up the phone and punched the numbers. I breathed deeply through my mouth and heard the phone ring. Please, please, no one answer. But someone on the other end picked up the phone. "Shit," I whispered, milliseconds before hearing my father's voice.

"Hello?" he answered.

"Hello Dad?" I said, trying everything in my power to maintain control of my voice. "Dddaaad?" Tears burst from my eyes and streamed down my face. "This is your son," and I couldn't say anything else.

"Are you okay?" he asked in as compassionate a voice as I'd ever heard him use.

"Not really," I answered, blinking and trying to clear my vision, wiping tears from my face. I breathed in through my nose, sniffled and tried to stop sobbing. I could imagine him frowning and rolling his eyes to the back of his head.

"Tell me what's going on. I want to help you no matter what kind of trouble you're in. I'm your father, and I'll stand beside you."

I couldn't believe what he had said, and the stream of tears became a flood. Between crying shudders I managed to tell him what had happened.

"It's okay, son. Alcoholism is a disease, and it's nothing to be ashamed of. I'm glad you're where you can get help. Is there anything I can do? Do you need me to fly there to be with you?"

"No," I said, regaining my composure. "I'll be okay. Thanks. How are you doing?" I asked, but awestruck relief prevented me from concentrating on his answer. We talked a few minutes then he called my mother to the phone. "Dad, I-I'm sorry. Are you sure she wants to talk to me?"

"I'm sure. She'll be glad to know you're all right and in a safe place."

The conversation with my mother lasted only a few minutes. They made me give them my hospital address and mailed a letter each week I remained at Beaumont. The content of their correspondence always started with, "We're glad your getting help," then sunk back to the same old superficial dialogue.

Another part of treatment at alcohol rehabilitation included group sessions. We sat in a circle while a therapist asked patients questions about their drinking. At each session, the therapist singled out one patient to take the "hot seat." The others asked questions or made accusations if they believed the person in the "hot seat" was being less than honest. This process attempted to identify the cause of the drinking. To me it amounted to another humiliating episode in my struggle for rehabilitation. I didn't want to be the person in the "hot seat," but eventually my turn came.

"So why do you drink?" the therapist asked, and I felt every pair of eyes in the room stab me. I stared at the floor, hating to be singled out. I wished I could have disappeared, but after a few minutes of trying to evade the question I murmured why I thought I drank. "I think I drink to hide my feelings of inadequacy from being adopted," I whispered.

The room seemed to groan with heavy silence as I clutched my hands and stared at the floor. The afternoon heat wasn't what caused the sweat on my palms. It was because I hated being forced to talk about my adoption. Relating adoption as the cause for my hospitalization reconfirmed to me that I was a mistake, bad, and defective.

The therapist took his time and waited to see if I'd say more. Sitting silently and continuing to stare at the floor, I looked at him when he started speaking. He looked me directly in the eyes, "No, you're wrong. There's more going on inside you than adoption. Your mind's so cloudy from alcohol that you're unable to see why you drank."

"No, that's not true," I burst out. "You asked me what bothers me and being adopted really bothers me. It bothered me when I was a kid and it still bothers me today."

The therapist scowled, shook his head and turned his attention to another patient. He never brought up adoption the remaining time I was in alcohol rehabilitation and I never said another word about it either.

Except for my sister I hadn't met another person who had been adopted. I never read books on adoption or attended adoption support groups. If I had, I would have discovered that many professional therapists discount or even totally reject the idea that adoption can be the source of emotional trauma.

The Army made me sign a contract saying I wouldn't drink alcohol for one year after completing the program—the last humiliation of rehabilitation. If I didn't sign the contract I'd have an immediate discharge.

On my return to Washington I had to take a drug called Antabuse designed to help prevent a drinking relapse. A person on Antabuse who consumes alcohol suffers a rapid increase in heart rate, red blotches on their skin and violent nausea. But I didn't care about the effects and started drinking a few days after returning to Washington. I drank beer slowly, trying to forestall the pills' effects, but red welts broke out all over my face and body, my heart beat wildly and I felt like throwing up. It didn't matter. Intoxication still provided my only relief from loneliness, so I quit taking the pills. The William Beaumont program hadn't changed me one bit, and I continued drinking as if I had never attended alcohol rehabilitation. Every night after work I'd drink myself blind and on Monday mornings couldn't remember the weekend. The only time I remained sober was during Army maneuvers where alcohol was prohibited.

My wife moved out after a few months of seeing no change in my behavior and filed for divorce. She didn't tell the Army about my continued drinking, and our divorce was final two years after we'd married. Divorce was the first time I'd learned a basic lesson that comparing one person to another will only result in unhappiness.

German or American?

Peter Friedrich, wer bin ich? Peter Frederick, who am I? German as determined by birth and blood, or American as influenced by upbringing and culture? Which is stronger—genetics or environment? The conflict of national identity threatened to tear me in half.

At the age of 30 I knew I didn't belong in the United States. In September of 1985, three years after leaving Germany, I decided to return and once and for all re-establish my roots. I believed I missed connecting with my heritage while stationed in Germany because the Army demanded too much of my time and energy. This trip would be different. It would mark the start of a new beginning. I didn't have an itinerary but planned to find a job that would allow me to live permanently in Germany. After finding a job I'd leave the Army and move back to my homeland, regain my original citizenship, and marry a German woman. This would put an end to my feelings of isolation. A desperate search to reconnect with my native land marked my last hope for finding the castle key.

An acquaintance—I no longer let people close enough to be called friends—drove me to the Seattle airport. He helped unload my luggage and before getting back in his car said, "Whatever it is you're looking for, I hope you find it in Germany."

"Thanks for the ride." I waved good-bye, picked up my luggage and walked inside the airport without responding to his statement. I didn't reveal that my trip to Europe was a search to make myself whole. That would have required admitting imperfection, and I would never admit to any weakness. Besides, he wouldn't understand. Most Americans, with blood diluted through intermarriage, lost the ability to trace their identity to a single nation. He couldn't comprehend because he didn't live the experience of belonging to a unique culture, language, race, heritage and history, links that forever tied me to Germany.

The plane landed at the Frankfurt civilian airport, and goosebumps rose on my arms on having returned to my beloved Germany. Retrieving my luggage, I headed to the train station located beneath the airport terminal. I wore civilian clothes wanting to look like my countrymen and vowed to live the next eleven days as a German. The metamorphosis needed to start immediately.

No child should ever be adopted by foreign parents, but my international adoption caused a special pain—adoption into a former enemy country. American propaganda had painted the United States as the moral savior of the world, a country that pretended to have the solution to every other country's problems. This pretentious attitude of superiority had one major flaw—the United States couldn't solve its own difficulties. I hated seeing American occupation soldiers walking through the civilian airport and glared at them with narrowed eyes and a clenched jaw. Images of destroyed German cities, the result of American bombings during World War II, burned in my mind. While growing up I learned the victor's version of history. Schools never mentioned the atrocities Americans had committed against my homeland. Only by conducting my own research did I learn about the American fire-bombing of Dresden in 1945. The raid lasted three days and killed over 100,000 German civilians, more people than in either the Hiroshima or Nagasaki atomic attacks. Americans secret the Dresden holocaust because that city, rich with art and history, had no military or industrial targets. The fire-bombs killed defenseless women, children and the elderly. Dresden represented only one of many unspeakable American war crimes, and the hypocrisy of the nation that appointed itself as moral savior of the world sickened me.

Arriving at the underground train station beneath the airport, I spoke entirely in German and ordered a one-way ticket to Wiesbaden. Boarding a train, I stared out the window, looking like a boy marveling at his Christmas morning presents. I smiled out at my present, the German countryside. Arriving in Wiesbaden, I checked into a hotel and unpacked. Though I hadn't slept in 24 hours, energy and excitement overpowered my need for sleep and I wanted to find Petti.

Leaving the hotel, I hurried through the downtown area to Petti's flat. America's plastic culture had seeped into Germany like stench pouring from a sewer. A McDonald's led the parade of "plastique Americana," and was joined by other franchise stores that now polluted my country's 1,000-year-old heritage. Americans justified their cultural genocide by rationalizing that money was more important than another country's society. I applauded the French for the courage to stand up to United States commercialism and keep their culture pure.

Darkness descended by the time I arrived at the subdivided house where Petti lived. But a different name had replaced Stöcker on the apartment directory; I rang the buzzer anyway. "Hello," a woman answered, through the intercom system.

"Hello. Is Petti Stöcker there?" I asked.

"No. I've never heard of the name," she replied.

I left the building and walked a few blocks to a phone booth at the Hauptbahnhof. A phone book at the train station didn't list Petti and directory assistance couldn't help. I felt sick at the thought I might never see her again. I'd have to wait until morning and then go to where she had worked.

A clock in the train station said a quarter-past-eleven, and hunger gnawed at my stomach. The restaurant in the Hauptbahnhof sat in darkness. No problem, I thought, and left to meander through downtown looking for another place to eat. After an hour of searching, I didn't find one open restaurant, and hunger pains made me fidgety. I rubbed my palms, breathed deep and felt my mouth water as I continued searching. After canvassing the entire city I discovered only beer halls and wine cellars open. But I didn't go inside because I had promised myself not to drink during the trip and returned to my hotel. After setting the alarm for 6:00 a.m., I crawled into bed with my stomach groaning. Ever since Ranger School, I'd hated being hungry and fell asleep remembering that some restaurants in the United States stayed open 24 hours a day, seven days a week.

At 4:30 a.m. I shot out of bed like a cannon, absorbed with thoughts of food and Petti. I showered, dressed and left the hotel to find breakfast.

German restaurants closed early but also opened early, and I ate a breakfast of fresh rolls topped with heaping slices of meats, cheeses and jams, washed down with orange juice and coffee. Now with a full stomach, I had only one thought and headed to the downtown business district.

Petti had worked as a receptionist for a large firm, her office on the ground floor. From her desk she saw the building entryway, and part of her job was to control access in and out of the building. I pushed aside the fear she might have left the firm and stared from the street into her office, longing to see the woman who had been my best friend and great love. I felt hopeful but helpless, the same feeling as falling through air before the parachute opens, as I pressed my face against the glass. Please be there, Petti, please be there. A woman inside had her back to me, but I would have recognized the brown hair and slender shoulders anywhere. Before I could ring the buzzer she turned around. Petti didn't expect me because we hadn't talked or written in three years. Her jaw dropped, then a huge smile spread across her face. She sprang out of her chair and rushed to the door. We embraced.

"What are you doing here?" she asked. "I thought you were in America."

"I came back to visit Germany and I wanted to see you." Her grip loosened around my shoulders.

She stepped back and looked at me. "Oh Peter." She searched my eyes and smiled. "I have to start work in a few minutes. Can you come back during my lunch break?"

"Whenever and wherever you want."

"Meet me here at noon." She gave me one last smile before returning to her office.

A few more hours wouldn't hurt after waiting three years. All morning I drifted in and out of stores, smelled flowers in parks and sipped coffee at an outdoor cafe. I wanted to tell Petti what I'd been unable to say when we dated—that I loved her. I'd never told anyone that I loved them. Fear of abandonment and rejection had imprisoned the words. Now I planned to tell Petti using the past tense and that helped loosen fear's power. Still, the thought of telling someone that I loved them, even in the past tense, gave me butterflies.

At noon I returned to her office, and we walked to a nearby square. Petti sat on a bench that faced a pool and looked at a fountain spraying water into a crystal blue sky. She pulled a sandwich from her brown leather purse.

"I made it before leaving for work this morning. Would you like a bite?" She offered her roll stuffed with cheese.

"No thanks, Petti. I ate a big breakfast and am not hungry. Would you like something to drink?"

"Sure, a Limonade. There's a kiosk around the corner." She pointed the direction before biting into the sandwich.

I came back holding two bottles of Limonade. "Thanks," she said, and took the bottle after eating the last of her sandwich. Petti turned toward me while we sat side by side but kept an arm's length distance. "Did you know I got married and moved to Mainz Kastel?" She forced a smile before putting the bottle to her lips.

A shudder ran up my spine, and I almost choked while taking a drink. "No," I replied, clearing my throat and setting the bottle on the ground. I kept my eyes glued to hers.

"I married my fiance' Heinz, the man I was engaged to when you came to say good-bye before leaving Germany." She paused and looked up at the broadleaf trees surrounding the square. "That was a long time ago." She slowly raised the bottle to her lips again.

"Petti, when I visited you before leaving, I had more to say than just good-bye. I wanted to ask if you'd come and visit me in the States. Did you know that?"

"No."

"I didn't ask because you told me about your engagement. So I said good-bye and left."

Petti didn't seem to hear what I'd said. "Heinz and I are very happy and plan to have children in a year or two, after we've saved some money." Her voice had a contented tone, and she sounded happy with her marriage. Her happiness pleased me even though my heart cringed with disappointment. Love's fire continued to burn, and part of me still wanted her.

"Petti, I'm not here to try and win you back. I just wanted to see you again."

A smile eased across her face. The same old sparkle danced in her hazel eyes. She gestured with the fluid arm and hand movements I remembered, and her beauty had grown more radiant over three year's time. Petti's energy, charm and attractiveness hadn't changed, but our interaction now had an unfamiliar and formal manner. The foot-and-a half separating us on the bench represented the change. "I know you're not trying to win me back, Peter."

Petti could always read me, better than anyone I'd ever known. I told her about meeting the woman from Georgia, the marriage and divorce. "She reminded me of you, Petti. I wanted her to be just like you. I loved you when we were going out. I wished I could have told you. I married the woman from Georgia hoping she would be you..." and I turned to look away before my sorrow turned to tears. I felt I had cheated both her and our relationship by keeping my love trapped.

"I know you loved me, Peter." She forced a smile, keeping her hands at her sides. "I have to go back to work."

"I'll walk with you."

"Thanks for coming and saying hello," she said at the entrance to her office building. We didn't hug good-bye, and I watched her walk inside the building. I never saw Petti Stöcker again.

Our meeting allowed me to let go of her; I wanted her happy, and she seemed content, and I had finally expressed my pent-up love. Why do I ruin relationships with people I love? I reflected on my boyhood and remembered the temper tantrum where I destroyed the model airplane I had painstakingly built. The pattern continued as an adult, except I destroyed love instead of models. Could I ever love a woman and stay in the relationship? My track record offered little promise, and I did not know how to change.

The next morning I sat in a train heading toward Bad Nauheim. The countryside sped by. This time I saw more cities and towns than forests and fields. Germany looked like one gigantic urban area interrupted by occasional tracts of nature. I didn't remember it being so crowded. Where were the wide-open spaces like in America?

The Middle Ages were still reflected in cities and towns. Narrow streets were originally built for carts not cars, centuries old architecture remained, clothes dried outdoors. The antiquated scenes left me with a sense of foreboding. Old things fascinated me, so the feeling didn't make sense. I had majored in history, but the passing scenes of antiquity filled me with gloom.

I shook off the melancholy, figuring my sadness resulted from having permanently said good-bye to Petti. I hoped visiting my mother would change my outlook, that it would mark a new beginning.

From the Bad Nauheim train station I walked to the sanatarium that was disguised as a yellow house. Inside, I moved past wooden people who sat hopelessly and took up space like artifacts in a museum. At the bottom of a set of stairs I arrived at a desk serving as a control point. A uniformed nurse behind the desk called Ilse Sander and minutes later my birth mother trudged down the staircase. We hugged for a second or two, and I stepped away, restraining my tears. I didn't want to hold back my emotions anymore. I wanted the tears to flow and hear my birth mother tell me everything would be all right, that she loved me and would take care of me. Instead, she launched a tirade about my not having visited in five years. She finished her lecture, and our interaction took on the same one-sided monopoly as during the first two visits. Ilse's lack of personal interest, coupled with her crudeness, yellowed fingertips from smoking rolled cigarettes and a preoccupation with what occurred 30 years before kept an insurmountable distance between us.

"What was my father's name? Who was he?" I asked.

"He was from Düsseldorf. He was a very bad man and died from alcoholism in the 1960s."

"What did he look like? Do you have a picture? Do I look like him?"

The last question infuriated Ilse Sander. "No, I don't have a picture. You don't look like him, you look like me." My birth mother and I resembled each other as much as Laurel looks like Hardy.

Again I admitted that I didn't like the coarse woman trapped in time's cage and absorbed with her past mistakes. Maria had told me that Ilse drank alcohol while pregnant with me. Why would a pregnant woman drink alcohol? I luckily had escaped physical deformities which pregnant women who abuse alcohol often pass to their children. This visit didn't begin a beautiful new relationship. Instead, I felt it marked the complete severing of ties between birth mother and son. I left Bad Nauheim with no desire to ever see Ilse Sander again. She had given me life and nothing more. And surprisingly, rejecting her brought relief rather than shame or guilt.

I ate alone in a restaurant that evening, alone and detached, the way it seemed I had lived my entire life. But this miserable lifestyle brought a strange solace—the comfort of familiarity. I had wanted this trip to end my loneliness, but I had yet to experience any changes. The following day, I took a trip to Nackenheim to see Liana whom I had dated my last few months in Germany. As with Petti, I hadn't written or called to inform her about my arrival.

I walked up the steps to the house where she lived with her parents and rang the buzzer. "Ja," a voice answered.

"Hello, this is Peter. I'm visiting Germany and came to see Liana. Is she here?"

"No." I recognized the voice of Liana's mother. "She doesn't live here anymore. Liana moved to New York City last fall."

Why would anyone want to leave Germany for the United States, and New York City of all God-forsaken places? I waited for the buzzer to sound that would unlock the door. The buzzer didn't ring, and Liana's mother didn't come to the front door.

I pushed the intercom button again. "This is Peter. Don't you remember me? We met a couple of years ago when I dated your daughter."

"I remember you. I'll tell Liana you visited the next time she and I talk. I have cleaning to do. Auf Wiedersehen."

"Wait a minute. I've travelled all the way from the United States to ..."

Loneliness returned on the walk back to the Nackenheim train station. This time it brought grief instead of comfort. A cloud of depression enveloped me as I waited on the platform. Why do I feel this way? I hate feeling isolated. Even when surrounded by people, I sometimes felt alone. How come I'm not changing while in Germany? God, are you punishing me? If you're punishing me, what was my sin? I don't want to be alone. I want to live, take part in life, have friends, do something useful with my life. Why am I always lonely and depressed? Why can't I connect with people? I sat on a bench, sunk in a hole of self-despair.

"Do you know when the next train for Wiesbaden arrives?" The German words contained an accent I didn't recognize.

I looked up to see a woman my age with blonde hair and blue eyes. She looked German, but she couldn't have been German from her accent.

"Yes, it comes in ten minutes," I answered.

"Thank you."

"Where are you from?"

"I come from Ravenna in Italy. I'm studying at the university in Mainz."

Monica Rossi wore a blue sundress, with white socks and brown sandals and carried a satchel at her side. I stood up and the top of her head came even with my eyes, her body looked sleek and trim, and make-up didn't hide her beautiful face. We talked until the train arrived, boarded and sat in the same compartment. Before going our separate ways, we agreed to meet for dinner later that evening.

We met at the Mainz Hauptbahnhof and walked to an outdoor cafe. I felt comfortable dressed in a short-sleeve shirt in the warm September evening. Monica wore the same outfit and threw a white sweater over her shoulders. She embodied the qualities I admired in German women: self-confidence, intelligence, independence and natural beauty. She lived in Nackenheim with her French friend and fellow student Natalie. They rented their apartment from Bernhem, Natalie's German boyfriend. We finished dinner, and I walked Monica back to the train station. She accepted my offer to meet in two days when I returned from Heidelberg.

The next morning I travelled to Heidelberg with hopes of finding a U.S. civil service job. But my plans didn't work out. I didn't qualify for any job openings; the personnel director provided little assistance, and I didn't have a clue on how to find a position with a German firm. My heart sank along with my plan to live in Germany.

On the walk back to the hotel I did what I swore I wouldn't. I went inside a bar and drank a beer. Alone in a dark corner, the beer triggered my alcoholism. It led to a second, then another, and another... Beer had long ago lost its euphoric effect. Now it only increased my depression. Stumbling out of the bar, I put a hand above my forehead to block the late afternoon sun. At a grocery store on the way back to the hotel I bought five, one liter bottles of beer. Five beers to take me to the place I wanted to go—nonexistence.

Staggering inside the hotel, I clenched a plastic bag holding my only solution to isolation and loneliness. The hotelier scrutinized me as I weaved past the desk. He watched me fall up the staircase as my five beer bottles tumbled down the steps. I crawled along the floor, picked up the bottles, then continued toward my room. Once inside, I locked the deadbolt, closed the drapes and left the radio and lamps turned off. Just enough light filtered through cracks in the curtains so I could see to open the first bottle. Slumped in a corner chair parked by the bed, I raised the bottle to my lips. In the silent twilight I closed my eyes and drank.

My drinking noises sounded like a sucking chest wound sapping the life from a dying man. I sat in a shadow world and stared into a void relieved by the senselessness alcohol delivered. It rid me of pain. After finishing the fourth beer and setting the bottle in a line on a table with the other empties, I heard muffled sounds from an adjacent room. Opening the fifth beer, I sat back in the chair, cocked my head toward the sounds and tried to discern the words next door. Intoxication acted as a filter and their words sounded far away, like someone speaking in a dream.

They spoke English, American English. They belonged to the country that had kidnapped me and robbed me of my heritage. I hated whoever occupied that room and wanted to yell for them to shut up and go back to America. I planned a speech: "Return to your plastic bankrupt culture. Go back to the land of idiots addicted to get-rich schemes. Get the hell out of Germany and quit polluting my country."

I put the bottle to my lips and took a swig before heading to their room to deliver my lecture. But the room rolled and pitched when I stood up, and I reeled as if on the deck of a ship caught in a violent storm. I felt I had to make my way to the Americans' room, but my knees buckled, and I leaned on the bed to catch my balance. Drunkenness proved too strong, and I fell forward onto the bed and passed out. Four empty, perfectly aligned beer bottles stood guard on top the desk as the fifth dribbled its foamy contents onto the rug.

I awoke fully dressed, still laying face down on the bed. With consciousness returned, I creaked my head sideways and saw the clock glaring 7:00 a.m. My head ached through a drunken haze, sandpaper coated my mouth and yielded a garbage pit taste. Pain seared my heart, and I hadn't forgotten the people next door. So I slithered off the bed and stumbled out the door, using the walls for support as I headed toward the community bathroom at the end of the hall. The door the Americans occupied opened just before I passed. I tried to remember the speech, so I could release my venomous hate. A woman came out of the room, a woman in her fifties. She had a familiar appearance and I stopped before starting my speech. The woman looked like my adopted mother, and my hate hissed away like air escaping a balloon. "Excuse me, ma'am," I said in English and sidestepped her, continuing to the bathroom.

Back in Wiesbaden that afternoon I called Monica and she asked that we meet at a restaurant for dinner. This time Bernhem and Natalie joined us. I immediately liked Natalie for her warmth, intelligence and attractiveness. Bernhem portrayed the typical German reserve, but he slowly warmed up and even managed to smile before we'd finished eating. The four of us talked entirely in German, discussing the arts, politics, literature and sharing experiences of travelling in different countries. Education became our common bond, and for the first time I appreciated my adopted parents' emphasis on academic achievement. After dinner we walked to a nearby discotheque to dance and have fun. I didn't drink alcohol, not wanting to make a fool of myself, but found it difficult. How could they *sip* wine, take thirty minutes to drink one beer and stop after two drinks?

People crammed the discotheque filled with steamy air. Sweat dripped from my face as we danced. Finally Monica suggested some fresh air. We walked along the edge of the Rhine River under a starlit night. I told Monica why I had come to Germany. She couldn't understand me. "You're American; you were raised in that country," she said. "You're trying to return to a foreign country to find something you can find anywhere."

"No, you don't understand. Germany is more than just a country. It's the only place where I can find happiness because I am a German. The salmon must return to where they were spawned. Nature is calling me back."

"Can't you be happy in America?" the Italian asked. I didn't have an answer.

The next day, Sunday, Monica and I went to a Sporthalle for exercise. I hadn't done anything physical during the trip though working out was as much a part of my life as eating and sleeping. We walked up the Sporthalle steps, and I hoped they'd have more than a swimming pool—maybe weights and a basketball court. Locked doors greeted us at the main entrance. The facility can't be closed at 1:00 o'clock in the afternoon. We circled the building and tried every door, with the same result. The Sporthalle was definitely closed. "How can this be, Monica? I'm dying to work out."

"I don't know. Let's get to a phone and see if there's another close by."

We walked to a nearby service station. The attendant said Sporthalles closed on Sundays because that's when Germans spent time with their families. His answer disgusted me. Gyms in the States always stayed open on Sunday. I needed to work out to get an adrenaline rush and relieve stress. Physical exercise provided the only positive energy in my life.

We decided to return to the Hauptbahnhof and walked toward a bus stop. One pulled in a block away, so we started running, gym bags banging against our sides. We arrived at the stop just after the doors closed.

"Thank goodness we made it," Monica said, between gulps of air.

The bus started to pull away, and I rapped on the glass at the front door, pleading for the driver to stop and let us on. He looked at me, shook his head no, and the bus roared away leaving me wheezing in a cloud of diesel exhaust. I kicked at empty air. "He would have let us on in America," I said between coughs.

"The driver would have let us on in Italy," Monica echoed.

The driver's refusal to let us board served as another example of parts of German culture which I didn't like. I wanted to eat in a restaurant at anytime and work out on Sundays. I wanted to see miles and miles of unbroken wilderness and dress any way I desired without people staring at my clothes. I didn't like being surrounded by antiquity all the time and longed for the warm hospitality of Southern culture.

Back in Nackenheim Natalie had dinner waiting. Bernhem, Natalie and Monica, people from three different countries, showed by example that they led good and decent lives. I wanted the same, to live a good life and be a decent guy, but I didn't know how. Every search for happiness ended in failure. I couldn't see anything good in my life and didn't know how to change. God, I wanted out of my sickening castle, but I couldn't find the key. My search for happiness in Germany was another dead-end.

I had experienced enough in Germany to know I wouldn't find contentment by simply living in the country of my birth. But before leaving, I had one last, bitter experience. The day before returning to America Monica and I travelled to Mörfelden to visit my grandfather's grave. We entered the cemetery, but his plot had a tombstone marked with a different name. I couldn't believe I'd forgotten the location of my grandfather's grave. Time must have muddied my memory. We searched every row in the area but couldn't find a tombstone marked with Peter Friedrich Sander. I was shaking as we approached an elderly man and woman and asked for their help.

"We're looking for the grave of Peter Friedrich Sander," I said, standing stiff as a board. "Do you know where he is buried?" My eyes begged a favorable response.

The old man and woman looked at each other and shrugged their shoulders.

Monica stepped in and asked the same question. She spoke better German and had a calmer manner. The Germans focused their eyes on the Italian as she explained what I wanted, then switched their gaze to me.

I stared straight into their eyes, elderly eyes that expressed compassion and understanding. Tears clouded mine as I silently pleaded that they tell me where my grandfather had been moved. Don't you know my grandfather was a good man? I was named after him and he's a connection to my past and a link to my heritage? I've come to pay my respects. I want to say hello to the man who took care of me the first year of my life. I stood motionless waiting for their answer.

"When did he die?" they asked.

"I can't remember the exact year, but sometime in the late 1950s."

"Unless a family member or friend paid a renewal fee his tomb could only remain in the cemetery for 25 years. If a renewal fee wasn't paid, his casket was removed and another put into the same gravesight. Germany's a crowded country and land is at a premium. We're sorry about you're grandfather," and they walked away.

What they said couldn't be, it just couldn't. I ran to the hut where the cemetery caretaker worked. He confirmed my fear that Peter Friedrich Sander no longer was buried in the cemetery.

The caretaker went back into his hut, and I felt my knees weaken. How could they remove my grandfather from his eternal resting place? Aches throbbed through my heart and tears of sorrow dripped from my eyes. My grandfather was gone, and I suffered yet another loss, the loss of a man who loved me. I'd never known such intense grief, and I clenched my teeth to stifle screams of agony. Pain wrenched my stomach, and I felt like vomiting. I wanted to fall to my knees, lie on the ground and pound my fists into the dirt. Monica put her arm around me and led me from the cemetery. "He's on the other side, Peter. It doesn't mean he's not with you." She stopped and used her hands to wipe away the tears streaming down my face. "A soul can't be captured in a casket. Your grandfather lives forever."

I sat silent in a railway car with Monica at my side on the return trip to Mainz. My hate toward Americans changed to a hatred of war. War's destructiveness had shattered my life. I wouldn't have been taken from Germany if there hadn't been a Second World War. I would have grown up in Kunzendorf and remained a German. I hated war, I hated being in the Army, I hated being American, I hated being adopted. I hated, I hated...

Peter Friedrich, wer bin ich? Peter Frederick, who am I? German or American? The answer was neither and both. I had German blood but an American mentality.

This trip allowed me to understand that a man can make his home where ever he chooses. If I wanted, I could live happily in America. My heart fought and pleaded, saying it wasn't true, that I was German, and only in Germany would I be content. In one of the few times in my life, intellect overruled emotion. Germany wasn't the key to my happiness. I couldn't deny what I had experienced, and my last hope for a key to the castle door died.

International adoption destroyed the connection to my heritage. It is only conjuncture to guess how my life might have turned out under different circumstances, but there is one certainty: If I had remained in the orphanage or had been adopted by German parents, I never would have suffered the loss of my national identity. If I had to be adopted by Americans, then they should have been of German descent.

The Cycle Repeats

Finding my birth mother, romantic relationships with women, service as an Army officer and the hope of reconnecting to my German heritage all proved illusions in my quest for contentment and happiness. I didn't know where else to search, and life without hope gripped me in its terrible fist. Only alcohol provided relief, so I continued to deaden my senses every night and weekend with booze.

I lost the ability to control my drinking. Instead of going to the gym, I drank. Mornings I'd swear never to drink again and emptied credit cards and cash out of my wallet before leaving for work so I wouldn't have money to buy booze at the end of the day. It didn't matter; I borrowed money from coworkers, saying I needed gas to get home. Everything I tried to stop drinking ended in failure: reading books, listening to cassette tapes, trying to find creative outlets as a diversion. I simply had no will power when it came to alcohol.

I made one last attempt to stop. Still careful to hide my drinking from the Army, I made an appointment with a civilian counselor, thinking therapy might provide an answer. The therapist said she needed power to help me stop drinking and wrote up a contract giving her the authority to inform the Army about my alcoholism if I continued to drink. In a fit of desperation, I signed.

One night after I'd gotten home from work the telephone rang. It rarely rang at home. Who could that be? Probably a telephone solicitor. I went to the kitchen and picked up the phone. "Hello?" I asked.

"Peter? This is your mother."

"Hi, How are you?" I asked, giving the standard mechanical reply.

"Not well. Your father's been diagnosed with cancer."

She spoke in her usual monotone, clinical voice. Won't she ever speak with emotion? Couldn't she express what she felt, or didn't she feel? I hated people who wouldn't talk honestly. Did she think his cancer was my fault? They aren't my parents. I hate her. I hate my adopted father. I didn't say anything and squeezed the phone, standing stone-faced.

"Peter, are you there? I'm calling to ..." and I slammed down the phone.

It rang a minute later. My adopted mother spoke again. "Peter? Did we get disconnected..." I hung up on her a second time.

The phone didn't ring again. My parents changed tactics and instead of calling, wrote letters that I ripped up before reading. Their only mistake was to love me when I hated myself.

I did go to a couple of therapy sessions. But instead of helping, I drank more and decided to stop seeing the counselor. A few weeks later my boss called me into his office. The therapist had called him. I denied drinking, but the Army began administrative discharge proceedings because I violated the William Beaumont contract where I had agreed not to consume alcohol after completing treatment. Still unwilling to admit a weakness, I fought the discharge.

But I knew the Army would win and prepared for life after the military by moving to a tiny one-bedroom apartment in Olympia, 20 miles south of Fort Lewis. After the Army I wanted to become a high-school basketball coach and was accepted into the Saint Martin's College teaching certificate program. A year after the start of discharge proceedings, the Army won, and I was issued an honorable discharge for, "Failure to respond to alcohol rehabilitation."

On the way home from Fort Lewis my last day in the Army I bought a shopping cart full of beer and a few groceries. I drove home, locked myself in the tiny apartment, drew the drapes shut, disconnected the phone and played my favorite Neil Young album. In my own private ceremony I took off the Army uniform for the final time. The last symbol of my worth landed on top of a pile of dirty clothes. Not knowing what else to do, I drank. And drank. And drank.

I had succeeded in transforming my inner castle to my outside world. Over the course of my adult life I had driven away every single person who loved or cared about me: birth mother, adopted parents, friends, romantic loves. Locked in a small apartment crammed with everything I owned, I drank beer after beer until passing out.

With a horrible hangover the next day, I shuffled to the refrigerator to grab another beer. The clock on the stove cried 3:30 a.m. as I struggled with shaking hands to open the lid on the can. I managed to pop it open and felt better after the first few swallows. My early morning breakfast was a couple of vitamins chased with a second beer. Then I drank until passing out a second time. I woke up sometime that night and did the same thing, over and over again. I lost track of time not knowing the day of the week, or if it was night or day. I didn't care about anything—people, working out, my future.

The shadow of two street drunks haunted me as I drank beer after beer after beer. Which fate awaited me: follow my father to an alcoholic death or live in an institution like my mother? Genetics proved stronger than environment, and as I drank, passed out, woke up and drank again, the family cycle came full circle.

Chaos ensued, and I limped out of bed after regaining consciousness. A grapefruit-sized bruise bulged from my thigh and a scarlet welt throbbed over my ribs. How did I get them? Then events from the previous drinking spree returned like images from a nightmare, and I remembered falling against a coffee table while trying to walk to the bedroom. My thigh hit a corner and my ribs bounced off the table's edge before I slammed face down on the floor. I didn't even remember getting up and finally making it to the bedroom.

My non-stop drinking continued, and I felt as if I spiralled through hell in Dante's *Divine Comedy*. Horror seized me when I finally ran out of beer. I frantically searched the refrigerator and pantry shelves, dumped grocery bags full of empty cans onto the floor and crawled on my hands and knees throughout the apartment—looking for a beer. But every can was empty. Crazed by an obsession to drink, I drove to a convenience store and picked up a case, slamming it on the counter.

"Can't sell it to you buddy," the man behind the counter said.

"Why not?" I asked, terrified. Why can't he sell me what I desperately need?

"Law says we can't sell alcohol until 6:00 a.m."

"What time is it?"

The man's eyebrows narrowed; he shook his head and frowned. "It's 5:15."

I left the beer on the counter, cursing the cashier and the law on my way to the car. I decided to wait in the parking lot until 6:00 and slumped back in the car seat even as the stench from my breath made me roll down a window. Scratching the side of my face, I felt stubble from not shaving since my last day in the Army. Wanting to make sure the whiskers were really mine, I looked in the rearview mirror and saw bags under bloodshot eyes, sunken cheeks and sickly white skin. Even so, at 6:00 I stood at the counter with a case of beer and opened a can as soon as I got in the car, not waiting to return to the apartment before pouring alcohol into my body. A beer commercial slogan ran through my mind, "It doesn't get any better than this."

This time alcohol had a different effect. The darkness I craved by passing out wouldn't come. I tried to guzzle a beer but it wouldn't go down. I tried to sip it, but my body couldn't absorb any more alcohol. I couldn't drink and couldn't pass out. What could I do? Caught in a merciless limbo between drunkenness and sobriety, I staggered to bed and collapsed, face first.

Pain contracted and expanded through my body with every breath, and a throbbing headache threatened to split my skull. Every part of me hurt; every muscle, every bone, every cell screamed in torment. Slowly and with great pain I rolled onto my back. Sweat poured out of me as if I had a high fever. Through a fog I heard my own forced breathing, gasps like a man comatose on a respirator. I reached past my shriveled stomach and touched my swollen liver. When did I last eat? I couldn't remember, but hunger pains were mild compared to the rest of my misery. Mustering the last of my strength I raised both hands above my chest and watched as they shook uncontrollably.

I had become what I had feared when first seeing my birth mother. My last bit of will to live slipped away, like a sunbeam grasped in my hand. Incoherent thoughts streaked by in unrecognizable patterns. Since I couldn't pass out and escape, and couldn't stand the torture, I merely shut my eyes.

It was March 29, 1987. I was thirty-one years old. My body, saturated with alcohol, ached and shook uncontrollably as I lay on the bed. Making an attempt to escape my plight, I concentrated on the only possible final solution. I rolled onto my back, interlaced trembling fingers, let my cupped hands fall on my chest, and I focused as I mumbled a prayer between cracked lips. I wanted out of hell and prayed to God for death.

One Day at a Time

I lay on the bed, quivering, drenched in a pool of sweat and hoping for a quick end. Unconsciousness remained at bay and I slowly opened my eyes to the bedroom's white ceiling swimming overhead. It seemed a whirlwind raged around me, and I hoped death would quickly come. Instead, for a short period, a calmness descended as if I was in the eye of a hurricane. The ceiling stopped swimming, and my thinking regained clarity. During this moment of peace I remembered a fragment of information from alcohol rehabilitation at William Beaumont Hospital. Instructors had said the kinds of meetings they forced me to attend in El Paso were also held in nearly every city and town throughout the United States. I wondered if Olympia had one, and I limped to the phone book, still hurting from the fall against the coffee table. A man answered a 24-hour alcohol help-line and offered directions to an 8:00 p.m. meeting. At a little after 6:00 in the evening I forced down a couple slices of bread and washed it down with a glass of orange juice. Then I limped to the bathroom, showered, shaved, brushed my teeth and hair. I put on clean cloths and drove to a meeting for reformed drunks.

I didn't want anyone to notice me and crept inside, sitting in a folding metal chair at the back of the room. I stared at the floor and twisted my hands in despair, waiting for the meeting to start. Someone tapped my shoulder, and I looked up to see an older man smiling. "I'm glad you're here," he said, his eyes sparkling. "I brought you a cup of coffee," and he handed me a small styrofoam cup. "It doesn't matter what you've done or where you came from, the important thing is that you're here with friends."

"Thanks," I whispered, and took the cup as the hot liquid splashed over its edges and onto my trembling hands. No one had smiled at me or said they were happy to see me in a long time. The man went to the front of the room as I wondered why he would welcome me. I must look terrible.

The thirty people in the room grew quiet, and someone read a passage from a book about alcoholism. The public could attend; there weren't any dues to pay, no one forced religion, there were no leaders and no membership forms to sign. I would have walked out at the slightest hint of a manipulative sales pitch, but the opening reading said that a desire to stop drinking was the only requirement for membership. After introductions, people spoke one at a time. They shared how alcohol had destroyed their lives and how they had learned to stop drinking after hitting bottom. Unlike the times when I attended meetings in El Paso, I listened closely and discovered their stories sounded much like mine. Once they took a drink they couldn't stop until blacking out. They talked about their early drinking and how booze initially took away their feelings of inadequacy, loneliness and guilt. But alcohol eventually turned on them too, costing them jobs and families, and others shared that drinking had put them in prison or mental institutions. Every person said that their life had improved once they put the bottle down and addressed the emotions behind their drinking. I didn't say a word but felt a bond with the people in the room. They drank like me, and I realized I wasn't the only one in the world with emotional problems. Hearing them talk about solutions gave me hope. They suffered like me but had found a way to work through their pain. The meeting lasted an hour, and a man handed me a meeting schedule as I walked out the door. "I hope you keep coming back," he smiled. "One day at a time."

I returned to the apartment, my littered cavern. Kicking cans aside to clear a path to the kitchen, I emptied the refrigerator of the remaining beer, pouring it down the drain. Then I tossed all the empties into garbage bags and dumped them in an outside trash bin. When I'd finished, I didn't know what else to do. For years I'd done little but drink while at home. People at the meeting said I didn't have to drink, that I had a choice and could make a decision to stay sober. They said I didn't have to stay sober all my life; I only had to stay sober one day at a time. In the morning I could make another decision to stay sober for that day only. I decided to stay sober until I went to bed, but I wasn't tired and the apartment felt claustrophobic. Then I wished I hadn't poured the beer down the drain. What can I do until going to sleep? I left the apartment and drove to a store to rent a video. I came home and watched the movie but still couldn't sleep. After another trip to the video store I fell into a deep sleep on the couch before the second movie had ended.

A dull headache greeted me when I awoke, and I felt like I had every other morning after a night of heavy drinking. I went to the kitchen and breathed a sigh of relief, realizing I'd thrown away all my beer the night before. I'd been sober for over 12 hours.

So I went to two meetings, one at noon and a second in the evening. People suggested I get a sponsor, someone who'd been sober awhile and could answer questions or lend support when the urge to drink struck. I had always prided myself on never needing anyone's help and lived the myth of the rugged American individualist, but illusions of self-sufficiency had crumbled in my desperation to stay sober. At the evening meeting I listened to a man talk about healing his broken relationships. I related to his story and decided to ask him to be my sponsor. After the meeting, I approached him as a thousand reasons raced through my mind on why I should turn around and run in the opposite direction. What if he said no? I'd be crushed if he rejected me. What if he was gay, what if he laughed at me...

But fear of drinking again squashed my fear of rejection. "Excuse me," I said, tapping him on the shoulder. "I'm new to all this, and I need a sponsor. Will you be my sponsor?"

He stopped and turned toward me. "I'd be delighted. My name is George. What's yours?" and he extended his hand.

"My name is Peter," I said, shaking his hand while staring at the floor, too embarrassed to look him in the eye.

"You doing anything now?" George asked.

"No."

"Good, I'm not either. Let's get a cup of coffee and shoot the breeze for a while." We walked to a nearby coffeehouse in downtown Olympia.

George stood 5'10" tall, had a thin build, dark eyes, short brown hair and a neatly trimmed beard. He might have been a little older than my 31 years and worked as a part-time actor and part-time therapist. George had a razor-sharp mind and didn't need coffee for energy. He hummed with enough energy for two people. We sat at a small table tucked in a corner, and despite his constant movements George talked with a reassuring calmness.

Between sips of coffee he told me how drinking once controlled his life and sent him spiralling into pitiful and incomprehensible demoralization. He laughed looking back on some of his escapades, and despite my misery I laughed along, knowing alcohol affected me the same way. George didn't monopolize the conversation and encouraged me to talk. He nodded when I told him I didn't know how to stop drinking and was sick of my life. "I felt the same way," he said, and didn't condemn me or offer any quick, pat answers to solve my problems. "I don't drink, one day at a time, and have been sober four years." George got sober while living on the streets and said I could get sober too. We exchanged phone numbers before leaving the coffee shop, and I rented two videos on the way home.

I went to two meetings every day for a month and often met with George. On the first Sunday of my new-found sobriety I also did something I hadn't done in years. I went to mass of my own free will. Before mass started I sat in a back-row pew of the quiet church and felt awe at being in God's presence. I remembered the indescribable love I'd known in the sixth grade when wanting to become a priest, the same love I had felt in the art gallery and when sitting on the hood of a jeep in a German valley. As I sat in that pew I felt God's love again burn in my heart and welcome me home. I closed my eyes, and it seemed as if I stood at one end of a pitch-black tunnel, looking down the other end at a man glowing in radiant light. He stretched out his arms, and the radiance changed into the shape of a brilliant cross. Organ music signalled the start of mass, so I stood up and used my fingertips to wipe away tears of joy.

Throughout the mass I reflected on my seemingly hopeless condition and understood God loved me at my worst and would help to improve my life. It didn't seem logical to trust in something I had once doubted, but I couldn't deny the presence of His love. My best efforts to find happiness had resulted in failure, and I certainly needed help to stay sober. I thanked God for bringing me to the meetings and for George, and asked Him to help keep me sober the remainder of this day.

I continued to meet with George at least once a week and talk about my difficulties. He'd share similar experiences and how he worked through problems, rather than give a patronizing textbook answer. George asked what I felt, and I trusted him enough to try talking about my confusion. I'd never done that before.

I'd learned to suppress feelings as a boy. American culture taught that men don't feel pain, and emotion proved a liability in the Army Officer Corps. But

I'd always felt, sometimes so deeply that it seemed to penetrate the marrow of my bones. Keeping my emotions buried amounted to trying to seal a pot of boiling water. At first I could only tell George that I hurt. But sharing my pain verbally helped relieve some of the pressure of pent-up emotions.

"Do you want some money for all the time you spend with me?" I asked at the end of one of our get-togethers.

George smiled, "No. You can pay me back by helping other people stay sober. Help make coffee before the meetings, clean up afterwards or say hi to someone who looks like they need a friend."

"I don't get it," I said. "You don't want anything in return for all the help you've given?" Nothing came free in America; everything had a price-tag in a culture dominated by greed.

"When I spend time with you, which I very much enjoy doing, it helps me stay sober too," George explained.

I remembered that when working with my Little Brother I felt good in a way I'd never before known. Helping others without expectation of reward gave me a feeling of self-worth. So I followed George's suggestion and took part in many clean and sober activities. Every Wednesday I chaired a noon meeting; I started working out again and played on an alcohol-free softball team. After three months of attending meetings I was ready to start talking about my problems.

I felt a tremendous gratitude toward George for helping me stay sober. I admired and respected him. Still, I had some misgivings, and after knowing him a few months he told me what I had suspected—he was gay. To George, being gay wasn't a big deal, and he didn't run around like a crazed fanatic demanding everyone treat him with respect because of his sexual orientation. He just wanted to live without anyone bothering him. But I told him I'd smack him if he ever made an advance toward me. He laughed at my stereotyped image and later on I rarely thought about his being gay. But it did make an impact on me. It broadened my life's perspective.

I met other gays after leaving the Army, and like George, they weren't radicals but people who wanted to live in peace. As with the Russians, what mainstream American culture had taught me didn't match reality. Combining my experiences with George and with the Russians, I learned first to get to know someone and then form my impression rather than prejudging based on someone else's values.

Four months passed, and I attended meetings daily and mass on Sundays, talked with George on a regular basis and stayed involved in nonalcoholic activities. Miraculously, I hadn't taken a drink during those 16 weeks. The obsession to drink had disappeared, and I no longer battled the compulsion to pick up a beer. My hands stopped shaking, headaches ended, dark circles under my eyes disappeared, no more cotton mouth, and my liver shrank back to its normal size.

People at the meetings said they would love me until I learned to love myself. I hated hearing them suggest that I didn't love myself. I thought I was fine after I stopped drinking but realized I felt ashamed about the way I still treated my adopted parents. Guilt ate at my insides, and I didn't have alcohol anymore to deaden the feeling. I asked George what he did when he felt guilty.

"There's more to sobriety than just not drinking," he answered. "I found it helpful to make a list of people I felt guilty, angry or afraid of. Then I wrote beside each person why I felt that way. I honestly looked at my side of the relationship and ignored any feelings of self-pity or how I thought others had wronged me. I can't control other people; the only control I have is over myself. People aren't going to change to make me feel happy. If I'm going to have peace of mind, then I'm the one who has to change."

George's proposal didn't suit me, and I decided to skip his suggestion. I didn't want to face my relationship with my parents and thought looking back on past mistakes would only make me feel more ashamed and discouraged. But the longer I put off his suggestion the worse I felt. I grew so uncomfortable that I finally followed his suggestion and wrote down my guilt, anger and fears.

George knew about my relationship, or lack of one, with my adopted parents. He'd often ask about them and I'd respond with a standard reply, "How should I know? We don't talk to each other." George never judged me but continued to ask. I finally admitted I felt ashamed about the way I had treated them but didn't know how to resolve the problem.

"They'd probably like to know you're still alive," he answered. "You could write them a letter and tell them what has happened since you hung up on them."

Later that week I did write my adopted parents a half-page letter and said I hoped they were well and asked them to write in return. In a few days the telephone rang and I wondered which of my new friends might be calling. I picked up the phone, "Hello?"

"Hello, Peter, this is your father and mother," they said, speaking on separate phones from their home.

Embarrassment prevented me from answering.

"We were thrilled to receive your letter and are very happy you're doing well. You're our son no matter what happened, and we will always love you."

"Thanks, it's good to hear you from you," I answered, remembering I hadn't asked for forgiveness in my letter.

"My cancer's gone into remission, and I feel as good as ever," my father laughed, and I could mentally see his beer-belly shaking.

"That's great news, dad." We spoke awhile longer and they told me they were encouraged by the fact that I no longer drank but were disappointed I'd left the Army. Of course I didn't tell them the reason I left the service. We never discussed problems or difficulties. They concluded their call with an invitation to visit, and I couldn't believe they hadn't given up on me. I now looked at my adopted parents with a new perspective—appreciation.

After I completed my list of guilt, fear and anger I asked George what to do next. He said I needed to share it with someone, that reading the list to another person would help get rid of my feelings' of destructiveness. George agreed to listen to me and said we could meet at his house on a Saturday morning.

I pulled up to his apartment and parked the car, as nervous as I was before stepping inside the Russian guardhouse. But this time I prepared to encounter my own dark side instead of an outside foe. George greeted me with a smile. "I'm glad to see you. Would you like a cup of coffee?" I followed him into the kitchen where he had brewed a pot. "Cream is in the refrigerator and sugar on the table," he said, handing me a cup.

We sat in his living room chit-chatting, and I twisted three pages of handwritten notes into a cylinder of paper. George didn't pressure me to start. This was my activity, and he waited for me to initiate the action.

"Are you ready to get started?" I asked, and felt my shoulder muscles tighten.

"Whenever you are," he smiled, speaking with an assured voice. "Would you like to begin with a prayer?" George didn't belong to any organized religion but lived a deep spirituality.

"Yes I would," I answered. We bent our heads as George listened to me ask God for strength and courage to change my life. I finished the prayer, and my sponsor got up from his chair and lit a candle. When he sat back down I started reading. Anger about adoption, guilt about how I'd treated my adopted parents and fear that I'd never be able to love another human being topped my list. Drops of sweat trickled down my ribs, and I licked my dry lips, forcing myself to read the entire list. George patiently listened and never interrupted. I finished and looked at him as he simply held a cup of coffee. Clenching my jaw, I waited for a lecture or to be asked to leave.

"Thank you for allowing me the opportunity to share in your life," George said, and continued by offering constructive feedback. We finished, and I walked out of his apartment lightheaded with relief at having shared my deepest self. Before starting, I had believed that if people knew what I had written they would reject and abandon me. George hadn't thrown me out of his apartment, and I learned my fears were not reality.

I went to a church to receive the sacrament of confession later that afternoon. A few people stood ahead of me, so I silently knelt in a pew at the side of the confessional, concentrating on the same list I had read to George and reflecting on how my behavior had hurt others. The last person in front of me finally exited the confessional, and I bit my lip and went inside. Kneeling beside a purple screen, the priest asked me to begin. He had to help me with the opening ritual since I hadn't been to confession in over a decade. I recounted my sins saying I truly felt sorry for what I'd done and needed God's help to lead a better life.

The priest didn't punish me further with a lecture on morality but said he thought I'd made a good effort to honestly search my heart. "For your penance..." and I braced for the mountains of prayers I'd be required to recite. Instead the priest said, "After confession say three Hail Marys and three Our Fathers. Over the course of the next week I want you to reflect on your life and at the end of seven days become thankful for three things that you've never been thankful for before." Then he absolved me of my sins and I knew God had forgiven me too when I felt His love enter my heart as I walked out of the church.

Trying to find three new things to be grateful for took me through the labyrinth of my life. I'd never been thankful for much, and the search took hours of careful reflection before I came up with them. At the end of the week, one of the things I thanked God for was my adopted parents. My emotions cried out that adoption was a curse and not something to be grateful for, but my intellect and spirit overruled the self-defeating emotions I'd had since childhood.

Self-examination, where I tried to search my faults, was a first step in taking responsibility for my life. I quit playing the victim role when I realized how my inappropriate behavior hurt others. Self-examination proved difficult and humbling, but discussing my flaws with George and the priest strengthened my desire to lead a better life. In its wake I gained something unexpected—a small measure of self-acceptance and self-respect.

Ever so slowly my perceptions started turning away from negative thinking toward positive growth and development. I tried to stop thinking about the unfairness of my early childhood and slowly began to appreciate the good aspects. This step-by-step process of healing began when I quit wanting to change the past and tried, as best I could, to live in the present. Instead of searching for happiness outside of myself, I tried to improve the way I lived. My demand for instant gratification always led me toward hell instead of making me feel better. I realized that I'd never find lasting happiness outside of myself, but contentment could come as a result of leading a good life.

I wasn't perfect and often made mistakes, sometimes taking one step forward and two back. But I'd pick myself up, brush off the dirt and keep going. The frightened little boy who thought no one wanted him was growing with a positive sense of self.

During the summer I went to the Evergreen State College near Olympia to lift weights in their gym. After finishing, on a whim, I dropped by the admissions office to see what courses the college offered. A woman putting brochures in a rack stopped to listen as I explained my background and she said a few openings remained in the college's Master of Public Administration program. So I stuffed a graduate catalogue and application form in my gym bag before leaving.

Later, I didn't know why thoughts of the MPA program constantly pestered me. Academics had never been high on my priority list, and I was already scheduled to start classes at Saint Martin's in the fall. Besides, my boyhood tapes were subconsciously playing: you're not smart enough to get a masters degree; your grades at Auburn were too low; you'll never pass graduate entrance exams; you can't; you can't... Fear still threatened to limit my ability to take part in life.

However, since becoming sober I'd learned to identify and express my fears. The Army had taught me to walk through physical challenges, and the meetings I now attended taught me to walk through emotional barriers. George listened to me recite reasons why I'd never get into graduate school but stopped me after I'd whined for five minutes, saying, "Why don't you just apply and see what happens?"

George provided the benefit of an outside observer's feedback on issues in my life. No matter how hard I tried I could never step outside my own perspectives, so I rarely met my potential. Without George's feedback I might never have applied for the MPA program. With his encouragement, however, I pushed aside fear of rejection and completed the application process. A few weeks later, a letter from the Evergreen State College arrived in the mail. I slowly opened the envelope:

"The graduate school at the Evergreen State College..." it was like reading a letter in a dream "...is pleased to inform that you've been accepted..." I couldn't believe what it said and re-read the letter. I whooped and hollered after double checking. I'd been accepted and immediately called my parents and George to share the good news. Then I stopped to say a little prayer and thank God for the opportunity ahead.

Being accepted into graduate school gave me options, something I'd rarely had until I stopped drinking. I could go to Saint Martin's and become a high-school basketball coach or go to graduate school instead. Having options was definitely better than being limited to a single choice. I chose graduate school because I figured a masters degree would eventually open more doors of future employment.

I flew to Florida at the end of the summer and spent a week visiting my parents before starting at Evergreen. They hadn't changed a bit but my perception of them had. They had forgiven me for my actions but didn't talk about it, sweeping the past under the rug as if it had never happened. I had gone from hating them to a grudging respect and admiration. My parents were still unaffectionate and superficial, but I knew I couldn't mold people into behaving the way I wanted. No one had ever taught my parents how to communicate openly, so they expressed affection by being good providers. I began accepting them for who they were rather than what I wished they'd be, and our relationship continued to improve.

Walking Along a New Path

Wanting to live closer to the Evergreen State College, I moved from the tiny apartment to an older home converted to a duplex near downtown Olympia. My spacious, new apartment spanned the entire second floor, and buckets of sunshine poured through its many windows to create a bright and cheerful environment. I unpacked my artwork, long buried in storage, and displayed paintings, sculptings and prints collected from my world travels. House plants, a slice of nature, grew lush and full in the abundant light, books filled two bookcases and a stereo played. What I loved most surrounded me—art, plants, books and music—treasures that stirred my soul.

One weekend morning I watered the plants, including one sitting on top of the television set, which blared a baseball game. Moving to the next plant, I heard a sharp pop followed with sounds like chicken sizzling in a frying pan. I turned around and saw the TV screen turn black as the baseball game disappeared into a small pinhole of light. Water had overflowed out the bottom of the plant and dripped into the television, causing it to short circuit. But I never repaired it or bought a new one and struggled through television withdrawal the following weeks. Eventually my mind cleared and I filled television's void with new and healthy activities, especially reading, and have never owned a TV since.

Loneliness continued after I stopped drinking and I had no crutches with which to escape the melancholy. Now, instead of escaping through self-destructive instant gratification schemes, I learned to accept periods of loneliness as part of normal life. If my depressing mood extended into self-pity I worked through the sadness by helping another person who struggled with alcoholism.

Then a second wave of guilt washed over me about the way I had treated my adopted parents. George suggested I make amends and try to set my wrongs right. "Look only at where you've wronged them. Remember, you're correcting your mistakes, and making amends doesn't mean criticizing the faults of others," he said. "Look only at your mistakes, not at those of your parents, and expect nothing in return. It doesn't matter what their reaction might be because you're cleaning up your side of the street and taking responsibility for your own past actions."

"I can't go to Florida and make amends to my parents. I don't owe them money. How can I make amends?" I argued.

"You can write a letter, but just saying you're sorry won't be enough," he answered. "The way to make amends is by living a new life and treating them in a healthy manner, not by saying your sorry and repeating the same old behavior again and again."

I quit arguing and sat down to write. I admitted I'd been a difficult child to raise and thanked them for providing a good home, especially for ensuring I received an excellent education. I wrote that I was trying to live a new and better life, then asked forgiveness for the hurt I'd caused them. The letter ended by asking if I could do anything to make up for my past mistakes.

My parents called a few weeks later but didn't mention my letter of amends. However, when my mother got off the line my father acknowledged receiving the letter. He said it was one of the most meaningful things he'd ever read. I told him I meant every word and asked again if I could do anything to repair the harm.

"No, I'm just proud to have you as my son," he replied.

I followed George's advice and made amends by changing the way I treated them. I maintained closer contact and from that time on wrote or called at least once a month. Our renewed relationship proved a miracle.

Support group meetings, like working out, became a regular part of my life, as vital as eating and sleeping. I eventually allowed myself to become vulnerable and talked with those I trusted about my fears, problems, hopes and dreams. They nurtured and encouraged me as I slowly worked through emotional difficulties one by one. My self-confidence grew and I finally ended my romantic loner fantasy, awakening to the reality that to enjoy a full and meaningful life I needed other people.

And I discovered a third dimension to my being, my spiritual side, and focused to enrich this most important part of life. My spiritual life grew as I attended mass on a regular basis, talked with others about God and read as many books on spirituality as I could find. My favorite authors were Thomas Merton, Saint Augustine, and Thomas à Kempis, a little-known monk from the 1400's who wrote *The Imitation of Christ*, a book that made God infinitely more relevant in my daily life. I uncovered books written by female mystics from the Middle Ages who wrote about a God that loved them at all times, without conditions. The God I gradually came to believe in was one of pure love who wanted greater things for me than I could imagine for myself.

My first step in recovering from the trauma of adoption had been to stop drinking. Then it became a difficult and slow process to heal boyhood wounds. My efforts to rid myself of the effects of childhood trauma amounted to escaping a pool of quicksand, and I became disillusioned, thinking I'd never move past the hurt. Like with my alcoholism, I realized I needed help to change my way of thinking.

With the support and guidance of my friends I turned to the same actions that had freed me from alcoholism. I asked God for help, revealed my pain, lived as best I could one day at a time and helped others.

I listened to how my friends handled their feelings of inadequacy and heard over and over again the need to take action. George told me simple cliches that nevertheless had a ringing truth, "You don't think your way into a new way of living, you live your way into a new way of thinking. Bring the body and the mind will follow." To heal from adoption, I had to take action. Reading books never got me sober, and knowledge alone would also never remedy my childhood pain. My friends told me to work through the inevitable setbacks, the feelings of despair and depression and no matter what, to keep on trying to change and grow. Healing from adoption happened slowly and only after I took positive steps to change. Despite the disappointment of not having an instant cure, I did feel better because I had hope.

Change meant doing things that allowed me to move through my fears. I always felt comfortable at work and on the basketball court, environments with clear boundaries for interaction, but felt awkward in social settings. The first summer of my sobriety I went on an evening clean-and-sober cruise where hundreds of people ate and danced as the boat steamed through Puget Sound. I introduced myself to strangers and engaged in conversations rather than sitting alone in a dark corner feeling sorry for myself. The entire night I watched a beautiful, tall woman with shoulder-length dark hair, in a sleek black dress. But I stayed away from her as insecurities whispered I didn't deserve women which I desired. But in trying to improve my life I'd discover again and again that my fears were not reality. Later, as I walked off the boat at the end of the cruise the woman in the black dress tapped me on the shoulder and asked me to join her for a cup of coffee.

I liked Gloria Melvin from the first time we talked. She had a kind heart, was 5'10", Catholic, of German descent and looked like a fashion model. Simple pleasures delighted Gloria and I found she didn't need to be entertained in a dating relationship. We dated for several months, and I felt closer to Gloria each time we met, until I realized our friendship had turned to love. When love surfaced I abruptly stopped calling or visiting. Despite my best intentions I once again fell into the same old behavior patterns. I saw Gloria through my childhood eyes and expected her at any moment to reject and abandon me. So to protect myself, I left her before she could hurt me.

What I had believed as a boy was cemented into my behavior patterns as an adult. I talked to others who had experienced similar fears, and they said they had finally changed their adult behavior by first changing their childhood belief patterns. I decided to try again with Gloria and called after a month of not seeing her. We started dating again, until I felt myself growing uncomfortable with her closeness and backed-off a second time. Fear continued to strangle our relationship.

Finally, I called her again and asked for a date.

"No, Peter, I won't go out with you anymore. I have to move on with my life and you're not able to be a part of it."

"Why?" I asked.

"I need a man who can share in my life and you're not able to do that because you're emotionally unavailable. I'm not willing to wait until you resolve your issues."

Gloria had the courage and honesty to tell me why she'd no longer see me, and I knew she was right. Afterwards, friends offered encouragement, reminding me that recovery from adoption was a process and that healing meant taking little steps, even if they proved painful.

My graduate studies experience at The Evergreen State College proved to be a journey through the jaws of intolerance, flying under the flag of political correctness. Evergreen's promotional literature emphasized diversity, but that proved untrue. The politically correct didn't welcome intellectual diversity. A vocal and aggressive group of administrators and faculty dominated the college and like a cancer, they ate at the health and vitality of the institution. They viewed big government as their engine to create a world to their liking, despised Christianity, viciously attacked European culture and crowned white males at the apex of things to blame. In classroom discussions I never once felt I could present a differing viewpoint in a non-threatening environment.

This was disturbing for several reasons. For one, it was a state college funded by tax payers dollars. But America's greatest treasure—freedom—came under attack at the Evergreen State College. If a free exchange of ideas and open debate of issues wasn't possible on a public college campus, then where in America could it occur? They condemned the Catholic Church and in so doing assaulted the nuns and priests who had raised me in the orphanage. I was lumped together with all Europeans when in fact the differences between Germans and other Europeans were as pronounced as the differences between elephants and mice. Their attacks were a replay of the dodge-ball incident, but this time the mob howled because I was a Christian male with European roots. This time I decided I wasn't going to be a doormat because recovery meant standing up to the disrespectful actions of others. I hoped that Evergreen's politically correct would one day meet their Russians in a guardhouse.

The MPA program required students to complete an internship, and in my spring quarter I decided to do my work in the sports administration field. I'd heard people at the gym talk about the college getting involved with some kind of an Olympic training program. So, hoping to land an internship in conjunction with the Olympic Committee, I made an appointment with the athletic director.

I walked into the airy office littered with books, wall plaques and trophies. Jan looked to be in her late 30's and greeted me with a firm handshake and warm smile. We sat facing each other without a desk or other barrier between us. She glowed with physical health and her green eyes danced while I reviewed my background and asked for an internship. Jan said the college was hosting the United States Olympic Academy XIII the following summer. "What's an Olympic Academy?" I asked.

She paused and smiled, ran a strong feminine hand through shoulder length silver-blond hair and continued, "The Olympic Academy is the annual education conference of the United States Olympic Committee. Each summer it rotates to a different college campus throughout America to further the philosophy and values of Olympism. This year it's at Penn State and next year it will be at Evergreen."

I said I was interested in working on the project.

Jan continued. "I'm also involved with an effort to build a permanent Olympic Academy here in Olympia. It will be patterned after the International Olympic Academy, a wonderful facility located in Olympia, Greece."

I knew from a life-long involvement with sports that the Olympics was the greatest event in the world. "How did Evergreen get to host the annual education conference of the Olympic Committee?" I asked.

"Dr. Joe Olander, Evergreen's president, is a member of the Olympic Committee's Education Council. Through his efforts Evergreen was selected to host the conference, and he's also involved in the effort to build a permanent U.S. Olympic Academy." She finished and handed me a packet of material on the Olympic movement. "Here, read this," she said, and stood up, walking me to the door. "While you're reading, let me think if there's a way to get you an internship that does more than meet an academic requirement. If you're going to do an internship with me I want it to be a meaningful and enjoyable experience."

Jan called a week later to schedule a second meeting. She said she needed help planning the Olympic Academy conference and asked if I'd be interested in working with her as part of an internship. "If you agree, I need to count on you from now until the conclusion of the Academy conference. I'm also working on getting your position funded so you'll get paid."

So I started my second professional job as the Academy Conference Coordinator and it marked the beginning of my Olympic experience. Jan became my first supervisor outside of the military and proved to be one of the most creative, positive and intelligent people I had ever met. I had always learned by watching others, and Jan stood out as a positive role model.

I accompanied her to meetings in Seattle where a private foundation worked to build a $25.7 million permanent Olympic Academy in Olympia, Washington. I walked into the world of developing a multi-million-dollar project.

A few weeks after starting to work for Jan she asked me to give a promotional speech about the Olympic Academy at a state-wide soccer club luncheon meeting. But since I'd never delivered a public speech and didn't like being singled out in a crowd, a knot grew and tightened in my stomach as the day of reckoning approached. The morning of the luncheon I nearly canceled, but recovery meant facing uncomfortable situations, so I dressed in a business suit and went to the meeting but couldn't eat my lunch. Fifty pairs of eyes seemed to grip me as I walked to the platform and set my speech on the podium. At that exact moment the podium light short-circuited, and I couldn't read my notes in the dimly lit room. I stuttered, repeated words, made up phrases and basically floundered as I wiped away sweat pouring down the sides of my face. Despite my horrendous talk people approached me after the luncheon with questions. Such is the drawing power of the Olympics.

Later, I accompanied Jan and Dr. Olander to Penn State for the 1988 Olympic Academy XII. The last day of the conference Jan was scheduled to speak about the Academy at Evergreen, and Dr. Olander would follow with a talk on efforts to build the permanent academy. Jan came down with laryngitis the night before and whispered that I'd have to take her place. I spent the entire night preparing a five-minute speech and the next morning found myself on stage beside Dr. Olander in front of 300 people. I never would have been able to give that speech if I had cancelled my earlier talk with the soccer club. It went so smoothly that I didn't even need my notes. Practice meant improvement.

A woman from support group meetings also went to Evergreen, and we had an impromptu conversation across a cafeteria table during a lunch. We talked about our families and I mentioned I'd been adopted. Her eyes narrowed into bullets as I described finding my birth mother. She took a deep breath after I'd finished and said she'd also been adopted. It was my first encounter with an adoptee other than my sister.

"I've been trying to find my parents for over a year," she sighed, pressing fingers against her temples.

"What's taking so long?" I asked, re-experiencing pain as I remembered my search.

"I can't find them, and I'm losing hope," she said, still rubbing the sides of her head and staring at the table.

"Oh, don't give up," I said, offering encouragement. "Persistence will pay off; I would have searched forever until I found my birth parents. Keep trying; you'll get a break."

"No, you were lucky. I don't know anything about mine, not even their names. All the documents about them were legally sealed at the time I was adopted, and every request I've made to reopen the records has been denied."

My jaw dropped with disbelief. "How can someone deny you access to information about your birth parents?"

"The judge I petitioned won't do it. He said he's simply following the law." She looked up with empty eyes. "That's the way it is in most states. Laws prevent adopted children, even when they reach adulthood, from opening their adoption records."

What could I tell her, that I was sorry? I encouraged her to keep trying, offered to listen if she needed to talk and left the table in shock. Freedom is prized above all else in American society, and I found it unthinkable that the government strips adoptees of their most basic right—to know their origins.

What is truth? Truth is that every adoptee has birth parents, and it is a lie to suggest otherwise. A second truth is that all people have inherent needs, needs driven by human nature. Deprivation of those needs causes suffering. Pain comes from hunger and an ache comes from not knowing one's parents. People instinctively move to satisfy both those needs. No one taught me that I should desire to find my birth parents, the desire came instinctively. And I suffered until the day I found my mother, just as the woman who had sat across the table was suffering.

Natural rights is the doctrine that individuals have certain rights by virtue of the laws of nature. The founders of the United States viewed laws designed to protect the natural rights of individuals as just. Laws that seal adoption records are unjust because they violate the natural rights of an adoptee.

Policy makers continually argue that government must rule in the best interests of the child. But I saw the pain of the adopted-child-turned-woman across the table and wondered, in whose best interest were her sealed adoption records?

Greece and Olympic Gold

Jan called me into her office a month after we returned from Penn State. "Sit down," she said, offering her usual smile, but the welcome contained a tenseness that betrayed a meeting of unusual importance. "We've got something significant to discuss."

I returned her smile and slid into the chair parked at the side of her desk.

"I've decided to make a career move," she said, looking me straight in the eyes. "I'm leaving Evergreen and moving to New England. I need a rest so I can evaluate where I want to go professionally. My last day with the college will be at the end of August."

Jan's announcement caught me by surprise. She had become a mentor, and I had grown found of the woman who gave me my first job after leaving the military.

"I called you in to discuss the leadership of the Olympic Academy. It's a prestigious event and one I hate to leave. One of my final duties is to make sure the leadership of the Academy transitions into good hands. Based on your performance, I thought you'd make an excellent director to head the Academy."

Blood rushed into my head, making my vision swirl. The news shocked me, and I sat open-mouthed on hearing her compliment.

"I talked with Dr. Olander, and he agreed with my recommendation that you be named the director. On behalf of the college president, I'm offering you the position."

"I'm honored," I said. "There's nothing more I'd enjoy than heading the Academy and I accept the offer."

She looked at me with her dazzling green eyes, smiled and nodded her head. In August 1988 I became the thirteenth director of a United States Olympic Academy and only the second ever to do so without a doctorate degree.

I now had ten months to prepare. My job was to plan and implement a program that examined the Olympic movement, so the Academy consumed my every waking hour. I loved the work and hurried to my office each morning. Twelve-hour days flew by and I spent many nights and weekends preparing. My work schedule soon became so intense that I postponed my graduate studies to concentrate solely on the conference. I made countless promotional speeches and met hundreds of people. My name and picture appeared in newspaper articles, and I spoke on radio and television. The entire time I asked God for humility and thanked Him for the job He'd given me.

But workaholism isn't a healthy disease either. Depression sometimes resurfaced when I was alone in my apartment at night or on weekends. Work provided an instant cure of busyness, and I'd drive to my office to distract me from my painful feelings. Depression disappeared minutes after I sat behind my desk and started thinking about the thousands of details associated with making the Academy a reality. But work, a temporary fix, proved a much easier route than taking the difficult steps that ensured a lasting recovery. Workaholism couldn't permanently heal my insecurities because the prestigious job of heading an Olympic event did nothing to change my boyhood perspective and emotions, which were still tender.

I lived, breathed and slept the Olympics. Working on the Academy, as much as I loved it, came with a price tag. My life slowly narrowed and the last few months before the start of the conference I found myself isolated. Workaholism had the same destructive effect as alcoholism. It reduced my life to a single component. I justified long hours of work by rationalizing that the Olympics were a once-in-a-lifetime opportunity and my job ended after one year. Until then, I had to give it my all.

The United States Olympic Committee each year sends five people to attend the International Olympic Academy located in Olympia, Greece. The IOA is a permanent facility located in the same location where the ancient Greeks held their Olympic games. I applied and was accepted as one of five American delegates to attend the IOA in 1989.

Selection to the International Olympic Academy opened a door. Possibilities often remained closed when I believed I didn't deserve good things, but in my recovery, I'd slowly developed a healthy self-esteem and believed good things could come my way if I worked for them. Taking action to move past insecurities freed me from fear and the door that opened with my selection provided me the opportunity finally to visit Czechoslovakia. Arrangements to travel to Czechoslovakia would allow me to visit Kunzendorf, the village where my German family once lived. This time the Army couldn't stop me, and I wrote Aunt Maria to ask if I could visit her before I went to Czechoslovakia. She wrote back saying she'd be delighted.

In late June, 1989, two days after the United States Olympic Academy ended, I arrived in Athens, Greece to join the 158 other delegates from 61 nations participating in the 29th Session of the International Olympic Academy. A welcoming committee of Greeks greeted delegates at the airport. They helped me process through customs before driving me to the President's Hotel in downtown Athens. The Greeks proved to be extraordinarily friendly people and I enjoyed their hospitality and warmth. At the hotel I received a delegate's package. Program literature came printed in three languages: Greek, the language of the host country; English, the world's language; and French, the official language of the International Olympic Movement.

The first official function of the Academy came the next day when delegates toured Athens' archaeological sites. That evening, just before sunset, the opening ceremony took place on the Hill of Pynx. The flags of each delegate's country encircled the ceremony area and a brass band played solemn music. From my vantage point I looked down from the Hill of Pynx to see the Acropolis cast in shadows. His Excellency Juan Antonio Samaranch, a Spaniard and President of the International Olympic Committee, gave the welcoming address. His talk and the speeches that followed had a common theme: in sight of the Acropolis where free assembly was permitted, delegates to the IOA became members of the Olympic family and were asked to give their ideas, feelings, effort and energy so that the tradition of tolerance, understanding and international amity, as created in ancient Athens, could continue to flow from the Hill of Pynx through Academy participants.

A reception followed and provided the first opportunity for me to mingle. The five Americans spent little time together, choosing instead to interact with delegates from other nations. Linda Williams, a black woman and part of the U.S. delegation, gravitated toward the Africans in the same way I searched out the Germans.

Losing my German heritage still troubled me. For months I had tried to find some benefit, something positive from the pain of inter-country adoption. My only solace was to look at the experience through a spiritual lens. I remembered a passage from the Bible, "For I will take you away from among the nations, gather you from all foreign lands, and bring you back to your own land." (Ezekiel 36:24) My suffering resulting from inter-country adoption had led me closer to God.

After speaking with the Germans I made my way through the crowd and introduced myself to as many people as possible. I now enjoyed socializing and felt comfortable in the crowd. This marked a significant personal achievement because I was interacting with hundreds of people in a social environment without the influence of alcohol.

We left Athens the next morning and travelled by bus to the International Olympic Academy. The IOA, a palace-like facility built near the outskirts of Olympia, stood adjacent to the ancient stadium where the Greeks of antiquity first held the Olympic Games.

Each morning at 6:00 I ran three miles with a man from the Netherlands and a Finnish pole-vaulter who each spoke excellent English. Thankfully, we didn't race, and the relaxing run became a time to share stories about athletics and our home countries. It reminded me of the male bonding I had loved so much in the Army, but this time it came without all the macho braggadocio. Classes filled our mornings and lecturers came from throughout the world to speak to Academy delegates. After lunch we broke into small groups of 10 to 15 people and discussed the morning talks and assigned readings. My perspective continued to broaden as I listened to people from other countries express their points of view.

Intramural sports took place after the afternoon seminars. Soccer was the most sought after, but not one of the Americans played. I participated in basketball and for the first time played under international rules.

Sports are a universal form of communication, transcending language barriers and national boundaries. A Russian played on my basketball team, and

I went out of my way to let him know I didn't hate him or his country. He was a fine athlete and played a good game. He seemed eager to become friends, and even though the language barrier prevented us from deep conversations, we still managed a friendship. We participated in the same seminar group and often kidded, arm in arm, saying, "Glasnost, Glasnost." We actually exemplified the power of the Olympic movement and through a common bond of athletics bridged differences two superpowers couldn't resolve.

I had been sober for over two years when I arrived in Greece, and my experience with the Olympics symbolized the 180 degree turn my life had taken. Three years earlier I had been training American soldiers to kill Russians. I thanked God for taking me off the path of death and destruction and putting me on one of cooperation and friendship.

Late in the evenings, around ten, groups of people walked the mile to downtown Olympia and shopped for souvenirs or ate and drank at the many outdoor restaurants and cafes. I'd always had an insatiable curiosity and joined groups of delegates at outdoor tables in Greece's late-night warmth to listen to stories from around the world. The delegates' common bond of sport became the vehicle for understanding, and as I first discovered in the wooden guardhouse, people have the same desires and needs no matter where they come from or what they look like.

The International Olympic Academy programmed socials every other evening. These allowed the delegations from each country to give a 10-15 minute performance highlighting a unique aspect of their culture.

The U.S. delegation met one afternoon to decide what we'd do for our social performance. We had trouble thinking of an act that would highlight a part of American culture. The United States is a young country without a distinct culture, and we had a difficult time agreeing on something uniquely American. We finally came up with the idea to put on a Star Trek skit. I was Captain Kirk and Linda Williams my first mate.

We pretended to land on a planet in a far away galaxy where the three other Americans played roles as the planet's inhabitants. Linda and I landed as the inhabitants stopped playing a game to argue over money, nationality and recognition. The crew of the *Starship Olympia* taught the inhabitants the noble ideals of the Olympic movement, and we ended our skit by each holding a single ring, then locking them together to form the five rings symbolizing the Olympics.

The International Olympic Academy stood as one of my life's most memorable and positive events. The academics proved stimulating, the athletics fun, my life's perspective continued to broaden, and touring and learning about Greece fulfilled my love of history. At the Academy I saw people from every race, culture, religion, sex, nationality, and political belief live together for two weeks in harmony and friendship.

But there was also another benefit. I believed I was being groomed for a position with the permanent United States Olympic Academy planned for construction in Olympia, Washington. I thought I had found my professional life's dream.

After completing the Academy, I flew to Germany on a Lufthansa jet. After landing in Frankfurt I took a train to visit great-aunt Maria before venturing to Czechoslovakia where I hoped to uncover more of my heritage and come to peace with my past.

Prelude to Czechoslovakia

When I stepped off the train at the Hannover Hauptbahnhof my great-aunt stood waiting with a smile, her blue eyes sparkling. Hieronymus had died in the eight-year period since I'd last seen her, and after his death she'd moved to Hannover to be nearer her children.

"Its so good to see you again, Peter," Maria said, rising on her tip toes to hug me.

"It's good to see you too, aunt Maria. You've always been kind to me," I smiled. She was in her eighties, but her physical beauty and emotional charm remained intact. "Thanks for allowing me to visit. It's been many years since we've seen each other."

"You are always welcome here. You're part of our family," Maria said, stepping back from our embrace.

Maria turned to a woman standing at her side, a woman who looked a little older than my 34 years. "This is my daughter, Christel," Maria said. Christel looked at me as if I were a museum piece but managed a smile when we shook hands. "Very pleased to meet you. My mother has told me much about you," Christel said.

We left the train station, and Christel drove to her home where I met her husband, Klaus-Dieter Dames, and their two small boys. I slept in a spare bedroom at their house during my three days in Germany since Maria didn't have room in her comfortable but small one-bedroom flat.

Before leaving the United States I'd researched my German background to understand why Germans had been deported from Czechoslovakia at the end of World War II. Gathering information wasn't easy since little is written in English on this dark period of our history.

Germans and Czechs had lived side by side since the Middle Ages under the rule of the Holy Roman Empire and later the Austro-Hungarian Monarchy. At the end of World War I Czech and Slovak nationalists succeeded in their goal of establishing an independent Czechoslovak republic incorporating three provinces: Bohemia to the west, Moravia in the center and Slovakia in the east. The new nation included Czechs, Slovaks, Poles, Hungarians, Ukrainians and Germans known as Sudetendeutsche. Sudeten Germans included such great names as the poet Rainer Maria Rilke, the geneticist Gregor Mendel, the industrialist Emil von Skoda and the automobile pioneer Ferdinand Porsche.

But the population mix of this newly created state spelled trouble. Seven million Czechs made up the largest single ethnic group. Second were Germans with three-and-a-half million people followed by two million Slovaks.

The Sudetendeutsche had lived for 700 years on the frontier communities ringing Bohemia and Moravia, lands adjacent to Austria and Germany. These German communities didn't want to live in a predominantly Slavic state and problems could have been avoided had the new nation's boundaries instead been drawn along ethnic and language lines. However, contrary to the right of self-determination, the Sudeten Germans never had an opportunity to express their desires in a national election.

The Czech and Slovak militia occupied the German Sudetenland and imposed foreign rule on a people who had lived in the land for over fourteen generations. Germans made up approximately one-fourth of the new state but were granted neither autonomy nor given a voice in Czechoslovak affairs proportionate to their numbers. They intensely resented having been turned into a minority overnight and once again demonstrated that every colonial people disdains a foreign ruler. Germans who publicly resisted Czech rule were killed or beaten.

Most public service jobs in predominantly German areas were occupied by Czechs, who for the most part spoke little or no German. The majority of state contracts for public works in German areas were also placed with Czech contractors instead of German ones. Furthermore, the official and exclusive use of the Czech language in the central ministries was seen as a form of discrimination. Slovaks and Poles living in the new state were provided the same privileges as the Czechs. This further outraged the Germans since they weren't receiving their economic and political rights in the same way as other minorities in Czechoslovakia.

The Sudeten Germans appealed to both the government in Prague and the League of Nations asking for political and social equality as well as some degree of autonomy in the German populated districts. The Czech state and League of Nations rejected all their requests for basic rights.

For eighteen years after the end of World War I all peaceful efforts by the Sudeten Germans to regain their right of self-determination failed. Then, with Hitler threatening the use of force, the 1938 Munich Agreement allowed three million Germans living on the borders of Moravia and Bohemia to secede from Czechoslovakia to Germany. Half a million Germans still lived within the borders of a reduced Czechoslovak state, but the new ethnic boundaries rendered the Czech state more homogenous by eliminating a large and discontented minority. This agreement was objectionable because it came with Hitler's threat, but France and Britain breathed a sigh of relief believing the Munich Agreement would lead to a lasting peace in Europe. Six months later, however, Hitler marched into the remaining sections of Bohemia and Moravia and World War II followed shortly after. The Sudeten Germans were not Nazis. But Hitler was an opportunist who had promised the Sudetens what they had been unable to achieve peacefully over an eighteen-year period.

Dr. Eduard Benes, the Czech president in exile during World War II, considered Germans who hadn't been happy under Czech rule to have been "traitors" to the Czech state, a nation that had existed less than 20 years. "We must get rid of all those Germans who plunged a dagger in the back of the Czechoslovak state in 1938," Benes declared. After the end of the Second World War he persuaded the western democracies to end 700 years of German presence in Bohemia, Moravia and Slovakia.

The Potsdam Conference in August 1945, signed by the United States and other victors, authorized the mass deportation of Sudetendeutsche from their homelands into Germany. The forced deportation of Germans immediately after the war occurred not only in Czechoslovakia, but also in Poland, the Baltic states, Hungary, Yugoslavia and Romania. Germans were also expelled from parts of Germany including East Prussia, Pomerania, East Brandenburg and Silesia to allow these territories to become part of Poland. The provisions of the Potsdam Conference said the deportations were to be effected, "in an orderly and humane manner." Fifteen million Germans were expelled from their homelands and two million died from beatings, starvation, disease, exhaustion or severe weather. These two million deaths consisted mainly of the elderly, women and children. In comparison, the number of German civilian deaths resulting from forced deportation is nearly four times greater than the total number of U.S. combat deaths in all of World War II.

Germans called the period of deportation the Vertreibung. They were not compensated for property left behind and deportations occurred quickly, without international supervision and under all weather conditions. The English author Victor Gollancz wrote in his 1946 *Our Threatened Values*:

> "If the conscience of men ever again becomes sensitive,
> these expulsions will be remembered to the undying shame
> of all who committed or connived at them... The Germans
> were expelled, not just with an absence of over-nice consid-
> eration, but with the very maximum of brutality."

These were the conditions under which Maria, Hieronymus, their children and my grandparents were expelled from their homes in the Sudetenland. Ilse Sander was 24 and living in Prague at the end of the war. I can only imagine the sheer agony my birth mother endured during the forced exodus. Knowing what happened to German civilians in Czechoslovakia helped me better understand my birth mother's tragic life and shed another ray of light on my early years.

There is no justification for the horrors committed by the Nazis during the Second World War. But the forced deportation of Germans from their homelands was a tragedy on an extraordinary scale, another outrage for which there can be no justification. Hate might have consumed me without my one source of consolation to help me come to terms with the Vertreibung. I remembered the words Jesus uttered while nailed and dying on a cross, "Father, forgive them for they know not what they do." Only by trying to pattern my life after the perfect example of Christ could I find the strength to forgive the United States, Russia, Czechoslovakia and other nations responsible for the Vertreibung.

However, the Sudetens recovered from the atrocities of mass deportation and helped contribute to the economic miracle of modern Germany. I shared their same resiliency, industriousness and strength to recover from the defeat of alcoholism.

Christel couldn't understand why I wanted to go to Kunzendorf. She was seven years old when forced to leave her home in Czechoslovakia, and the Vertreibung brought back terrifying memories. But Maria understood my need to visit the lands of my ancestors. "Oh, let him be, Christel," Maria said. "Peter needs to walk the ground where our family once lived."

I had outgrown the illusion that I'd find lasting happiness by searching outside of myself and knew visiting Kunzendorf would not mark the beginning of eternal joy. Still, I felt called to travel to the town of my ancestors in much the same way as one visits a loved one's grave.

The second night of my visit Maria invited me to her flat to talk about my trip to Czechoslovakia while Klaus-Dieter prepared coffee in the kitchen. We sat at her dining room table and Maria showed photos and told stories of her days in the Sudetenland. She was born and raised near Kunzendorf and was 39 when forced to leave her home. After the war the Czechs changed the name of every Sudeten town and village from German to Czech to eliminate any symbol of a German presence. Maria believed Kunzendorf had been renamed to Kúnčice.

Kunzendorf was more a village than a town, and Maria suggested I try and find a Czech man named Herr Dressler. He knew my grandfather and might tell me stories about Peter Friedrich Sander. She said people in central Czechoslovakia wouldn't speak English and probably not German. To help me overcome the language barrier she wrote a list of questions in German, then in Czech, that I could give to people in Kunzendorf. It had been 43 years since she'd left Czechoslovakia, but she spoke in Czech while writing on the paper, showing she'd retained her second language. I read the questions: I am American and cannot speak Czech. Please speak German with me, I can understand German. Where does Herr Dressler live? Thank you for helping.

Maria said my grandfather had established a dowry for my mother. It consisted of land, a house, money and other valuables, but the dowry fell into Czech hands and my grandfather never received compensation. Herr Dressler might have taken the dowry, and Maria cautioned me, that if I found him, not to talk about stolen German property. Maria needn't have worried. I wasn't after money but only wanted to see the land of my ancestors.

Maria unfolded a map of Czechoslovakia and traced her withered finger over the outer edges of Bohemia and Moravia. "This area was the Sudetenland," she said, then pointed to the capital, Prague. "Such a beautiful city," she reminisced. I watched her slide her finger eastward to a town called Bělotín. "This is the closest railroad station to Kunzendorf. From there you can take a bus to Kunzendorf." Then she wrote the directions.

Maria gave me a copy of a Sudetenland geography book that included a section discussing Kunzendorf:

"In northern Moravia, one kilometer from the Czech language border, lies the town Kunzendorf once inhabited by Germans. Surrounding the town are 500 hectare of agricultural land and 20 hectare of forested land.

In 1939, 400 people, each owning 8-25 hectare, lived in the 74 houses of the town. There were two restaurant owners, two tradesman, one butcher, one blacksmith, two seamsters and one shoemaker. Many inhabitants worked in construction, the railroad or in nearby industries.

The town owned a school which opened in 1856 and was rebuilt in 1935 with two grades. The school was administered by Oberlerher Sander. Until 1938 the people of Kunzendorf went to church in the neighboring Czech community of Speitsch. In 1938 a long desired wish materialized for the people of Kunzendorf to become part of the German parish and afterwards they attended mass in a nearby chapel erected in 1717 in memory of the Black Plague. Also in Kunzendorf were one voluntary fire department created in 1898, German cultural organizations and agricultural town groups.

World War One: 10 died and two were missing

World War Two: 13 died and 13 were missing

The Vertreibung: two killed

Klaus-Dieter joined in. He seemed a thoughtful man and had been listening closely while Maria talked. Klaus withdrew a match from his coat pocket, lit a pipe and said he'd never been behind the Iron Curtain. He thought it would be fascinating to visit a communist country because of their different way of life. "The people there have a different mentality because of their political ideology," he said, rubbing his neatly trimmed brown beard. "It would be interesting to try to understand how they perceive the world."

"I'm excited to travel to a communist country," I said. "While I'm in Czechoslovakia I want to immerse myself in their culture. I want to compare American propaganda to the reality of a communist state."

Klaus-Dieter, Christel and Maria drove me to the Hannover Hauptbahnhof. They helped me purchase a ticket to Prague then a return ticket to Frankfurt where I'd fly to Seattle. I shook hands with Klaus-Dieter and Christel, then hugged Maria, and before stepping into the train thanked them for their generosity and kindness. I could never repay my German relatives except to treat others in the same fashion.

The Final Outward Search

The journey included a stop at Nürnberg where I had to change trains before continuing to Prague. During the three-hour layover I secured my luggage in a locker and left the station to stroll through the walled, medieval section of the city. The streets were nearly empty on late Sunday afternoon, and I rounded a corner nearly tripping over a bum who sat cross-legged on the sidewalk with his hat laid in front of him, begging for money. I stopped to talk with the ragged, filthy man whose fate I had barely escaped. Despite his downcast condition he looked up at me and laughed, "I'm alcoholic," he said. "You can talk with me as long you'd like."

I smiled back, reached inside my wallet and handed him a few Deutsch marks. "I hope you have better days," I said, and the beggar thanked me as I walked away.

A few blocks farther I came across a group of small, brown nuns gathered outside a church. Their blue and white habits drew me toward them. Part of me had never forgotten the kind sisters who raised me in the orphanage.

"Hello sister," I said in German to a tiny nun with wire-framed glasses standing near the edge of the group.

"Hello young man. Nice of you to greet us," she answered in perfect German.

"I've always appreciated the good work of sisters. I'm travelling to Prague by train and have a layover, so I decided to take a walk. What brings you all here?"

"Our cloister immigrated from India ten years ago today. We're going to celebrate our anniversary with a mass in a few minutes."

"Can I join in your celebration?"

"We'd be delighted," she answered. "You should go inside as the mass will soon begin."

I opened the thick wooden door and entered a windowless, ancient church with only a handful of people scattered inside. A center aisle divided twenty rows of wooden pews and the tapping of my shoes against the concrete floor broke the silence as I walked toward the front. Clusters of white candles set on the altar and alongside the stone walls illuminated the interior with soft flickers of light. I stopped to genuflect before sliding into a pew, knelt on a hard wooden keeler and made the sign of the cross. A life-size figure of Christ nailed to a cross rose from the head of the altar. Wooden carvings of the Stations of the Cross, worn from the ages of time, hung on each side wall, and a marble statute of the Pietà, where the Blessed Virgin held the dead Christ in her arms, stood in a small alcove to my right. Statues of Saint Joseph holding the infant Jesus and another of Mary flanked the altar. Otherwise the church stood bare. The fragrance of incense mixed with the musty smell of time lingered in the air. It brought back memories of the sixth-grade when I used to sneak into church and pray before statues of Christ, the Blessed Virgin and the saints.

Still kneeling, I closed my eyes and silently talked to God, thanking Him for sparing me the misery that would have come had my birth mother raised me, for giving me a good home with my adopted parents and for pulling me out of the darkness of alcoholism. I thanked God for excellent health, a good mind and the ability to feel deeply, which for many years I'd tried to deaden with alcohol. "Your will, not mine," I whispered and crossed myself a second time before sitting on a hard wooden pew.

Soft music started to flow from the rear of the stone church and filled the interior with tender tones. I looked back and saw a teen-age boy and girl playing a violin and a flute. The sounds intensified my gratitude, and I felt connected to an unseen force of pure love. In the few seconds that followed I understood God loved me more than I could comprehend, and I wiped tears of joy which streamed down my face as the nuns and a priest filed by.

On the crowded night train to Prague I sat in a compartment with five Germans in their early twenties who pulled bottles of schnaps, beer and wine from their luggage as soon as we pulled out of Nürnberg. I turned down their offers of drinks and couldn't help but smile remembering days when I would have been smack in the middle of their party. The Germans, who'd travelled to Prague before, were returning to Czechoslovakia for a vacation. They said the train would stop at the border where passengers would have their travel papers inspected, and every foreigner would be required to exchange money into Czechoslovakian Krona. My compartment mates advised me to exchange only the minimum required, an amount determined by the length of one's visit, because Prague's black market offered double or triple the official exchange rate.

Daylight came an hour after we crossed the border and I stared out the window to look at my ancestors' land as the train rolled through the countryside. The train pulled into Prague a little after six in the morning, and I felt exhausted, having not slept due to the non-stop noise of the Germans' merry-making. All I wanted was to find a hotel and sleep.

On the crowded concourse going toward the center of Prague's main train station, I listened to a public announcement with a woman's expressionless voice in a language I'd never before heard—Czech. I could decipher other languages spoken by people in the station: Slavic, Russian, Polish, Hungarian, Rumanian. People in the station looked different than Germans, shorter and squatter, and dressed in plain, drab-colors. Information signs posted throughout the station were printed in Czech, Russian and other Slavic languages. Czech words were long with few consonants and strange punctuation marks. No signs were printed in German, English or other west European languages.

Plenty of soldiers drifted throughout Prague's Hauptbahnhof, and the athlete-warrior part of me sized them up. How would we have fared on opposite sides in a war? Quickly pulling out of the competitive mind-set, I exited the train station, following signs to a taxi stand. At least twenty people stood in line ahead of me, so I set my luggage on the sidewalk, sat on a suitcase and waited. There were no taxis and only a few cars and busses on the streets. Except for the desire to sleep I wasn't in a hurry, having only a skeletal itinerary. I'd always traveled without a rigid schedule because it allowed opportunities to mix with the local population and experience their way of life.

An hour passed, and I'd managed to wait to the front of the line when a beat-up and rusted black Mercedes stopped at the taxi stand. The driver got out and helped load my luggage and those of a man and woman who'd been waiting behind me. The couple piled into the back seat as I climbed into the front, and the driver sped away. A couple of days' beard plastered the driver's face, who looked as if he'd just woken up and hadn't combed his thick, dark hair. But he drove like a madman, fast—but not as fast as Germans—and recklessly, very unlike the Germans who always maintained perfect control of their cars. I didn't feel safe with his driving ability nor with the mechanical condition of his 1960's vintage Mercedes, if it was his, since I didn't know if Czechs could even own property. He said something while grinding gears pulling up a steep hill, and the couple in the back seat responded. The driver looked at me as if expecting an answer. I responded in German that I wanted to go to a hotel. The driver answered in difficult to understand German because of his thick Czech accent. I asked that he repeat himself. After several tries, where each time he spoke louder as if it would help me understand, I grasped he'd first take the couple in the back seat to their destination, and then he'd drive me to a hotel.

He dropped off the other passengers then asked, "You have German marks?"

"No," I lied. "But I have American dollars," I said, speaking slowly and clearly, enunciating every syllable so he could understand.

"That good," he beamed as we whipped around a corner. "I give 20 krona for every dollar."

I looked hesitant, more from trying to decipher his speech than his exchange rate. When I didn't respond he tried a different approach. "All hotels full in Prague. But I get you hotel room. I know hotel manager. It good hotel; you able to walk downtown."

I remained quiet, trying to analyze his offer. I had absolutely no idea where we were and couldn't get my bearings because few buildings had signs, and the streets all looked the same. The driver increased the pressure of his sales pitch, "I get you hotel, you give me $200 for 500 Krona. That 25 Krona for dollar. Very good exchange rate. Best in Prague."

I didn't know the hotel situation in Prague but wanted one within walking distance of downtown and his exchange rate was two-and-a-half times better than at the border. "Okay," I answered. What else was I going to do if all the hotel rooms really were full?

After a fifteen-minute ride, the driver pulled in front of a four-story building marked with a small hotel sign posted over double-wide glass doors. He turned off the ignition, and the engine sputtered and popped before shaking to a halt. The taxi driver opened the door and had both feet on the street before leaning back to ask, "How many days you want stay?"

"Five to seven days," I replied.

"Good, I come back."

The driver returned, got in the beat-up Mercedes, slammed the door shut, and I feared the entire car might fall apart. "Everything good. My friend have one free room. Only for you. Ten minutes we go inside. You have American dollar? Two-hundred dollar? I give you 25 Krona for dollar. You get hotel room. All hotels full. Very good deal."

I took my wallet out of my jeans and raised it to my chest when he quickly pushed my hand below the windows of the car. I nodded my head saying I understood while pulling out four $50 dollar bills. No one who might be watching could see us exchange money when I kept my hands on my lap. His face lit up when he saw the money, as if the horse he'd bet on just finished first. The driver slid 5000 Krona into my hand while looking nervously outside the car windows. We finished the exchange, and he helped carry my luggage into the hotel foyer, ignoring everyone inside. Then the driver left without saying good-bye.

I handed the hotelier at the front desk my passport and said in German that I planned to stay in Prague for a seven-day vacation. He gave me a room key and told me to retrieve my passport from the front desk whenever I left the hotel and to drop it off when I returned.

After walking up three flights of stairs I opened the door to my room with a single queen bed, private bath, no television and a radio with only two stations. A man continually talked on one station so I kept the radio tuned to the other that played classical music. After a hot shower, I set my portable alarm clock for two in the afternoon, and collapsed in the bed.

The alarm never woke me, but at four in the afternoon annoying sounds of accordion music catapulted me out of bed. Slamming off the radio, I dressed and ate an early supper in the hotel restaurant before walking downtown, which true to the taxi driver's word, was only a few blocks away.

Narrow cobblestone streets led to a magnificent building, Czechoslovakia's Museum of Natural History, positioned at the end of a major boulevard. A huge statue of Saint Wenceslas on horseback, a king who ruled Bohemia and Moravia in the Middle Ages, stood between the museum and boulevard. Walking to the front of the statue, I looked down the crowded boulevard as energy pumped through me. I'd reached my dream of visiting the land of my German ancestors. A few minutes later the adrenaline subsided, and I walked down the boulevard gawking at everything. Hours later an outdoor cafe offered a welcome rest stop, and I took a seat to order a cup of coffee. Living in the Pacific Northwest had turned me into a coffee connoisseur, and the waiter brought a tiny white porcelain cup filled with thick, syrupy liquid and plenty of grounds. It tasted bitter, so I ordered a second cup but found to my displeasure that's how Czechs drank their coffee.

Darkness had descended on Prague by the time I left the cafe and headed back to the hotel. Despite the late hour, men and a few women walked by themselves on the streets of Czechoslovakia's largest city. It offered a scene I'd never seen in any large American city. Americans, though always intent on ensuring individual rights, couldn't provide the most basic right of all—a life free from fear.

A discotheque sign glowed above a doorway, and I decided to look inside, still wide awake after having slept the better part of the day. I descended a flight of carpeted stairs and entered a small club playing recorded Czech and German songs. A few couples danced to the upbeat music; the clientele ranged in age from twenty to fifty and dressed a couple of steps above the casual jeans I wore. Liking the two-to-one ratio of women to men, I returned to the hotel, changed into the one suit I'd packed, and backtracked to the discotheque.

I scooted up to the bar and ordered a cola. Nursing my drink, I surveyed the surroundings and spotted two women sitting with a stout, olive-skinned man at a table in an enclave. The women looked about my age, and the man might have been ten years older. One of the women was quite attractive and smiled. I walked to her table to strike up a conversation. The music blared, so she stood up, and we faced each other inches apart trying to talk.

She was Czech and spoke German but not English. It took me a couple of tries to get her first name correct, Zdena, and I could never correctly pronounce her last name, Mrkvànkovà. The woman and man sitting at the table were Zdena's companion and her Italian boyfriend. Zdena and I danced and talked until she glanced at her watch and told me she and her friends had to leave since they started work early the next morning. Zdena got up from the table and asked me to follow her outside where we drank in cool air and a delicious quiet.

"I'm happy to have met you and am impressed with the beauty and culture of Prague," I told Zdena, smiling into her blue eyes.

"Thank you. I am pleased you like our city," she answered using a hand to brush back her shoulder-length blonde hair. Without the blaring noise of the discotheque music I heard a Czech accent as she spoke German. Zdena possessed the natural European look I found incredibly beautiful. She wore little makeup, a touch of perfume, earrings, a pearl necklace and watch with a slender wristband. She seemed independent and strong but at the same time kept her graceful femininity. From the way Zdena talked and carried herself, I could tell she was educated, mature and cultured. My instincts told me she could be trusted.

"Are you sure you can't go and have a drink somewhere before you go home?" I asked, not wanting her to leave.

"No, I have to go because I must get up early for work." She shook her head in disgust after glancing at the Italian who was passionately kissing her companion.

"Okay, but first I have to tell you why I'm in Czechoslovakia. Prague is only my first stop, after that I'm going to visit a small town in northern Moravia. Don't you think its strange that an American would want to go to such an out of the way place?"

"Why do you want to go there?"

I briefly shared my story explaining my desire to visit Kunzendorf.

"What was the name of the village you want to visit?" Zdena asked as her forehead wrinkled with curiosity.

"Kunzendorf, but it was renamed after the Germans left. I can't remember the Czech name, but I have it written down in my notes back at the hotel."

She looked at me without blinking and said, "We call it Kúnčice. I know this because I was born and raised in Valašské Meziříčí, a small town five kilometers from Kúnčice."

What were the odds? Over a million people lived in Prague and I met someone who grew up two-hundred miles away, in a town near Kunzendorf. I knew it was more than coincidence and thanked divine providence. Zdena and I agreed to meet later in the week.

I spent the following days walking through Prague, savoring the experience of being in a city over 1,000 years old. In addition to visiting art galleries, museums and cathedrals, I kept my eyes open, trying to see how ordinary people lived. Shops weren't as well stocked as those in America, and lines formed at the entrances of food stores. Behind the Iron Curtain I never once heard English. I wouldn't have been able to communicate had I not spoken German.

Zdena and I met a few nights later, and we ate in an elegant restaurant overlooking the Vlatava River. A stringed quartet played music as Zdena and I talked about our lives, the United States, Czechoslovakia and Germany. The bill for a five-course dinner came to less than five dollars, and we left the restaurant so Zdena could give me a walking tour of Prague.

We finished the tour near midnight and walked back to the restaurant. An old woman in rags, pulling a cart filled with all her worldly belongings, hobbled toward us from the opposite end of a dimly lit and deserted street. I handed the destitute woman a few Krona as we passed.

"That was nice of you," Zdena said.

"I'll never miss the money, and the woman obviously needs it. It bothers me to see people living in wretched conditions," I replied. "God loves that poor old woman, and I hope she knows happier days in her next life."

The woman pulling the cart was the only street person I saw in Czechoslovakia. It pointed to another difference between the United States and Iron Curtain countries. "Americans look down on communist countries, but at least people have a place to sleep in your country," I told Zdena. "America is a rich country, but in every city there are thousands of homeless people."

Zdena worked as a banker and didn't believe me as I challenged her image of the American paradise. "Are there really so many homeless people in America?" she asked. "I thought it was just communist propaganda when I heard that some people in America don't have shelter."

"No, it's true," I answered. "It's a disgrace."

We arrived at a taxi stand where we'd end our evening. "When do you plan to go to Kúnčice?" Zdena asked.

"I'm not sure, in a day or so," I answered.

"If you wait until the weekend I'll go with you. My mother still lives in Valašské Meziříčí. I can stay with her and you can sleep in a hotel. Then I'll take you to Kúnčice. It will be easier if I'm with you because people in Moravia don't speak English or German. Our second language is Russian, and it will be difficult for you without a guide."

I didn't hesitate giving her an answer. "I'll wait until the weekend, and I'd be very pleased if you'd come with me."

We met at Prague's train station after Zdena finished work on Friday afternoon and boarded a train for the journey. The ride passed quickly, and I sensed traces of romance stirring beneath our budding friendship. Zdena tried to answer all my questions about the passing countryside, the passengers on the train and the Czech mentality. We arrived in Valašské Meziříčí, a town about the size of Mörfelden, and walked to a hotel where Zdena helped me check into a room. As in Prague, I had to hand over my passport and explain why I'd come to Czechoslovakia. Zdena did all the talking since the hotelier didn't speak English or German. His eyes lit up when he opened my passport and saw I was American. He gaped at me as if I had just stepped off of a spaceship, and Zdena said I was the first American he'd ever seen.

I set my luggage in the hotel room and returned to the lobby to walk Zdena to her mother's apartment complex. She said she'd meet me at the hotel in the morning, and we'd take a bus to Kunzendorf. Back in my hotel room before going to sleep I knelt beside the bed as I did every night and thanked God for another day without a drink. That night I extended my thanks for the opportunity to visit Kunzendorf and for meeting Zdena.

In the morning we took a bus from Valašské Meziříčí to a village about a mile from Kunzendorf. That was as close as we could get. We would have to walk the remaining way because Kunzendorf didn't have weekend bus service. White puffs of clouds billowed in the crystal blue sky, and the warm temperature made me wish I'd worn shorts instead of jeans. Northern Moravia is farming country. Rolling hills, covered with fields of crops and patches of woods, lined the road to Kunzendorf. No billboards polluted the quiet serenity of the beautiful countryside, and we walked on the narrow paved road only once scampering to the side to avoid a passing car. A small sign stood along the roadway outside of Kunzendorf with Kúnčice printed in large bold letters. I ran to the sign, slapped it with the palm of my hand and, much to Zdena's dismay, started to dance.

"I've waited 10 years for this day," I laughed. "I'm celebrating reaching my goal. Do you want to dance with me?" I laughed again, extending my hand and continuing to dance as if in a discotheque.

Zdena stared at me with her mouth wide open and shook her head no.

I didn't care and continued my celebration because, unlike the day I met my birth mother, this was a happy occasion. Zdena didn't understood my joy in arriving at the end of my family history rainbow, the pot of gold that meant the search to uncover my roots was over at last.

I stopped dancing, and we continued walking to the village. Kunzendorf could be seen from one end to the other and at the second block I saw the school my grandfather administered. I walked around the building and peered through windows, but drawn shades prevented me from seeing inside. All the houses in Kunzendorf had gray stucco exteriors and, where Americans would plant lawns, these villagers planted vegetable gardens. The air smelled rich with earth and fertilizers, and not one car was parked on the main street. Zdena asked a woman hanging laundry on an outdoor clothes-line if she knew Herr Dressler. After a few exchanges, Zdena looked at me and beamed, saying Herr Dressler lived in Kunzendorf and we then walked to his house.

We turned on a side street and arrived at a large house with an attached barn where several men worked outdoors. Zdena talked to one of them who quickly disappeared inside the house and returned, accompanied by an old, bent-over man who walked with a cane. "That's Herr Dressler," Zdena whispered, and we walked toward the aged man. I felt no animosity toward Herr Dressler and had only come to uncover more of my roots. The two Czechs talked for several minutes, and I guessed Zdena explained the purpose of our visit. Herr Dressler looked up at me, keeping one hand on the cane and extending the other. I shook the hand of a man who knew my grandfather, and he invited us inside. We met his wife who asked us to sit in a kitchen nook and brought bottles of warm lemonade to drink. The three Czechs talked and were only interrupted when Zdena paused to translate. I felt out of place not understanding the language and wished I could have spoken Czech.

Herr Dressler said he missed his friend, Peter Friedrich Sander, after he left Kunzendorf and sent Frau Dressler to rummage through boxes of photos. She couldn't find any pictures of my relatives and returned to the kitchen empty handed. Zdena translated a couple of questions for me, but I didn't learn anything new. I suppose my presence resurfaced old memories the Dresslers would rather forget, and I felt uncomfortable during our twenty-minute stay.

We left the Dresslers and walked out of the village on a dirt road splitting fields of waist-high corn. A trail, overgrown with weeds, led from the road to a chapel constructed during the Black Plague. The doors were locked, and peering through yellowing window panes, I saw only a bare interior. I had nothing more planned, so we left Kunzendorf.

I had retraced my German family history as far back as I could, and there were no more people to meet, villages or countries to search. I had done everything humanly possible to reconstruct my origins and felt relieved knowing my outside search was forever over.

On the way back to Valašské Meziříčí I asked Zdena why she wasn't married or didn't have a boyfriend. "You're smart, kind and beautiful. It seems plenty of men would be interested in you."

She answered after taking a deep breath. "Men are interested in me, but I don't want just any man. I need a man who is intelligent, responsible, has a good character and one who will commit to me. This type of man is very rare to find."

I nodded my head in agreement and wondered if Zdena and I might have met under considerably different circumstances if the Germans hadn't been expelled after the war.

We left Valašské Meziříčí for Prague on Sunday afternoon, and I departed Czechoslovakia that night. Zdena proved a perfect tour guide, and without her assistance travel in Moravia would have been extremely difficult. I thanked her for all she'd done and we exchanged addresses. I felt sad looking out of the railroad car window with Zdena standing and waving good-bye on the dock as the train slowly rolled out of Prague. I don't know why, perhaps part of me still dreamed... how different my life would have been if only...

The Inner Journey Continues

On the return flight to the United States I looked forward to seeing familiar surroundings, friends and my Siamese cat that I had rescued from the pound. I adopted my blue-eyed beauty as a kitten about the same time I started working for the Olympic Committee and named her Venus, the Roman goddess of love and beauty. At the prison for abandoned felines she meowed sadly and jabbed a paw out of the cage as if pleading for help. Our bonding began when we took morning walks in a nearby patch of woods. I'd meander down the dirt trail sipping a cup of coffee and Venus would run ahead, sniffing bushes, darting after insects or chasing small rocks I tossed in her path. She stayed outdoors whenever I left the duplex and ran to greet me, her tail pointed straight in the air, when I pulled in the driveway. I'd open the car door and Venus would jump in my lap to welcome me home. She slept at the foot of the bed every night and pawed my face in the morning to tell me she wanted breakfast. I always spoke to her in German, so great was my affection for her. Before leaving for Europe, I asked my friend Janice to kitty-sit while I travelled to Greece, Germany and Czechoslovakia.

Janice picked me up at the Sea-Tac airport, but her strained voice signalled something was wrong. She answered my concerns by saying things were fine but stopped on our walk to the baggage carousel and asked, "Can we go to the airport lounge and get a drink?" I knew something had happened to Venus but waited to let Janice tell the story.

I sipped a latte and watched Janice quickly down a bourbon and coke. She finished her drink, set the glass on the table and stared at the ice she poked with a straw. "Venus ran away while you were gone. Oh, Peter, I'm so sorry." She looked at me with eyes coated in tears. "I looked everywhere for her, posted "lost cat" signs throughout the neighborhood, went door to door asking if anyone had seen a Siamese cat, but Venus disappeared. I feel terrible." She motioned the waitress for a second drink.

"That's not going to bring back Venus," I said waving off the waitress. "Listen, you went out of your way to care for Venus and to pick me up at the airport. You've been very kind, and I'm grateful for all you've done. It's not your fault Venus ran away. What's done is done and it's okay, Janice. Now let's go."

We stood up from the table and walked out of the lounge. "Thanks," she said. "I was so worried you'd be mad at me. I'm really sorry."

I wasn't angry at Janice but felt a tremendous sadness with the loss. Perhaps it's overly sentimental to grieve a pet, but my adoption background always intensified the sorrow of any loss I suffered. I loved my cat, and looking back on the night when I drove Venus to Janice's, I remembered how she cried and meowed, locked in her kitty cage. I had felt as if I were breaking a pact of trust and was abandoning my cat. When we had arrived at Janice's before my trip, I had carried Venus to an empty room and held her in my arms, stroking her soft hair and whispering she'd be okay. After Janice's news, I now felt as if I had betrayed a creature that trusted me.

But Venus was only the first in a series of losses at that time. My father's cancer came out of remission while I was in Europe, and his health quickly deteriorated. My mother called a week after I returned and told me my father was dying. I caught the next plane to Florida, but he died before I made it home. My mother, even after losing her husband of thirty-five years, continued to conceal her emotions and resisted my condolences. I wanted to give her a comforting hug, but she still avoided physical closeness, and our life-long pattern of isolation continued. My sister behaved in the same manner and resisted my attempts to discuss grief and loss, choosing instead to talk about the funeral arrangements and recall happier days.

A parish priest said a requiem mass for Francis Xavier Dodds, and afterwards, my mother, sister and I boarded a black limousine and led the funeral procession to a national military cemetery at Pensacola Naval Air

Station. Out of the limousine, my sister and I flanked my mother on the walk to the front of the casket as other mourners trailed behind under the hot Florida sun. An American flag covered my father's casket and six uniformed members of a military honor guard stood at attention to one side. The priest gave his final remarks, offered last prayers, and as my father requested, sang the Irish song, "Oh Danny Boy." He finished singing, and the military honor guard pointed their rifles into the sky and rendered one last salute to the infantry colonel who had served his country for twenty-two years. They fired thirteen volleys, and when the last echoes of gunfire fell silent, a lone bugler played *Taps*. The bugle's melancholy notes spread throughout the military cemetery and fell on thousands of identical white tombstones that marked the graves of deceased American warriors. When *Taps* concluded two soldiers crisply removed the flag and folded Old Glory into a triangle. They marched toward us and stopped directly in front of my mother. One handed her the folded flag of the United States of America and said, "A grateful nation wishes to thank you for your husband's service, ma'am." She had reached out with trembling hands and took the Stars and Stripes, then burst into tears for a few seconds, one of the few times she had ever allowed herself to cry. I kept my hands at my sides, resisting the urge to console my adopted mother. My sister continued to stand dry-eyed and motionless. The funeral ceremony ended, and the remains of the Dodds family solemnly walked to the waiting limousine.

I had wanted the ceremony to include the casket being lowered into the grave so I could reach down, grab a handful of dirt and throw it over the coffin as the last act of saying good-bye. But the service was clean and sanitary and didn't include this meaningful symbolic ritual. As the limousine drove away I looked out the window and saw two grave diggers, two complete strangers, wheeling the casket to my father's final resting place.

After the man who raised me died I contemplated what I might have done differently while he still had lived. I'd made amends a year before and knew I'd done everything in my power to mend our relationship. After his death I never wished to go back in time and say or do things differently. I remembered my father with gratitude and respect but still never felt close to him or loved him. Never did I shed tears of grief after his death, and the sad truth is I missed Venus more than I missed my adopted father.

A third loss after returning from Europe was due to political in-fighting. The United States Olympic Committee killed the permanent Olympic Academy project. The death of that project ended my dream of working for the Olympics. The Olympic Committee selects former Olympic athletes to fill its managerial and administrative positions, and I lacked that prerequisite. I served as director of the Academy and circumvented Olympic Committee hiring policy only because it was a temporary job. After returning from Czechoslovakia I'd lost Venus, my adopted father and my dream job. I had no other choice but return to college and complete my master's degree.

During my final quarter of graduate school periods of loneliness returned with such potency that I often plummeted into depression. I couldn't understand why. I worked out and attended support group meetings regularly, continued to develop my spiritual life, helped others struggling with alcoholism and tried to live a decent life. Still, most often on Sunday nights, I'd sink into a depression so powerful it felt as if I were trapped in an empty, pitch black chamber. It seemed I groped my way through darkness but couldn't find the walls and feared the chamber had no limits.

When depression took hold I saw myself merely enduring a gloomy existence where my life had no meaning, purpose or value. Depression took away my hopes and dreams, and nothing I did broke the crushing darkness. I experienced a complete sense of hopelessness and helplessness. Alcoholism taught me my limitations, and I knew I had to ask others for help. So instead of clinging to old behavior by ignoring the problem or trying to solve it on my own, I buried my pride and reached out for help. Being miserable had lost its appeal. The need to interact with others instead of playing the melancholy loner again proved essential in breaking through barriers that prevented a satisfying life.

George had moved away from Olympia and I'd found a new sponsor whom I told about my loneliness and depression. The healing process started as soon as I honestly talked to another human being about my difficulties. I asked my new sponsor if he had any suggestions.

"I don't know," he answered. "Deep issues often surface after the chaos of alcoholism is taken care of. What you're experiencing isn't unusual. Lot's of people pass through a similar period after a few years without a drink. Sometimes repressed anger, anger you've blocked from your consciousness, causes depression. Maybe that's surfacing, so you might want to try and identify any deep-seated anger."

I doubted my sponsor's guidance and sought a second opinion from an acquaintance who worked as a therapist. He repeated that repressed anger can cause depression, and I quit fighting after hearing the same advice from two different people.

Every day I set aside a period of quiet time to reflect on my life and try to find the source of my anger. I walked back through the years looking for someone or something that caused a rage so deep that I blocked it from my consciousness. It wasn't easy. Again, I realized I needed more than human help and asked God for insight. The answer slowly emerged over a period of weeks and turned out to be one I didn't want to accept—I hated my birth mother.

The disclosure revolted me. How could a man hate the woman who brought him into the world? I didn't want to face the truth. If I had deep-seated anger it must be directed somewhere else, but further meditation proved fruitless. My inner voice, the part of me that never lied, clearly said I raged at my birth mother for having abandoned and rejected me. What could I do? Grasping for happiness in an attempt to deaden pain didn't work, and I had no choice but to confront the primal wound.

Shame and guilt ate at my insides as I told my sponsor about my discovery. "Thanks for sharing," he said. "Never deny your feelings even if your mind screams otherwise. You had no way to deal with the rage except to deny its existence. Take time to let yourself feel and then take action to resolve your anger."

"I have to get rid of it," I answered. "Somehow I'm going to let go of the past."

My sponsor and I talked for hours, and he offered several suggestions on how I could come to terms with my birth mother. I decided to write Ilse Sander a letter—a letter I'd never mail. I hadn't seen her in ten years and didn't know the address of the yellow house in Bad Nauheim. Still, I wrote as if she would read the letter, but instead I would read it only to my sponsor.

I couldn't start writing until I reached a point where rage didn't consume me. My only recourse was to reflect on the life of Christ and try to follow in His footsteps. Jesus loved everyone no matter what they did, and I had

to do the same. With Christ's love guiding the way I began with a saluta-
tion to Ilse Sander and hopes that she'd found emotional and spiritual
peace. I acknowledged her extremely difficult life saying I didn't know if I
would have survived the Vertreibung. I went on to thank my mother for
giving me life. The letter then turned to my own weaknesses, and I admitted to plenty of mistakes and could only ask forgiveness from those I'd
hurt. I finished by forgiving her for failing to mother me and signed Peter
Friedrich Sander. I meant every word I wrote.

A few days later I called my sponsor to set up a meeting. We met at a
park overlooking Olympia's harbor, and I read the letter as if I were saying
the words to Ilse Sander. My sponsor took the papers after I'd finished and
said my anger was no longer a secret or a burden. "You can get on with
your life now," he said as we walked out of the park.

My periods of depression ended after that day. Forgiving my birth
mother for giving me up for adoption marked the end of a long inner
journey just as Kunzendorf concluded my outer search. They were both
destinations I needed to reach in order to heal.

No Greater Love has a Man

Finally, I completed my graduate degree and entered the job market. The college's computer center stayed open twenty-four hours a day, seven days a week and students could use the terminals on a first-come-first-serve basis when classes weren't scheduled. It became my second home as I typed responses to job applications, wrote cover letters and resumes. During this period I occasionally saw a co-ed who nearly took my breath away. Whenever I saw her I'd stop what I was doing to appreciate her striking beauty. She stood nearly as tall as me, walked with a graceful sway and carried her slender frame with confident assurance. Golden strands streaked through her thick brown hair that was brushed straight back, without a part, and fell to the middle of her back. She captured the European look and embodied my ideal.

Sometimes she caught me staring, and I'd snap my head in another direction so I wouldn't be embarrassed. Did she find me annoying or was she displaying an interest? I decided to approach her the next time our paths crossed.

Behind a terminal one afternoon near the front of the windowless room, preparing job applications, I'd finished a cover letter and hit the print command on the keyboard. Printers were located in a different room, so I went to retrieve my document. On the way my heart rate raced when I saw the tall and beautiful woman sitting behind a terminal in one of the back rows. Her fingers flew over a keyboard, and she didn't look up when I passed by. Butterflies flew inside my stomach as I planned how I'd approach her.

On the way back from the printer I stopped by her terminal. "Hi," I said looking at her.

She stopped typing, glanced up, and her face flushed red. "Hello," she said, fighting a startled expression and managing a weak smile. A perfect set of almond-shaped green eyes stared at me, and high cheek bones gave way to a narrow mouth and well-defined jaw-line.

"I've seen you around campus and wanted to introduce myself. My name's Peter Dodds."

"I"m Tiffany Baack, nice to meet you."

I tried to remain calm and carried on a conversation to determine if she was interested in me. I fought to keep my body relaxed and hoped my voice didn't betray my rumbling nervousness.

"I'm studying psychology and want to help troubled teens after I graduate," Tiffany said. "How about you?"

My intuition told me she would go out with me but I had to concentrate to find the right words. The same panic I'd always felt the split-second before leaping from an airplane when parachuting shot through me as I asked, "Would you like to go out on a date sometime?"

The seconds seemingly stretched to an hour before she responded, "Sure." I exhaled, and a smile covered my face.

We met at the computer center a few days later to begin our date, but it wasn't an extravagant affair. My mother's birthday was a few weeks away and we went to a mall to shop for a present of fine chocolate.

Tiffany dressed casually—a light colored-cotton skirt and blouse, black patent leather shoes and ankle high white socks—very natural and very feminine. She wore only a touch of makeup and I caught traces of her fragrant perfume as we walked to my car. She reminded me of German women, and with the last name of Baack I felt an attraction based solely on her national heritage. Long legs smoothly carried her 5'11" frame and our nearly identical gaits allowed us both to walk at a natural pace. Tiffany spoke articulately and I quickly picked up on her intelligence, but she showed no signs of snobbishness. She seemed considerate of others, emotionally secure, had a positive outlook and pleasant disposition. I'd never felt so comfortable with an almost total stranger. Awkwardness, so often that un-wanted third party on a first date, didn't appear as we shopped at the mall.

We dated on a regular basis and what began as a physical captivation broadened into a mental and emotional attraction. I genuinely liked Tiffany from the very beginning, not because I hoped for a romantic affair but because I enjoyed, admired and respected her.

I participated in the June graduation exercises as the final event of my Master's degree experience. The night before graduation the College Alumni Association held a dance, and I volunteered a couple of hours to sell tickets at the door. Tiffany helped me and it turned out to be a raucous affair with an unruly crowd. Rowdy drunks didn't want to pay the cover charge, people attempted to sneak booze past us, and plenty of underage kids tried to lie their way through the doors. I wouldn't have brought Tiffany if I'd known there would be so many rude and vulgar people, but she didn't mind. She once worked as a cocktail waitress and knew how to handle drunks and rogues with polite firmness.

"I'm sorry you have to put up with so much crap from people," I said during a lull.

"Oh don't worry," Tiffany answered. "This isn't anything I haven't encountered before."

I never would have guessed she had a tough side, but it shouldn't have surprised me. Tiffany had also worked as a white-water river guide and was no wall flower. My admiration and respect for her continued to increase. After our shift ended we danced, laughed and talked to friends. The dance finished, and we walked outside and stood underneath a roof staring at a heavy downpour.

"My umbrella isn't doing much good in the backseat of my car," I joked. "Why don't you stay here, and I'll run, get the car and bring it back to pick you up."

"Wait a minute," Tiffany answered, and she reached out to grasp my hand.

"What are you doing?" I asked, but she bolted into the pouring downfall pulling me along. We sprinted to the car hand in hand with rain streaming down our clothes.

"Hey, watch out for that puddle!" she yelled, running me into ankle-deep water, and my footsteps splashed waist-high waves onto both of us.

"This weather sucks; I had enough of this in the Army," I yelled, hearing my shoes squish with every step.

"I can't go any further; let me go," she laughed, trying to slow to a walk.

"C'mon, this is what you wanted, so this is what you're getting," I laughed, slowing to a jog and using my free hand to wipe away water running down my neck.

We arrived at the car out of breath, and between gasps for air yelled into the pouring darkness. "Yeeeaaahh! Yeeeaaahh!"

"I've always wanted to do that," she said, standing beside me as I opened her door. Before stepping inside, she looked at me and shook her hair like a dog drying after a bath. "Thought a little more wouldn't hurt you," she giggled and bent over to wring her soggy hair as I smiled and wiped the drops off my face. We drove out of the parking lot with the radio blasting, the car seats dripping like soaked sponges, windows fogging from the heater as we laughed hysterically.

After graduating from high school Tiffany had traveled to France to study. Her time in France matured her, broadened her life's perspective and contributed to her European flair that I adored. International travel became common ground and we shared endless stories about our overseas experiences.

"I did something else besides go to school while I was in France," she told me one afternoon. "I've known you long enough so I feel comfortable in telling you."

"What did you do?"

"I modelled when I lived there. But I don't like to tell people."

"Why not?"

"People expect me to behave a certain way, or be a certain kind of woman after they find out I was a fashion model. I don't want to be anyone's image; I just want to be me."

Tiffany also liked to ride horses. She seemed to float on top of a horse as it galloped across fields. Her parents owned two and she sometimes brought me to the stable when feeding them. The horses behaved like spoiled children, not cooperating with Tiffany as she coaxed them to their stalls where they tried to eat the other's food. I smiled, watching Tiffany treat them like the obstinate brats they were. Smells in the stable brought back pleasant memories, and I remembered the same smells in a German valley while sitting on the hood of an Army jeep.

Tiffany had become my best friend, and from that foundation blossomed a profound love. At the same time, old thoughts and emotions surfaced when I realized I loved her. I felt myself wanting to pull away as with every woman I'd ever loved. Lifetime patterns don't magically disappear, and my relation-

ship with Tiffany would end if I repeated old behavior. I thought back to
Gloria Melvin and remembered what she told me when ending our relationship, "You're emotionally unavailable." Could I change a lifetime of learned
behavior and break the cycle of pulling away from women?

My relationship with Tiffany became a symbolic experience that
showed how I had changed emotionally, mentally and spiritually. My
imagination saw the transformation:

Tiffany rode a horse other than those of her parents, one only
I could see. Riding on this horse Tiffany pierced the invisible
realm of sentiment and arrived at the surreal world of my inner
being. Beneath shimmering moonlight, my love glided atop her
mount as it galloped through a primeval forest along a damp,
earthen path. She rode effortlessly, long hair and loose fitting
white garments flowing in the wind as the rhythmic clatter of
racing hoofbeats broke the stillness of cool night air.

Rider and horse arrived at the edge of the great forest
where Tiffany pulled to a halt just inside the trees. She
leaned forward in the saddle to survey the scene in front of
her—the bleak landscape of my ravaged spirit and the
smoldering ruins of a shattered past.

Urging the horse forward Tiffany edged out of the forest
and came to a tiny village illuminated with the shadowy
light of burning torches. The village consisted of four
outdoor stages lined up side-by-side on one side of a dirt
road. The inhabitants were actors and actresses who performed tragedies at each of the different settings. Tiffany
rode into the village and stopped alongside the first stage.
She looked at a destitute German woman who sat beside the
platform and clutched a nearly empty bottle of booze.

"Why are you crying?" Tiffany asked.

The elderly German woman looked up, exposing a dirty
face caked with streams of tears and sobbed, "I lost my only
child when he was one and couldn't get him back. I wanted
to raise him, watch him grow and have him care for me now

that I'm old." The woman resumed her downward gaze, removed a wrinkled tinfoil package from inside her coat and began rolling a cigarette.

Tiffany rode to the second setting where a man as broken as the woman shuffled from the front to the back of the stage with his head bowed. He too was German and moved slowly and only with great effort. Tiffany couldn't see the man's face, but his ragged clothes and painful movements showed he'd lived a hard life. The black specter of death shadowed the pathetic man, and Tiffany cried out, "Stop! Turn around and come forward."

The man stopped but didn't turn around. He raised his head as if sniffing the air and then continued limping toward an empty horizon.

A group of young children played a game at the village's third stage. Still mounted on her horse, Tiffany watched as the children stopped their game of dodge-ball and formed a semi-circle around one of their mates. The frightened and isolated boy stood facing his tormentors with feverish eyes, looking for a way to escape as the others began their taunts.

The rider and horse arrived at the last stage where a married American couple dejectedly talked about the emotional behavior of their son. "We've given love and tried our best to provide him with a good home, but he doesn't respond. What can we do?"

Tiffany had seen and heard enough and galloped out of the village as the morning sun cracked the eastern sky. Night had turned to day when Tiffany arrived at a meadow with my castle in its center.

She dismounted and stared at the menacing fortress. A blanket of silence covered the castle and meadow, even the air stood still. Drawing in a breath of daybreak's air Tiffany patted the horse and whispered "good boy" before heading toward the castle. She walked across the meadow until stopping in front of walls that had held me prisoner for thirty-five years.

"Peter? Peter? Come out, come and enjoy life," she shouted. "Leave your emptiness behind and come to me where you can experience friendship and love." Tiffany reached within her breast pocket to withdraw a heavy iron key and threw it over the wall.

I sat inside the castle on a cobblestone walkway and listened to Tiffany's pleas as the key sailed over the wall. It hit the cobblestone with a shrill clank and skidded a few yards before coming to a halt near my feet. Doubts about leaving the castle clouded my mind as I picked up the key and juggled it in my hand. I've finally been given a key to leave this cursed place, but do I have the strength to change a lifetime of isolation?

A ray of sunlight gleamed through the door's keyhole as I walked toward the castle's only exit. I slid the key into the rusty keyhole, gave it a twist and heard a clink as the latch unlocked. Loneliness had become comfortable because it was all I knew. Should I risk leaving miserable but familiar surroundings?

I pushed against the massive door with both hands, heard a sucking noise and felt it give. I'll never again be rejected or abandoned, locked inside this castle. Do I have the courage to leave my protecting walls in the hope of finding love?

The door resisted when I pushed, so I leaned into it with a shoulder and shoved with all my strength. I groaned, shoved harder, and finally the door swung open. From inside the castle's darkness I saw Tiffany standing in the sunlight. She waved for me to join her, and I walked out of my self-made prison.

Freedom from the castle came only after I'd done the work to recover from adoption: having faith God could heal me, seeking the help of others, admitting my faults, making amends, helping others and seeing good in every person. Searching for happiness outside myself had led only to emptiness, but I found contentment when I tried to live a good life. My adult behavior changed after my distorted childhood emotions had been replaced by healthy self-esteem.

This time I did more than simply stay in a relationship. For the first time I decided to commit myself to it. Committing to a relationship allowed me to experience joys that had previously remained hidden. Making a self-promise, and adhering to it, made me feel good about myself and formed the basis of a healthy relationship.

One summer afternoon we hung out at a waterfront park, enjoying the sun.

Boredom struck after a few minutes of tanning, and we got off our blanket to walk through the park grounds. We arrived at a tract of freshly mowed grass the size of a football field. The lawn had been watered recently, and grass clippings stuck to our feet and ankles. We ran and danced across the field dressed only in bathing suits, enjoying the sun's warmth pressing against our bodies.

Tiffany sprinted ten yards ahead and suddenly stopped. She turned in a crouch and looked very serious while motioning me forward with her index finger. "Come here my darling," she said with a fabricated British accent.

I walked toward her, wondering what she was up to. When we were close enough to touch she kicked a knee in the air and slammed her foot into a puddle hidden beneath the grass. Then Tiffany bolted as muddy water and slimy grass splashed me from the chest down.

"Run, but you can't hide," I laughed, giving chase. I caught Tiffany and held her arms behind her back.

"Let me go; let me go. Aaagghh. Help!" she screamed, struggling to break free.

"So you can give it but can't take it my little pretty," I said, picking her up and dumping her in pool of glop.

She sat in the swamp looking like a helpless puppy. "You're mean," she whimpered. "What did I do to deserve that? Come here and help me up." She extended a hand, leaving the other in the mud.

I crept toward her like a cat stealthily approaching its prey. When I reached out for her hand she hurled a handful of mud against my bare chest. I kicked the puddle and Tiffany had just enough time to turn her head before a wave of muck washed over her.

"Aaagghh! You play dirty, now help me out of this mess. I'm serious this time." She extended a slop covered arm. I reached down to help her, but instead she yanked me into the grimy pool. I promptly dunked her head into the ooze. We laughed and played in the muddy field under a hot sun until we looked like two swamp creatures from a horror movie. Finally, we called a truce, washed off with clean water from a nearby hose and left the park. I hadn't played since my days as a lieutenant in the Army.

Tiffany took in the world and molded what she saw to her own ideas. Self-confidence allowed her to express her views even when others disagreed.

Unlike me, she handled confrontation in a healthy manner. We sat in her living room one night after dinner, and the conversation turned to abortion.

"I think a woman should have the right to choose whether or not she has an abortion," Tiffany said, as if giving the daily weather report.

My body constricted and a flash of heat whipped across my face. I leaned forward in my chair and stared at her. "I can't believe you said that. How can anyone support the murder of unborn babies?" I asked in a voice that would have frozen water.

"That's not what I said. I said a woman should have the right to choose." The infliction and tone in her voice hadn't changed from her previous sentence.

"You support legalized murder?" My eyes narrowed into bullets and my voice went up an octave. "I've heard all that crap before. There's one argument pro-abortion people make that drives me crazy. Do you know which one?"

"No," she answered, as if telling a waitress she didn't like her eggs scrambled.

"It's the argument that women who live on the streets shouldn't have babies because their offspring do nothing but drain society and never amount to anything. My birth mother lived on the streets. Do you think I should have been aborted? Do you think my life is worthless?" I shot out of the chair and stomped to the door. Rage blinded me as I groped for the knob.

"I don't want to talk anymore. I'll call you later," and I pushed the door open.

"Wait a minute," Tiffany said in a self-assured and calm voice. I stopped in the doorway but didn't turn around as she got out of her chair and walked toward me. She stopped directly behind my back, reached past me and pulled the door shut. I stared at the closed door and felt Tiffany take my hand. "I don't want you to leave yet. Come back here with me," and she led me to her bedroom.

"Lie down on your back and be still," she said as softly as a flowing stream. I laid on her bed and Tiffany turned off the light. She crawled on to the bed and blanketed me with her body. "It's not good to leave in such a troubled state," she whispered in my ear. "Wait a few minutes before going." She wiggled her hands under my back and pressed her head against the side of mine.

Minutes ticked by and neither of us spoke. The heat of her body and rhythm of her breathing slowly melted my anger. It's what I'd wanted from my adopted parents when I was a boy but then I didn't know how to identify or express my needs. Tiffany taught me it's possible to disagree and still love. We spent the night together and before leaving in the morning I kissed her at the doorway.

Back at my duplex I checked the telephone machine for messages and heard Tiffany's voice. "Hi Peter, it's me," the tape played. "Thanks for last night, and I can't wait to see you again. I hope you have a grrreeaaat day and I'll talk to you soon. Bye."

I smiled, listened to her message a second time and walked to the kitchen to pour a cup of coffee. "This coffee tastes grrreeaaat," I said out loud, imitating Tiffany.

My feelings had swung like a pendulum. With Tiffany I knew joy and happiness as intense as my darkest depression.

I'd never told any woman that I loved her, so I wasn't sure I could tell Tiffany how I felt about her. I would wait for her to tell me first. But I waited for words I'd never hear. After several months of dating, subtle signs signalled Tiffany didn't love me: she didn't display pictures of me at her trailer, talked increasingly about her last boyfriend, and she often asked for time alone. My inner voice, the part of me that never lied, murmured our relationship would soon end. Rather than challenge Tiffany in an attempt to forestall the inevitable, I remained content to enjoy our remaining days together.

After a week apart, Tiffany called and asked to come over. I knew the purpose of her visit and, with a sinking stomach, waited the 40 minutes it took her to drive to Olympia. Her car pulled into the driveway, and I peered out the kitchen window to watch her park. She walked up the outside flight of stairs and I greeted her before she could knock.

"Hi," I said stepping back from the doorway.

"Hi," she answered and walked inside. We didn't hug or exchange our usual greeting where I lightly kissed her lips.

"How was the drive? Do you want something to drink?"

"No traffic, and I'll skip the drink but thanks. Can we go into the living room?" Our conversation hadn't included one touch, a sure sign to me our relationship had taken a drastic turn.

We walked past the plants, artwork and books into the living room. I sensed a firmness in Tiffany like the night she worked the door at the alumni dance. We sat on opposite sides of the sofa, and I looked at Tiffany, waiting for her to start. I braced for what I knew was coming.

"I'm glad we can talk Peter. I went away last week to be by myself so I wouldn't have distractions and could think without interruptions. I thought about my life and about you."

Everything except Tiffany sank into oblivion. My body tightened as if expecting a blow and I heard the distant pounding of my heartbeat. Tiffany breathed regularly, talked in her normal voice, sat in a relaxed manner and didn't show any emotion except that she'd made up her mind.

"I've tried to love you. I have forced myself to love you but it's just not there for me. I can't pretend any longer, and I have to tell you how I feel."

Numbness paralyzed my body even though it felt as if I'd been smacked in the face. I stared at Tiffany, and she seemed to be sitting at the end of a dimly lit tunnel.

"This relationship isn't working for me, and I'm going to have to move on without you. I'm sorry, Peter. I'm really sorry."

It was my greatest fear come true—to love another person and then for them to leave. No tears swelled in my eyes. I couldn't feel a thing. I knew I had to say something but my lips seemed glued together and my parched tongue stuck to the roof of my mouth. With great effort I managed to say, "Thanks for telling me, Tiffany. Do what you feel you need to do."

I expected her to stand and leave, but she stayed for a few hours. It surely wasn't easy for her to tell me face to face how she felt, and it made me appreciate her maturity. Even when she was breaking off our relationship, I continued to admire and respect Tiffany.

"I'm going to go now," she said, and I walked her to the door. Shock began to give way to pain and the American in me struggled, the part where males are taught no matter how bad they hurt never to show their feelings. Tiffany stood at the doorway while tears formed and slowly trickled down my cheeks. I turned my face to try and hide the pain, but Tiffany knew.

"Come here," she said, walking toward me. She put her arms around my back and hugged me. "It's okay, Peter. You'll be okay," she said over and over again.

"It hurts to lose you." That was all I could say, nothing else registered.

"I know," she said, and slowly broke away and walked out the door.

My love for Tiffany was unconditional. I didn't plead, coerce or try to manipulate her into changing her mind when she ended our relationship. I wanted her to be happy even if I wasn't going to be part of her life. All I could do was let her go. As much pain as I endured, my inner voice said letting go was the right action to take.

I stared out the window watching Tiffany drive away and felt my heart crack. She came to teach me about life and love, and after I learned her lessons, our paths split. If I never know love again it will be bearable because I have experienced love in its truest form, a love that took me to the upper limits of my existence.

But Tiffany made one last appearance:

> She picked me up and we rode toward my castle on the horse that only I could see. Inside my heart we rode through the primeval forest, past the village and out to the meadow with my castle at its center. I dismounted, and Tiffany leaned down from her saddle to plant a final kiss on my lips before she rode away and forever disappeared.
>
> The sound of hoofbeats fell silent and I stood alone in the meadow staring at my castle. Darkness and misery loomed inside the open door. Should I go back inside the castle after having been abandoned and rejected by one I loved?
>
> Voices from my early childhood echoed deep inside the castle, "Any person you love will leave. You can't love because no one will love you in return."
>
> But then I heard another sound, the truth of my inner voice, and it drowned out my fears. "There is One who always loves you, no matter what you do and no matter what you experience. You will always be loved by the One who made you; that One is God."
>
> I was no longer a child in a man's body.
>
> I turned away from the castle and walked through the surrounding meadow to continue my inner journey.

Appendix 1

There is no greater sorrow on Earth than the loss of one's native land.

—— Euripides, *Meda*, v. 650-651

Adoption is a sensitive issue that always involves fundamental concerns for the rights and well-being of the child. These concerns are magnified in the case of international adoption, which not only severs the child's ties to biological parents and extended family, but can also entail a loss of social, cultural and national identity.

The phenomenon of international adoption has persisted in the United States with little regard to the rights of the foreign-born adoptee. Unfortunately, inter-country adoptions are seen by most Americans as a solution for families needing children rather than children needing families.

The Convention on the Rights of the Child was adopted by the United Nations General Assembly on 20 November 1989 and entered into force on 2 September 1990. It is regarded by most child rights experts as the standard by which adoption procedures should be judged. As of 18 August 1996, 187 countries had either signed the Convention or become States Parties to it by ratification, accession or succession. International concern to safeguard the rights of children offered for inter-country adoption is reflected in renewed efforts to provide suitable alternatives within the child's home country. *Article 8* of the Convention ensures the child's right to preserve her or his identity, including nationality, name and family relations. International adoption is to be considered only when all possible means of giving the child suitable care in her or his own social and national setting have been exhausted.

The United States is one of six countries yet to sign the Convention along with Somalia, United Arab Emigrates, Cook Islands, Switzerland and Oman.

In 1992, with growing concern about international adoptions, a meeting of child welfare experts was held in Manila, Philippines on "Protecting Children's Rights in Inter-country Adoptions and Preventing the Trafficking and Sale of Children." The recommendations of the Manila conference emphasized the need to encourage local alternatives to international adoptions, beginning with social services to help keep families together. Among comprehensive recommendations, the meeting cited the need for:

- economic assistance to parents and families (i.e. food and clothing) to help keep families intact;

- counselling to help stop abuse and conflicts within families;

- family planning education and services to help prevent unwanted pregnancies;

- support for single parents, and single mothers especially.

The Manila conference recommended that if a child cannot be raised by her or his parents, care within the extended family, with support if necessary, should be the next goal. If this is not possible, efforts should be made to secure domestic (in-country) adoption. Only when all such alternatives have been exhausted should international adoption be envisaged.

Those who desire to help children in economically deprived, or war-torn countries, have alternatives to international adoption. The United Nations Children Fund (UNICEF) in 1993 published a comprehensive guide for providing services to children in conflicts. The guide makes a number of recommendations for protecting children:

- every effort needs to be made to maintain family unity and avoid separation of children from their families;

- efforts to reunite families should be made as soon as possible;

- unaccompanied children should receive emergency care and be provided a legal guardian;

■ placement decisions for the care of children should assure long-term, nurturing relationships; children should be cared for within their own families, communities and cultures, and their language, culture and ethnic ties preserved.

World Vision is an international partnership of Christians whose mission is to work with the poor and oppressed to promote human transformation, seek justice, and bear witness to the good news of the Kingdom of God. Since its founding in 1950 World Vision has grown to be the largest privately funded Christian relief and development organization in the world, helping children and families in more than 100 countries.

World Vision is not an adoption agency and does not facilitate adoptions. It works to help children become productive citizens in their own countries. Child sponsorship promotes positive and lasting change by using sound community development principles with programs in nutrition, education, health care, agriculture, and vocational skills training for children, parents and their communities.

For more information, contact:

United Nations Children's Fund
3 United Nations Plaza
New York, NY   10017

World Vision
P.O. Box 78481
Tacoma, WA   98481-8481
telephone: 1-800-423-4200

Appendix 2

Resources for Adoptees, Birth Parents and Adopting Parents

The following lists, by no means exhaustive, organizations that may be helpful to adoptees in a search for birth family and provide emotional and practical support.

United States

Geborener Deutscher (a newsletter for German-born adoptees)
805 Alvarado DR. N.E.
Albuquerque, NM 87108

Adoptee's Liberty Movement Association
P.O. Box 727, Radio City Station
New York, NY 10101-0727

American Adoption Congress
1000 Connecticut Avenue N.W., Suite #9
Washington, D.C. 20036

Council for Equal Rights in Adoption
356 East 74th Street, Suite 2
New York, NY 10021-3919

The Musser Foundation
P.O. Box 1860
Cape Coral, Fl 33910

National Adoption Center
1218 Chestnut Street
Philadelphia, PA   19107

Washington Adoption Rights Movement
5950 6th Avenue South, Suite 107
Seattle, WA   98108-3317

Adoptive Parents for Open Records
P.O. Box 193
Long Valley, NJ   07853

Canada
Parent Finders, Metropolitan Toronto Area
2279 Yonge Street, Suite 11
Toronto, Ontario   M4P 2C7

Parent Finders Edmonton
#49-52307 Range Road 213
Sherwood Park, Alberta   T8G 1C1

Searchline
63 Holborn Avenue
Nepean, Ontario   K2C 3H1

Parent Finders, National Capital Region
P.O. Box 5211, Station F
Ottawa, Ontario   K2C 3H5

Adoption Disclosure Register
Ministry of Community & Social Services
2 Bloor Street, 24th Floor
Toronto, Ontario   M4W 3H8